Insights into Labor Issues

THE MACMILLAN COMPANY
NEW YORK · BOSTON · CHICAGO · DALLAS
ATLANTA · SAN FRANCISCO
MACMILLAN AND CO., Limited
LONDON · BOMBAY · CALCUTTA · MADRAS
MELBOURNE
THE MACMILLAN COMPANY
OF CANADA, Limited
TORONTO

Insights into Labor Issues

Edited by

Richard A. Lester
PRINCETON UNIVERSITY

Joseph Shister
YALE UNIVERSITY

New York
The Macmillan Company
1949

INTRODUCTION

PUBLIC interest in labor issues has expanded with the growth in union membership. Labor is front-page news. Unfortunately, understanding of labor problems has not increased with the newspaper space devoted to strikes and organized labor. In some respects, abundance of published information and views has served to perplex rather than to enlighten the public on labor questions.

The country is rapidly becoming aware of the urgent need for more light on labor relations and issues in collective bargaining. It is no exaggeration to say that labor relations represent our most critical domestic problem and that perhaps the very survival of democratic capitalism rests on our ability to develop practical solutions to various labor problems.

In recognition of the vital role that human relations play in our economy, universities and colleges have been expanding their staffs and resources for research in the economic, psychological, social, and political aspects of labor. This volume represents some of the results of such research and indicates how understanding may be enhanced through analysis of underlying factors and how new insights may be gained through the application of new methods and approaches.

The chapters in this book grow out of the special studies and experience of their authors. In general, the contributors are labor economists who obtained their Ph.D. degrees during the decade prior to Pearl Harbor, benefitted from practical experience during the war, especially with the National War Labor Board, and have been interested in the application of economic analysis and social science techniques to the field of labor. A statement of each author's training and experience follows Chapter 13.

Each essay is an independent contribution. No attempt was made to "coordinate" the essays or to present a common point of view. The purpose is simply to present worth-while analyses or investigations of important labor subjects.

Significant implications for union, management, or government policy are to be found in each chapter. With the increased importance of collective bargaining in our economy, it is essential that policy-makers appreciate the evolving patterns of collective bargaining discussed in the essay by Harbison, Burns, and Dubin. Equally necessary for policy purposes is an insight into the new techniques of bargaining, the meaning of which Kassalow explores, and the character of our labor movement, the determinants of which Dunlop examines.

Recently much has been said about collective bargaining under multiple-employer arrangements and the unionization of salaried employees. The experience of San Francisco, the area with the most highly developed multi-employer bargaining in this country, is thoroughly analyzed in the essay by Kerr and Fisher. The problems involved in the organization of individualistic professional employees for purposes of collective bargaining are interestingly explained by Northrup. Lessons can readily be drawn from both essays.

As collective bargaining has spread to larger segments of the economy, it has become increasingly desirable to distinguish the role of bargaining from other aspects of labor-management relations. Chamberlain demonstrates the dangers inherent in attempts to interject bargaining into the settlement of grievances, which involves application and interpretation of existing collective agreements. Shister analyzes union-management cooperation on production problems to discover what conditions seem to be necessary for the success of a program for joint effort to reduce production costs.

As recent experience has so forcefully demonstrated, wages are a key factor in collective bargaining. Truly remarkable have been the developments in wages during and since World War II. Lester applies economic analysis to the problem of wage differentials, pointing out the implications of his studies for both economic theory and practical wage policy. Roberts indicates the marked changes that have occurred in the American wage structure and their meaning for future labor developments. Belfer and Bloom effectively demonstrate that strong trade unions and recent trends in union policy require significant modifications in traditional economic theory, if economists and industrialists are to make sound analyses of the effects of economic change under existing conditions. Reynolds examines the character of the labor market, especially the supply of labor to the individual firm, and draws important conclusions for wage theory and industrial policy from his analysis.

Continued full employment, affording workers ample job opportunities, is generally recognized as a prerequisite for the maintenance of democratic capitalism in a world veering toward socialism and communism. But full employment in a free society requires restudy of the role of collective bargaining in wage determination and involves the assumption of new responsibilities and policies by trade unions. Forsey examines the issue of planning and control of wages, labor mobility, and trade union policy under conditions of full employment in peacetime. Long studies the question of change in the size of the nation's labor force under different economic conditions, especially when the economy approaches full employment. In order to avoid inflation and unforeseen labor shortages that may upset full employment planning, it is essential to know how the labor force adjusts, and whether it does vary much, with changing incomes and employment.

These remarks indicate the pressing problems with which the essays in this volume deal. The purpose of the book will be achieved if its contents serve to indicate the value of economic analysis for a correct understanding of labor issues, help to stimulate further research in the field of labor, and contribute to the development of more intelligent policies in industrial relations. It cannot be stressed too often that, in the human aspects of American industry, the nation badly needs more light and less heat.

Four of the essays (those by Northrup, Reynolds, Forsey, and Harbison, Burns, and Dubin) represent revisions, adaptations, or further development of material originally published in journals or reports during 1946 and 1947. For the granting of permission to use such material previously published, the editors wish to thank the *American Economic Review*, the *Quarterly Journal of Economics*, the *Canadian Journal of Economics and Political Science*, and the Industrial Relations Counselors, Inc.

TABLE OF CONTENTS

PART THREE: LABOR AND FULL EMPLOYMENT

PART ONE
Labor Relations

CHAPTER ONE

Toward a Theory of Labor-Management Relations[1]

by *Frederick H. Harbison, Robert K. Burns, and Robert Dubin*

RESEARCH in labor-management relations is expanding at an impressive rate. The number of articles on labor subjects appearing in professional journals is at an all-time high. During the past three years, furthermore, at least ten universities have set up new research organizations in the industrial relations field, and many more are being planned. Prior to the war, the labor economists were for the most part the only scholars with a major interest in this field; today, however, they are being joined by a rapidly growing group of psychologists, sociologists, and political scientists who are making significant contributions to thinking on labor-management relations.

What will be the outcome of this burst of new energy and interest in this field? Will new discoveries be made leading to a more scientific explanation of labor relations, or will the end result be a conglomeration of unrelated pieces of research which will confuse rather than clarify an admittedly complex area of social science? The answer, we feel, will depend on the extent to which the various specialists in this field relate their individual research projects to some framework or series of frameworks which have promise of leading ultimately to a general theory of labor-management relations. Researchers in this field should have some points of common reference, some idea of what questions are most crucial for study, and some sense of participation in helping to build up a consistent

[1] This is an adaptation of Professor Harbison's paper published in the *American Economic Review* (Proceedings, May, 1947).

3

and well-integrated body of knowledge in this very live and important field for study. Toward this end we are proposing here, for the purpose of creating more interest and concern in the care and planning and integration of research, a tentative framework for the study of labor-management relations.

The main objectives of research in labor-management relations should be, first, to analyze the impact of a strong labor union movement on the business enterprise system, and second, to measure influences of the relationships between unions and employers on social and political institutions of the nation. Mere statements of objectives indicates that study of labor-management relations is of crucial importance for an understanding of the broader and more fundamental problems of how to make mass democracy work in the atomic age.

Our American business enterprise system consists of small businesses owned and run by an entrepreneur with only a few employees, and also of mass production enterprises employing hundreds of thousands of workers. Some companies are in fact as well as in theory controlled by stockholders; some are "management controlled" or "banker controlled"; others are dominated by a single individual. Our business enterprise system is composed of a conglomeration of different types of business organizations. Yet, it is a *system*—a mixture of competitive and monopolistic forces—that somehow or other provides the goods and services which our society demands. It is a well-known fact, of course, that there is a high degree of concentration of economic and political power in the hands of so-called "big business." Giant corporations such as U.S. Steel, General Motors, General Electric, International Harvester, and other leaders in their respective industries or trades have a very profound effect on the social, economic, and political life of the nation, and in many respects set competitive patterns to which hosts of other businesses must adjust or conform.

In addition to a system of business organizations, we also have a labor system, a *union movement*. Within organized labor there are many different types of union organizations, large and small. The very large unions, such as the United

Steelworkers, the United Automobile Workers, the Teamsters, and the United Mine Workers, have well over half a million members apiece. Some international unions, on the other hand, have as few as a thousand members. Then there are "independent" unions of various sizes and types, which are subject to various influences. Some unions are run from the top down; others operate from the bottom up. In the aggregate they constitute our union movement, which is now a very powerful and dynamic force in this country. Directly or indirectly this union movement affects the thinking and action of practically all employers, organized or unorganized. The nonunion employer is constantly aware that a union will be in position to organize his plant unless he meets or betters wages and working conditions prevailing in organized establishments and solves some of the problems of human relations in his organization.

In both the system of business organization and the union movement there are elements of competition and monopoly, of bigness and smallness, of personal struggles for prestige and position, and of concentration of far-reaching economic and political power. In this context, the study of labor-management relations is in reality the study of the influence and impact of these two heterogeneous systems on each other.

CRUCIAL QUESTIONS

There are two categories of extremely pressing, yet for the most part unanswered, questions. First, there are problems relating to the implications of large power concentrations in the hands of private groups. Can large-scale unionization operate within the framework of the present private enterprise system, or must it bring about some modifications in this system? Will the modifications be in the nature of joint economic planning of basic industries? Will concentrations of power in big unions, which parallel similar concentrations of power in big business, inevitably result in some form of bilateral monopoly? Are there automatic or natural limits, inherent in our present economic and political organization, to the exercise of power by large unions and large employers? What social controls through governmental action, if any, should be placed on the accumulation and exercise of such power by either side?

Another set of questions involves the balance of power between individual unions and managements and the resultant kind of union-management relationship which develops. These questions have to do with issues centering in the plant, whose resolution leads to conflict or cooperation, and stability or instability. Under what circumstances do cooperative relationships develop between employers and unions? What changes in human relations accompany the working out of harmonious union-management relations? What social skills are necessary to make such relationships work? What are the limiting factors on union-management collaboration, and, if collaboration is achieved, how stable is it likely to be? Where conflict rather than cooperation prevails, is there an effective basis for mutual survival in labor-management relations?

It is these and related questions for which we seek an answer. The framework for research set forth herein may suggest a new approach for the study of some of these problems.

TYPES OF RELATIONSHIP

In searching for answers to these questions, one needs a framework and methodology for development of a general theory of labor-management relations.[1] Such a theory must give proper weight to all of the motivating forces (social, psychological, economic, or political) which determine the policies and actions of employers and unions. It cannot rest on the assumption that actions of workers, unions, and employers stem entirely or even mainly from economic motivations.[2]

---

[1] The term "labor-management relations" we define as the relationships between union officials and employers, and the relationships between employees and management which stem directly or indirectly from union-employer relationships. This definition will include union-management relations in *organized* plants and also employee-management relations in *unorganized* plants to the extent that such relations are influenced directly or indirectly by what takes place in organized plants.

[2] Many studies of union-management relations rest upon assumptions that employers are interested only in profits and workers think of little else but

It must recognize as principal variables many factors which labor economists have heretofore banished to that intellectual no man's land where other things are always equal.

Obviously, it is impossible to study at one time the interplay of all variable forces which determine broad relations between unions and employers throughout the economy. For practical purposes, it is necessary to break down the study of labor-management relations into small segments. But such segments must be part of a carefully conceived and well-integrated, over-all plan of research, based upon a consistent body of theory as well as objective reporting of facts.

It is feasible, we believe, to break down the study of labor-management relations into segments by studying different types of such relationships. A conglomeration of unrelated case studies of labor-management types, however, in itself would not lead to a theory of labor-management relations. In order to develop a theory, it is of primary importance to understand the interrelationships between union-management types, the manner in which such types conform to general patterns, and the forces which account for the patterns which are set. In reality, labor-management relations as a whole make up a *constellation* of interrelated types and patterns which are joined together by a complex of social, economic, and political forces. If we can develop a method for determining characteristics of these types and then work out hypotheses concerning their probable interrelationship within a

wages. Research in the field of "human relations in industry" has demonstrated that workers, union leaders, and businessmen are motivated by social, psychological, or political influences as well as economic factors. We refer here to the various well-known works of outstanding exponents of this school such as Elton Mayo, F. J. Roethlisberger, Benjamin Selekman, Burleigh Gardner, William F. Whyte, and E. Wight Bakke. Too often economists have ignored the rich literature in sociology dealing directly with economic aspects of social life. Max Weber, Emil Durkheim, Karl Manheim, Georg Simmel, and in this country, Talcott Parsons, Louis Wirth, Everett C. Hughes, W. L. Warner, and others have much to teach economists who read their works. Even the "human-relations-in-industry" group has often paid little attention to its intellectual predecessors. At least the first third of the Western Electric researches (*Management and the Worker*) represents a kind of intellectual provincialism, overcome only when the data dictated a new approach and this was found in the works of sociologists and social anthropologists like Malinowski, Durkheim, and Simmel.

broad constellation, we will have a basis for at least a tentative formulation of a general theory of labor-management relations.

In defining a type of labor-management relationship, we should analyze three general sets of characteristics: first, the forces (economic, social, psychological, or political) that determine the policy decisions and actions of management on the one hand and union officials on the other; second, the structure of power relationships within management and within the union; third, the balance of power between union and management. It should be possible, then, to classify observations of human, economic, and political behavior with reference to these three general categories. The first of these categories of analysis we call for purposes of simplicity "the forces influencing decision-making." These are of two kinds: factors relating to the framework within which decisions are made and factors stemming from the prevailing structure of attitudes, reactions, and beliefs. The remaining two categories relating to existing power relationships we term "the structure of power."

FORCES INFLUENCING DECISION-MAKING

To understand union and management decision-making, it is necessary to analyze the existing framework which delimits the scope of decisions and influences their character and effects. This framework is a configuration and a composite of many types of influences—economic, social, political, and psychological. These may be termed the "framework factors." Each should be studied separately and in relation to its interaction with the others. Let us take one of these, the economic framework, and examine it in some detail. It should be understood that parallel expansions must be made of the other framework factors as well. Space limitations prevent our doing that here.

Economic Framework Factors

There are several aspects of the economic framework, within which union and employers bargain, which influence their decisions and help to condition their relationship to one another. Some of these are: (*a*) the nature and character of the product market; (*b*) the nature and character of the labor market; and (*c*) capital requirements and cost conditions in the plant and industry.

(*a*) *The Nature and Character of the Product Market.* In a locally competitive market, the union may be welcomed and its bargaining power increased because of the union's role as a stabilizing force. This is particularly true in industries such as cleaning and dyeing, and residential construction, which are usually characterized by low capital requirements and effective free entry. From a functional point of view, the union can prevent wage competition between companies and help to police selling prices and to stabilize the industry. In such cases, employers may become dependent upon and cooperate with a union in order to achieve competitive stability in terms of wage rates, and to a lesser extent, competitive equality in terms of labor cost and product prices. Joint decisions in collective bargaining, as well as the policies formulated by the union and the employer, will tend to be made within this cooperative frame of reference.

Where the local market is imperfect or monopolistic, the employer may have greater natural bargaining power relative to the union, and more ample financial reserves and staying ability. However, such bargaining advantages may be offset by unexpected but important factors which influence management decision-making. For example, continuity of operations is of critical importance in certain industries, such as daily newspaper production. More than two-thirds of all daily newspapers are located in one-newspaper towns and cities. The great majority have no direct local competitors and many are profitable financially, and strong and formidable in terms of collective bargaining power. However, they are almost completely dependent upon the union for a supply of skilled labor. In addition, their product—the news—is highly perishable. Their tradition of "never missing an edition" is strong and pervasive, and this factor, somewhat more sentimental than economic in character, has weakened and reduced in part what otherwise might be a relative preponderance of management bargaining power.

Another factor which may limit or offset greater bargaining power of an employer is immediate public demand for uninterrupted supply of a product or service. Public utilities, where a local producer is the major supplier of a commodity or service demanded by the community, are an example. In a collective bargaining situation, the employer may seek at all costs to avoid strikes and shutdowns. He may buy labor peace at the price of above-the-market wage adjustments and contract concessions that could have been resisted by utilizing his potential reserves of collective bargaining power. He may consider it essential to build and maintain favorable employee opinion as well as a favorable attitude toward the company on the part of the general public and particularly the government. In any case, he will have an incentive to make collective bargaining work, and this in itself may contribute to a more stable union-management relationship.

Where the market for the product is national, it may either be subject to a high degree of monopoly control or be highly competitive. If it is monopolized, producers may be in a better position financially to make concessions in collective bargaining. This will tend to influence their decisions, particularly where the added cost can be passed forward in the form of higher prices. The only limiting factor need be the elasticity of demand for the product. Of course, monopolists that are unionized do not face the problem of having cost and price standards undercut by nonunion firms or nonunion competition. This means that a high degree of monopoly control of the market in itself tends to simplify the union's problem of establishing standards over the entire market area. At the same time, it should also be recognized that a monopolist with an inelastic demand for his product based upon difficulty of product substitution will have unusually strong bargaining powers. He may be willing to take a long and costly strike knowing no substitute products exist which will encroach on his market while production is halted. His anticipation, under such circumstances, of the outcome of the strike is defeat of union demands. Thus, the monopolist may not always be willing to collaborate with unions at the economic expense of the buying public.

Where there is intense intra-industry competition, employers and unions are confronted with important problems and decisions relating to competitive wage-price relationships. The union faces difficult problems in extending organization and union standards throughout the market particularly where there is a proliferation of producers, both large and small. Unless and until this is done, decisions by union employers will·be strongly influenced by competitive conditions in non-union areas. Moreover, the union will always fear the rearguard danger that union shops, operating usually at higher wage rates in relation to nonunion competitors, may be disadvantaged and tend to slip out of union control, migrate to nonunion areas, go out of business, reduce wage standards, or otherwise unstabilize existing collective bargaining relationships.

(b) The Nature and Character of the Labor Market. Where skilled labor is required, it is generally easier for the union to gain control of the labor supply. This increases the bargaining power of the union and, of course, influences its decisions. In such instances, employers tend to become dependent upon the union, particularly where the union, by extensive organization, has established firm control over men in the trade and has supplemented this by tight control over jobs through union shop and closed shop contracts. Where employers are dependent upon the union for supplying men and where their situation is such that they feel the direct impact of union power, it will be to the employer's advantage to establish and maintain amicable and effective working relations with the union. In short, there may be a strong incentive for such employers to make collective bargaining work.

If the labor required is largely semi-skilled or unskilled, an employer may be less dependent upon the union for supplying labor. Other worker replacements may be readily available except in times of severe manpower shortages. There may also be possibilities of substitution through technological developments of a labor-replacing or labor-displacing type. In making its decisions and policies, the union may recognize its inferior bargaining position. It may decide that it can best increase its effectiveness by prudent administrative policies and practices that tend to offset relatively weaker organizational and bargaining power.[1] The union, therefore, may have an incentive to cooperate both to avoid conflict and to promote stable relations.

Bargaining power in the hands of the employer is, of course, enhanced where there is concerted action among the employers of an area with respect to collective bargaining issues. Well known is the widespread policy by which companies determine their wage rates according to "area averages." Such concerted action includes as well the determination of company policy in other issues according to "area practice." That development was, of course, accelerated under the War Labor Board policies which applied the "area standard" as one of the principal criteria in stabilizing wages and in determining other issues. We cannot underrate the importance of this doctrine in management thinking for it sets significant top limits on concessions which individual employers may be willing to grant to a union. The same kind of bargaining advantage is secured by a company which is the principal employer of labor in a given area, i.e., where there is monopsony in the labor market.

Confronted with either concerted employer action or monopsony, local unions may seek to offset the employers' advan-

---

[1] In this connection it is characteristic for the union to seek a union rather than a closed shop, for example. It must also be recognized that the initial disadvantaged position of the union, as a product of the character of the labor market, leads to other moves to strengthen the local union's position. Before mass organization of workers such local unions were weak in bargaining power. But affiliation in international unions, themselves larger and more powerful than some individual businesses, gives back to the local union some of the bargaining strength, which, if only the influences of the labor market were operative, it would not have.

tage by bargaining on the basis of an industry pattern or the application of national standards. In assisting the local, the international union may provide skilled negotiators, statistical and research data, strike funds, and the like. Under such conditions, the resolution of collective bargaining disputes may depend in part at least upon the difference between the area standards of the employer and the national standards that the union seeks to establish.

(c) *Capital requirements and cost conditions.* Decision-making by the employer and the union will also be influenced by the nature of capital requirements for the industry. This may include the aggregate amount of capital investment in plant, the total amount of capital investment per worker or per unit of output, and the extent to which the investment is fixed and permanent or may be rather readily disinvested or shifted elsewhere. Where a steady capital inflow is required for growth and replacement, the decisions of both parties in collective bargaining (but particularly management's) may be influenced by the extent to which its actions may affect confidence of investors and thereby limit the supply of capital.

The influence of capital requirements has its greatest significance in terms of cost conditions and the degree of adjustment that may be possible as a result of increases in wages and other costs occasioned by collective bargaining. Unit labor and capital costs may be either high or low, flexible or inflexible, and decreasing, increasing, or relatively constant. Consequently, the effects of cost changes will depend on the circumstances, and the decisions of both parties will be influenced or affected by such conditions. For example, where the capital costs are high relative to labor costs and product prices, the cost adjustment required by higher wage rates may be less important than maintaining full utilization of capital equipment and high output by avoiding costly interruptions in production. In other words, stable, uninterrupted production, based on stable union-management relationships, may be the major requisite to maintaining a strong competitive position in an industry. Wages and other money costs under the labor agreement in many instances may be of secondary importance to management.

A high proportion of labor costs in an industry may limit somewhat, under given product demand conditions, the ability of a union to increase wages. However, the union may be in a better position to extend organization, obtain recognition, and establish wage standards if, in conjunction with management, it helps to eliminate wage and price cutting through a stabilization program which "takes wages out of competition."

The Structure of Attitudes, Reactions, and Beliefs. Another important determinant in the decision-making process is the structure of attitudes, reactions, and beliefs that prevail within the union and management groups. Let us look briefly at a few of the more important elements that influence attitude formation and decision-making.[1]

Both unions and employers are concerned alike about their respective rights, privileges, and opportunities. If these are seriously challenged, or the balance is shifted or changed, feelings of insecurity are aroused which may affect and greatly influence attitudes and actions. Of course, important changes in attitudes often develop out of the bargaining process itself. The reactions of each party to the proposals and counter-proposals of the other tend to influence attitudes and beliefs and to modify the actions of each.

The union as a group, and its individual members, for example, are generally interested in three types of job security. One is the general availability of jobs as a whole. Broadly defined, this is a community-wide problem—one of social security which may be handled in part through collective bargaining but ultimately through broad governmental action. Another is the security of various jobs in the production process. This is primarily a form of security associated with technological change. The third kind of security is individual

---

[1] Space limitations do not permit a systematic treatment of other elements that should also be considered. These include, among others, the interaction of the individual, his group, and other groups; types of leaders, their attitudes and motivations; individual and group goals and ends and the means for attaining them.

possession of the job. This is basically a matter of individual and group rights, power, and control. For security and other reasons, individuals and the group that represents them are actively interested in technological developments that affect the job itself, and managerial methods and policies that affect the handling, promotion, and demotion, transfer, layoff, and discharge of individuals on the job. Similarly, security of management rights, enabling management to manage and discharge responsibilities and obligations which it feels are within its sole jurisdiction, affects intimately and deeply management's structure of attitudes, reactions, and beliefs.

The extent to which individuals in a group achieve expectations which they consider reasonable helps to determine the group structure of attitudes and beliefs. These expectations encompass a whole configuration of demands relating to the physical and mental well-being and morale of group members. They include such matters as satisfactory terms and conditions of employment; adequate opportunities for correction of grievances and removal of dissatisfactions; individual recognition and dignity; effective communication and understanding of common problems; opportunities for participation by the individual and the group in decisions affecting them as a means of providing outlets for creative energy; and satisfying and congenial relations with supervision, with fellow-workers, and with union officials in terms of rights, privileges, and duties.

The achievement of what are considered reasonable expectations is also an indication of the adjustment of the group to the existing economic, social, psychological, and political environment. If the degree of adjustment is unsatisfactory, changes will develop in the group structure of attitudes, reactions, and beliefs. Such changes in turn will influence the action of the group.

THE STRUCTURE OF POWER

The welding together of the union and management systems of decision-making into a relationship which governs the actions of one toward the other forms the second set of characteristics of a labor-management type. If we assume that the labor-management relationship is partly a power relationship, we can address ourselves to such questions as these: Where does the power lie? How is it acquired or from where is it derived? Over what areas does the power of each side extend? How is it used? What are the consequences of its use? These power relationships can be divided into two analytical categories for the purpose of study: (1) the internal power relationships within the management and union groups; and (2) the balance of power between the management and the union. The analysis of the consequences of the use of power is applicable to both of these categories of power relationships.

In discussing the first group of power relationships, for example, we should consider such things as the power of the individual company executives to make decisions. Whom do they have to consult? What pressures are brought to bear upon them? What are the legal or economic limits on the use of this power? What economic factors tend to limit or to enlarge their power? Likewise, on the union side we should look at the power of the union officials with respect to the rank and file, the struggle for control between opposing factions, the prestige of the union with the workers, and effects of the market on the power of particular unions.

An even more crucial problem is the analysis of the balance of power between management and the union. In some union-management types the power of the union is so great that it can force its will upon management. In others management has the upper hand. In still others, the power may be fairly evenly matched. In all cases it is necessary to determine the extent to which one side has the power to initiate action or dictate policy.

TYPES OF LABOR-MANAGEMENT RELATIONS

By focussing attention on these two sets of characteristics —the factors which account for decision-making and the structure of power—it may be possible to distinguish consistent labor-management types.[1] To be sure, the characteristics of these types cannot be defined as *precisely* as the chemist defines the properties of elements. Yet, even where we know only a few of the more important motivations on the union or management side in particular case types, it is possible to find a logical explanation of joint actions taken by the parties and to develop perhaps a reasonably accurate guide for prediction of their future course of action.

For example, in a study of the relationship between the UAW (CIO) and the General Motors Corporation we have found a very clear-cut motivational pattern on both sides. The insistence of the corporation on protection at all costs of its managerial functions has its roots in the conviction that the union is striving to undermine the authority and status of management and has as its ultimate objective the destruction of private enterprise. The union officials who deal with General Motors seem to be convinced that full production and full employment in the automobile industry can never be assured unless social controls are exerted over big business enterprises such as General Motors. These leaders advocate that the union, and if necessary the government, should participate in shaping the major policies of General Motors and the automobile industry to ensure protection of the economic interests of both the workers and the public.

General Motors, accordingly, identifies its tough policy in keeping the union at arm's length with an ideological battle for preservation of free enterprise and the American way of life. The UAW (CIO) identifies its fight for joint economic planning with a crusade to usher in a new era for the common man.

The conflict between the corporation and the union, therefore, is a clear-cut manifestation of a power struggle between those forces advocating unrestricted freedom for private enterprise and those forces advocating some form of planned econ-

---

[1] In preliminary research undertaken by the Industrial Relations Center of the University of Chicago during the past year several different case types have already been analyzed in some detail.

omy. These opposing economic and political philosophies are more than academic beliefs in the minds of the parties. They are connected with the preservation of status and authority, if not the survival, of both the management and union officials involved.

Within such a motivational framework, the union-management relationship appears to be consistent. The corporation looks upon collective bargaining as a means of *containing* the union within the narrow area of wages, hours, and conditions of employment. The union looks upon the collective bargaining agreement as little more than a first step toward social and economic planning. Both sides, of course, have an interest for different reasons in making the contract work. As we might expect, matters such as grievance procedures, seniority rules, working hours, and even wage determination appear to have been disposed of by give and take through collective bargaining. The real conflict, which appears to have no basis of solution, centers on what collective bargaining should be and should include. The clash of interests here seems to color even the day-to-day relationships from top to bottom, and comes into sharp focus in struggles over negotiations of new agreements (as in the strike of 1945–46 over the wage-price-profit issue).

In the cases of two other automobile companies, a small novelty manufacturing concern,[1] and four small steel fabricating companies, we have been able to distinguish other types of labor-management relationships with sharply different managerial and union motivational patterns, resulting in an entirely different kind of collective bargaining.

In the case of the Studebaker Corporation, we find a collective bargaining relationship with the UAW (CIO) of quite a different character from that at the General Motors Corporation. Basically, with respect to money matters, the "big three" of the auto industry, and in particular General Motors,

[1] See *"From Conflict to Cooperation:* A Study in Union-Management Relations," by William F. Whyte and Associates, Committee on Human Relations in Industry, The University of Chicago, published in *Applied Anthropology,* V, No. 4 (Fall, 1946).

set the pattern for Studebaker collective bargaining. This is accepted by both the local union and management as setting the upper limits of union money demands and company concessions.

However, the dependence upon the General Motors pattern ends there. The Studebaker relationship is characterized by cooperation. This company and the local union center collective bargaining on problems rather than on principles. The result is that neither side is concerned particularly about the scope of collective bargaining.

The collaboration between union and company at Studebaker is not based upon dominance of collective bargaining by either one side or the other. Matching the clearly defined management functions or prerogatives which the union recognizes as being the role of management, there is an equally well-developed set of "union prerogatives" which center on job control. Thus, for example, from the union point of view, this local has one of the most satisfactory seniority agreements in the auto industry. In addition, there is a highly developed sense on both sides of the importance of making the union a party to decision-making on factors which affect the work force.

It is clear from our study of this situation that the power balance is fairly evenly distributed between company and union. The corporation stands firm at certain points in its relationship with the union, notably on the question of stabilizing unit labor cost. It has the advantage of being the principal employer in South Bend, and its history within the past fourteen years of having weathered severe financial crises makes clear to the community and its workers the potential insecurity of jobs. On the union side there is considerable evidence that the use of direct economic power in forwarding particular demands is always latent. Both union and management officials have the feeling that strike action or other uses of economic power would be resorted to by the union, given issues of vital concern to the membership.

The result of this relationship is that the company demands

and gets stabilized unit labor costs. Part of this feature of
company advantage results from the incentive system of wage
payment which has recently been extended to cover indirect
labor. A notable aspect of the incentive system is the degree
to which the union participates in its operation. At the same
time the company benefits from the industrial peace which
makes Studebaker unique in the automobile industry in this
regard. The no-strike record is a valuable asset to the company from the standpoint of continuity of operations, and
plays no small role in the public relations program of the
corporation.

From the union standpoint, the strongly entrenched union
prerogatives and the degree of union job control give stability
to the union as an organization. At the same time, the union
can take a long-range view of its relationship with the corporation since it is not continually fighting to maintain its status
and power vis-à-vis the corporation on a daily basis.

To sum it up, within the limits of free action on both sides
of the bargaining table, against the background of the general
forces operating in the economy and over which this local
union and management have no control, fear has largely been
minimized for the Studebaker workers. This has been accomplished through joint company-union action addressed to local
plant problems and the forging of a union-management relationship that is an effective tool in establishing a congenial
atmosphere for their solution.

Although it is possible to classify labor-management relations by types, it is certainly true that some cases are apt to
be unstable. For example, today the labor-management relationship in the novelty company mentioned in footnote 1, page
18, falls into a "union-management cooperation type." Two
years from now, it may have been transformed into one of
labor-management conflict because of a change in the motivations of one side or the other. Accordingly, in analyzing
union-management types, it is important to look for the elements of stability or instability in the particular relationship
being studied.

Varied Types and Their Interrelationships

Up to this point we have discussed merely the tools (methods and concepts) which can be employed in a study of labor-management types. In order to understand the dynamics of labor-management relations we postulate that the labor-management types conform broadly to patterns, and that some types constitute generating centers which have a profound influence on other types. The types fall into three general categories: (1) generating types which have a direct influence on other types, (2) satellite types which are dependent to some extent on generating types, and (3) semi-isolated types which are more or less self-contained.

Let us first consider the generating types. Here are three examples: (1) General Motors and the UAW (CIO); (2) U.S. Steel and the United Steelworkers (CIO); and (3) the bituminous coal industry and the United Mine Workers (AFL). These types of relationships represent great concentrations of power. Through collective bargaining among themselves, and possibly negotiations with the government, the parties determine the wages, working conditions, and conditions of employment of the hundreds of thousands of employees in these basic industries. Literally thousands of other employers and unions in the same or related industries, furthermore, are influenced in their relationships directly or indirectly by the decisions reached in these great labor-management nerve centers. Thus we call these centers of concentrated power "generating types."

In order to determine the structure of power in labor-management relationships throughout the country it is necessary, obviously, to find out where these concentrations of power are, how the power relationship is developed into a workable arrangement between the parties, and the nature and extent of the influence of such centers of power. In itself this will require considerable exploration and research. The three examples cited above are influential national nerve centers. There are other important generating types of labor-management relations which are nerve centers in a particular region, market, industry, or work classification. These are important to study also.

The next task is to study the relationship of satellite types to the generating types. Let us first look at a few examples of satellite types. The relationship between the management of the Studebaker Corporation and Local 5 of the UAW (CIO), although different in very important respects from that existing between General Motors and the International UAW (CIO), is nevertheless dependent on what takes place within the General Motors empire. The base wage rates at Studebaker are set with reference to the General Motors rates. To a large extent the "market climate" for automobiles is determined by General Motors and the other two dominant automobile manufacturing concerns. Broad union policies, furthermore, are determined in no small measure by what concessions can be secured by the union from General Motors.

As a rather unique situation representing cooperation between a union and a large company, the Studebaker relationship does not conform to the General Motors type. Yet, because of its dependent position in the industry, the Studebaker relationship tends to adjust to a climate created by the General Motors relationship.[1] To date we have discovered several different variations of satellite types which adjust in this fashion to generating types.[2]

Finally, recognition must be given to a category which we describe as semi-isolated types. In terms of the economy as a whole or the extent of the market these do not constitute nerve centers or power concentrations. Their influence on other types of labor-management relationships, furthermore, is not very great. At the same time they are not influenced signifi-

---

[1] Our initial studies of labor-management relations in GM and in Studebaker, of course, go into these points in much greater detail.

[2] For example, the relationship between the Jones and Laughlin Steel Corporation and the USA(CIO) bears most of the earmarks of the relationship between U.S. Steel and the same union. In this connection, we have examined in a preliminary way about fifteen different situations in the basic industries which appear to fit into the classification of *conforming* satellite types.

cantly by what happens in the generating types. The relationships between the union and the management are more or less self-sufficient. For example, we have been examining lately the union-management relationship in a small novelty and manufacturing concern dealing with an AFL industrial union. It appears to be capable of settling its own affairs and is relatively immune from the influence of decisions made on the outside regarding such matters as wages, working conditions, union security, or management rights. We have also observed that the very mature type of relationship which exists today in the men's clothing industry is surprisingly self-sufficient and in many respects independent of what goes on in other manufacturing industries.

CONCLUSION

Within the framework outlined in this chapter fundamental research should proceed in two directions. First, there is a great need for case studies of different types of labor-management relationships in which the principal social, psychological, political, and economic factors which determine each individual relationship are carefully analyzed. Such case studies can be conducted in all parts of the country by interested research specialists in industrial and human relations. They should deal with situations in small plants as well as large industrial empires and with relationships between single unions and single employers as well as those involving regional or industrywide bargaining. Second, the development of the concepts dealing with types of union-company relations— generating types and satellite types—calls for the cooperation and combined thinking of many scholars in the field. In this way it will be possible to develop a theory of labor-management relations which should provide a basis for predicting the probable course of such relationships and a guide for recommending appropriate measures for improving them.

The approach which we have suggested can be criticized on many scores. It will be difficult to get reliable interview information on the factors which motivate workers, business managers, and union leaders. It is difficult to classify complex kinds of relationships between unions and employers into types. We will find, furthermore, that such relationships may have a habit of changing type. This approach also calls for interdisciplinary collaboration among scholars and considerable joint planning of research between institutions, which is always difficult. Then, too, we should recognize that it is impossible to determine *all* of the characteristics of any labor-management type, and certainly we will have departed from this world before we can define *all* of the types which exist. It is far better, however, to face up to total problems than to study only neat little facets of problems on which statistics or facts are easily obtainable. As labor economists we have an obligation to attempt to throw some new light on the crucial problems of our time in the field of industrial relations.

CHAPTER **TWO**

Multiple-Employer Bargaining: The San Francisco Experience[1]

by *Clark Kerr and Lloyd H. Fisher*

IN the San Francisco Bay Area,[2] the traditional single-employer agreement is now the exception rather than the rule; the "master agreement" is the predominant instrument of collective bargaining. Three-fourths of the employees covered by labor contracts in the City of San Francisco work under the terms of master agreements. This area is unique not only in the extent of multiple-employer agreements, some of which are also multiple-industry, but also in their intensity of application.

Modern industrial development conduces to large-scale organization. What is a little less obvious, but more central to the present discussion, is that the absence of large-scale enterprise is no obstacle in industrial relations to unitary decisions covering a number of companies. San Francisco, an area marked by the predominance of medium- and small-scale firms, has witnessed unitary decisions in labor relations by management, not through the coagulation of ownership but through deliberate and rational self-organization of separate ownerships. Notwithstanding the fact that the small enterprise is the characteristic San Francisco firm, the areas of labor

[1] The authors wish to acknowledge the helpful suggestions, which they were not always wise enough to accept, made by Rudolph Thumann, General Manager of the United Employers, George Bahrs, President of the San Francisco Employers' Council, and Paul Heyneman, Vice President of Eloesser-Heyneman.

[2] When reference is made in this discussion to San Francisco, it equally applies to the entire industrial area, including particularly Oakland, unless otherwise specified.

and industry that respond to a single decision are large.

It is evident that some of the same problems tend to exist whenever collective bargaining is carried out on a large scale. However, the employers' association differs from the single large enterprise in that it usually acts as a single entity only in matters affecting the labor relations of the constituent firms. Price, production, and marketing policies are more or less independently determined.

WIDESPREAD DEVELOPMENT OF MASTER AGREEMENT

The associational structure which now characterizes collective bargaining in San Francisco has largely developed since 1934.[1] Subsequent to this date the master agreement type of collective bargaining mushroomed into dominance. The particular historical event most closely associated with the modern development of the multi-employer contract was the waterfront and general strike, followed by a period of intense organizational activity by the unions. The waterfront strike was for ends beyond those of the ordinary strike. Its essential aim was to shift job control from employers to union. In this it was successful. It was followed by the "march inland," led by Harry Bridges of the Longshoremen's Union. The unionization drive spreading from the waterfront was paralleled by similar efforts from other centers of union power in the city. San Francisco historically had been one of the strongest centers of trade union influence in the United States. Following 1934, the power and aggressiveness of the union

---

[1] Cross, in his definitive history of organized labor in California, shows the first informal association of employers to bargain with a union in San Francisco was organized in the newspaper industry in 1851 (p. 23). The oldest continuous master agreement in the city was first signed in 1902 between the Draymen's Association and the Teamsters' Union (p. 248). (Ira B. Cross, *A History of the Labor Movement in California* [Berkeley, Univ. of California Press, 1935].) In a study made in 1915, Cross concluded: ". . . it is clear that collective bargaining based on joint or trade agreements was an accepted fact in practically all lines of trade in San Francisco. . . ." (Ira B. Cross, *Collective Bargaining and Trade Agreements in the Brewery, Metal, Teaming and Building Trades of San Francisco, California* [Berkeley, Univ. of California Publications in Economics, 1918], p. 343.) These earlier master agreements, with a few exceptions, were discontinued during the decade 1920–30.

movement expanded, and its strength locally could hardly be matched in any other metropolitan center in the United States.

More specifically, the waterfront stimulated the San Francisco pattern of bargaining. Two of the earliest and most important employers' associations, the Waterfront Employers' Association and the Distributors' Association of Northern California, developed out of relations with the Longshoremen's Union. The San Francisco Employers' Council, the over-all citywide association of employers, was first organized by a shipping company official and the president of the Waterfront Employers' Association. Originated on the sprawling waterfront of San Francisco, this system of employer bargaining quickly spread to other local industries and surrounding areas, and found acceptance.

Contemporaneously with the expansion of union strength came a deterioration in the position of the employer. Union tactics of picketing and conducting boycotts were given greater legal sanction, while employer resort to the injunction and yellow-dog contract was circumscribed. The National Industrial Recovery Act and the National Labor Relations Act placed unionization efforts under public protection. In San Francisco these developments hastened the demise of the San Francisco Industrial Association, a belligerent employers' association of classic type. The San Francisco Employers' Council, the principal sponsor of multiple-employer agreements, was its successor.

The master agreement in San Francisco developed largely because union recognition had become an acknowledged necessity, and the organizational strength of the unions had surpassed that of the individual employers. The strategic position of the employers had deteriorated and the position of the unions improved. The organization of employers' associations was a rational act to prevent a further deterioration, and if possible achieve improvement, in the bargaining position of employers.

The association of employers was a defensive move and the master agreement, in the early stages at least, was a formal expression of this defensive action.[1] One of the primary aims of the San Francisco Employers' Council is stated as: "To promote the recognition and exercise of the right of employers to bargain collectively." [2] In San Francisco, which had an entrenched and aggressive labor movement, employers were fighting for the right to bargain collectively at a time when elsewhere in the United States it was labor which was trying to establish this principle.

One of the most important modern master agreements in the San Francisco area, the contract between the International Longshoremen's and Warehousemen's Union, Local 6, and the Distributors' Association of Northern California, had its origin in a lockout by recently organized employers designed to force the union to bargain collectively with the association. The technique employed was inspired by union tactics. A boxcar was partially loaded by executives of the Woolworth Company. The union proclaimed it "hot." It was sent from one warehouse to another for completion of the loading. As one group of organized workers after another refused to load the "hot car," establishment after establishment closed down, until a virtually complete lockout of all members of the local had been effected. Negotiations were resumed only with the recognition of the association as the bargaining agency for the employers.

A further illustration, among many, was the demand for a master agreement by a newly formed association of hotel and restaurant employers. Here again the issue was a demand that the union recognize the right of the employers to bargain collectively. The aim was to replace another type of multiple-unit "agreement"—the "shop card." The shop card system is a unilateral master agreement under which a well-organized union, commonly although not necessarily craft in

<hr />

[1] Employers' associations have historically been organized initially for purposes of defense. Hoxie, for example, observed: "The employers' association movement was in the beginning primarily defensive." (R. F. Hoxie, *Trade Unionism in the United States* [New York, Appleton & Co., 1920], p. 201.)

[2] San Francisco Employers' Council, *Articles of Incorporation and By-Laws* (1938).

form, sets a price on labor unilaterally. The shop card system is analogous in its essential features to the commodity market with quoted prices. The commodity, in this case labor, is offered at fixed terms. No contract is negotiated and the terms are enforced entirely by the monopoly position of the union. The requirements for the development of a shop card system are a strongly organized union and unorganized or weakly organized employers. The shop card technique is a counterpart of the employer domination of the market, widely characteristic of an earlier period of industrial relations.

The hotel and restaurant employers sought to turn this unilateral system into a bilateral one with a master agreement. The employers' association, availing itself of the absence of a contract, instituted a sharp reduction in wages in all its member establishments when the union struck against a single member, with a guarantee of immediate restoration of the cut upon recognition of its right to bargain collectively for its members. This right was obtained and a master contract signed. The master agreement type of bargaining, however, has been difficult to maintain in this industry for much the same reasons that the shop card was at one time an accepted device. The multiplicity of small, almost itinerant employers, the tradition of "side deals" with individual workers, and the resultant obstacles to group interest, have made an employers' association in this field the least cohesive and permanent in San Francisco. The over-all master agreement has been abandoned and several agreements, negotiated by smaller groups with more homogeneous membership, have taken its place, although many establishments belong to no association. This is one of the few cases in recent times where a master agreement once established in San Francisco has failed to survive.

The master agreement did not appear until after the fundamental question of recognition was settled. It is not easy to conceive of a master agreement developing without the concession that there are somewhat autonomous spheres within the industrial commonwealth and that one of these spheres belongs to labor and another to management. The master agreement is fundamentally a treaty between a group of employers more or less related to one another by common problems and a group of employees bound by certain common interests. In this treaty, as in others, the recognition of sovereignty is implicit.

EMERGENCE OF ADMINISTRATIVE EMPLOYERS' ASSOCIATION

The employers fought to establish the master agreement principally to prevent strong unions from using whipsaw tactics successfully against them by gaining different concessions from different employers, and then standardizing the several separate agreements at the most favorable level of concessions on each individual issue. The master agreement was an "anti-whipsaw" technique as it has generally developed in San Francisco.

One employers' representative has stated the master agreement arose as a result of the decision to "sit it out rather than slug it out." In order to "sit it out" successfully the cost had to be reduced for the employer and increased for the union. The master agreement system achieved this result. "An injury to one is an injury to all" became the motto also of the employers.

The single employer faced with a strike lost his market to his competitors. The union, with the rest of its members working for the competitors, was in a strong position. The unified employers' association, insisting on a master contract, made any strike an industrywide, areawide stoppage. The pressure on any one employer was reduced since all his competitors were likewise shut down, and the union had all its members unemployed and the cost to it greatly increased. The strategy of the employers also included the use of public opinion. Onus for a strike is usually laid at the door of the union, not the employer. If one employer is struck, the effect on the public is likely to be insignificant and little public concern is aroused. An industrywide, areawide strike which shuts down all sources of supply may vitally affect the public. Public opposition to the cessation of the flow of goods or services finds expression in condemnation of the union. The cost to the union again has been increased. The bargaining position of the employers, by lowering their individual costs and raising the costs to the union, is greatly augmented. The master agreement was a strategic device for securing this end result.

Employers' associations, once collective bargaining is accepted, are of two types, or at least of two degrees. There are those more or less formal associations that engage in the negotiation of contracts. The act of mutual identification occurs approximately once a year when representatives of the separate firms comprising the industry, or a substantial part thereof, bargain jointly with the union. The result is ordinarily an agreement expressed in a series of identical contracts executed separately between the individual employer and the union. The loose structure of the employers' organization and the low degree of mutual identification suggest that each employer is explicitly reserving the right to bargain individually, or to negotiate a distinguishing clause which will better meet his own preferences or necessities. This type of negotiatory employers' association appears to result most frequently from a nonmilitant union and nonmilitant employers. It is dependent for survival on this balance of nonmilitancy. If one side alone becomes more militant, it is likely to break down into domination by that side. If both become equally militant, a more complete mutual identification of employers results and a genuine administrative association emerges, constantly on the alert to defend or attack against the union.

This second, more formal type of industry association explicitly adopts the slogan of "solidarity." Like a trade union, its cohesive force stems from the need for united action in the face of a common threat and the conviction that employers must "hang together or hang separately." Obviously the stronger the union, the more persuasive the argument.

San Francisco employers shortly discovered that whipsaw tactics could be used by sophisticated and ingenious unions during the life of a contract, as well as during its negotiation.

Through job action or the processing of individual grievances, improvements in job rates or conditions were obtained from individual employers, and the standardizing process repeated. This changed the character of the association into the administrative type. Joint action, rather than taking place periodically during disputes over contract terms, became constant. The joint negotiating committee gave way to the permanent administrative institution. It is this combination of multiple-employer agreements and administrative employers' associations, united under a joint council, which distinguishes the San Francisco pattern of industrial relations from the customary pattern thus far developed in the United States.

The most influential employers' associations in the San Francisco Bay area are of the administrative type. They feature full-time professional negotiators and labor relations experts for the interpretation of contracts and handling of grievances. A small staff of experts working for the association replaces the industrial relations managers of the individual firms. The professional negotiators, or a small committee working with them, carry the power of attorney for all members of the association and can make contracts binding upon all members. The San Francisco Employers' Council recommends to each of its member associations that a self-renewing power of attorney be granted by the individual firm to the association, subject to formal cancellation only at the expiration of its term.

LOCUS OF DECISION-MAKING POWER

All master agreements involve a shift in the locus of decision-making power. This is particularly true when they are managed by an administrative employers' association. On the employers side, the decision-making function moves from the individual firm to the association of employers, and on the union side from the shop unit or plant unit to the local or perhaps the international.[1] Such shifts in the location of

---

[1] This latter shift in locus of authority occurs without the master agreement, although the master agreement emphasizes the reduction of local autonomy. Shister states: "It has been shown that even where collective bargaining is conducted at the local level, the local in question is not always

decisive authority involve important and difficult problems. They involve the necessity of subordinating individual requirements and choices to some concept of collective welfare and the corollary requirement of developing the machinery for reconciliation of differences among employers and among the several plant units of employees. The effect of centralizing decisions, at least in San Francisco, generally seems to have turned collective bargaining, in a particularly pronounced way, into a political and legal institution, with formal procedures replacing informal ones and institutional relationships replacing personal relationships. Flexible personnel policies are supplanted by a legally defined system of rights and duties. Grievance procedure is vested in professional personnel. Differences of opinion are referred to the final authority of the contract, regardless of other considerations of equity. While these tendencies are evident also in single-unit bargaining, the extension of the agreement to a multi-unit area greatly augments them.

There are distinctions between the employers' association and the constituent employers who compose it. The employers' association acquires an institutional character and an identity somewhat distinct from that of any of its member firms. It becomes interested in its own survival as an institution and must provide against internal conflicts which would threaten its dissolution. Both for the sake of survival and in order to perform its functions best, each association must establish the rules by which common decisions are reached. In San Francisco the majority of associations provide each member with a single vote. There are associations, however, in which voting strength is distributed according to the number of employees or volume of business. In others, a majority vote carries, provided the majority also represents two-thirds or three-fourths of employment or business volume. The last two arrangements appear to occur when one or a few large

completely free in bargaining. Control by the national office, in one form or another, is usually present to restrict the complete freedom of the local." (Joseph Shister, "The Locus of Union Control in Collective Bargaining," *Quarterly Journal of Economics*, LX [August, 1946], 544.)

concerns are found in conjunction with a very substantial number of much smaller concerns, which might otherwise out-vote the dominant enterprise or enterprises. Every effort is ordinarily made, however, to reach decisions by unanimous votes, since complete unanimity is desired in resisting union demands or in supporting a program of action.

Unanimity of action has normally been achieved. This is partly because of the common interest of employers in disputes. Their problem of achieving unanimity is somewhat less than for most unions. Employers are engaged in an attempt to maximize profit over some period of time and this involves an effort to minimize costs per unit, including labor costs. Unions, being primarily political, nonprofit institutions have no such singleness of purpose. Except in the restaurant industry, few employers, once members of associations, have later withdrawn, and few associations have shown outward signs of internal dissension. One test of cohesion has been the efforts of unions on occasions to break associations. Unions have chosen employers who were considered vulnerable because of lack of reserves, the sympathies of their working class customers, efforts to maintain a reputation for "fairness," or chain operations which could be attacked elsewhere simultaneously, and have sought to separate such employers in the hope of securing a favorable bargain with them that could be extended elsewhere. With few exceptions, the associations have met this test of solidarity. In the bakery industry, the entire industry has locked out its employees when one member was struck. In the department store industry, "buycotts" have been organized to offset the effects of picketing on a single store, and member stores have cooperated in recent years to supply items in short supply, such as nylons and white shirts, to any store threatened by union action, leaving it to the public to make the picket line ineffective.

Any tendency of the large firms to dominate or to discriminate against the small firms has not yet been evident. While the associations, regardless of formal voting procedures, have apparently been more responsive to the desires of the more powerful member firms, the smaller firms have not been ignored. The master agreement has not been used as a device to set conditions that they could not meet or that were to their competitive disadvantage. This may be the case in part because the larger firms need the smaller firms. If any large number of small firms were outside an association, the pattern set by them could hardly be resisted by the association if more favorable to the union. Likewise the small firm, weak by itself, finds it advantageous to retreat into the "walled city" of the master contract where protection exists.

On occasion employers' associations have found disciplinary action necessary against recalcitrant members and have vigorously defended their sovereignty. In 1941, for example, in the midst of a hotel strike, one of the major San Francisco hotels, the Sir Francis Drake, withdrew from the association and signed a separate agreement with the union. The San Francisco Employers' Council issued a special bulletin to its members calling upon them to support all picketed hotels and likewise secure the support of their business correspondents. A unanimous resolution of the membership of the Council provided in part as follows:

It further appearing that said Sir Francis Drake Hotel, notwithstanding its solemn commitments to its fellow members of said association, has now in secret negotiations concluded a separate agreement with said unions in spite of said written commitments and its obligations to other members of said hotel association; and whereas the integrity of joint commitments between employers engaged in industry-wide bargaining is absolutely essential to such a system of labor relations;

Now, therefore, be it resolved, that the San Francisco Employers' Council condemn and deplore the action of said Sir Francis Drake Hotel in repudiating its obligations and commitments to other employers, and that this council call upon its members and the public to support in every possible way these hotels which have been prejudiced by the unfair action of the Sir Francis Drake Hotel and who are still resisting the efforts of the unions to encroach upon the right of employers to select suitable employees and to determine their qualifications.[1]

[1] San Francisco Employers Council, Membership Meeting, November 5, 1941.

Within several weeks the Sir Francis Drake changed ownership, was released from its contract by the union, and returned to the association. Such disciplinary action has, however, seldom been necessary.

Cohesion and universality are both compelling needs of
the type of association which has developed in San Francisco.
These associations need cohesion in order to withstand union
attacks. This implies a restricted, well-chosen membership
selected on the basis of strength and uniformity of purpose.
At the same time they must necessarily enroll most, if not all,
of the employers in the same contract area if they are to function best. Otherwise the employers outside the association
can by their actions set the pattern for the organized group.
Subject to these contradictory compulsions the choice usually
has been in favor of universality, with the occasional exclusion of what are known as "weak sisters," provided they are
neither too numerous nor too large. This group of less re-
sistant firms, if party to the association, causes internal conflict and reduced solidarity. The associations also must be
concerned with the "lone wolf" who, while not necessarily a
weak bargainer, prefers to pursue an independent course outside the association.

A literal application of the doctrine "an injury to one is
an injury to all" is seen in the handling of grievances. The
grievance belongs to the association rather than to the individual employer against whom it is alleged. In some associations, settlement of grievances on the plant level is virtually
prohibited. One association representative, asked what kind
of grievances remained within the jurisdiction of the individual employer, replied that the employer would probably be
free to meet a complaint about the condition of toilets but all
other matters would lie within the jurisdiction of the association. This is the counterpart of the union claim that all
grievances filed by individual workers are the property of the
union, for fear that some employee may accept a settlement
which would be unsatisfactory to the union and be used else-

where against it. Similarly the employers' associations seek
to ascertain that no one employer will settle a grievance on
terms unacceptable to other employers.

Mutual identification has proceeded to the point that the
association has sometimes become the sovereign body in industrial relations, and the individual employer exercises only the
functions reserved to him by the association to which he belongs. The San Francisco Employers' Council, sponsor and
chief exponent of the master agreement, has developed a grievance procedure reflecting this premise. When a grievance is
introduced against an employer, an employers' grievance committee is organized from employer members of the association
holding the contract. Any such employer may serve on this
committee, except the employer against whom the grievance is
charged.

This system seems to have reduced the number of grievances to a minimum. Standardization of rates and conditions reduces the possibility of unfavorable comparisons by
employees of one plant with those of another and thus shuts
off an important source of grievances. Likewise the difficulty
of winning a grievance against a single employer, backed by
the association, reduces the inclination to file grievances.

Job evaluation is used in some associations to assure that
no single employer will set standards which the others will be
forced to emulate. Standard job descriptions are prepared for
each position. Contractual rates become maximum as well as
minimum rates for these jobs. The association has the right
to inspect the books of the individual members to ascertain
whether the proper rates are paid for each title. It also has
the right to interview individual employees to determine
whether they are properly assigned to the job titles which
they carry. While these are extreme cases, more frequently
it is only rates for "premium" men and merit increases that
are reviewed.

A further development of the administrative type of association is the weekly or semiweekly conference of association

staff members with the union for constant review of problems arising under the contract. The operation of the contract is under the constant surveillance of the association.

TRADE UNIONS AND THE MASTER AGREEMENT

A trade union is not solely a business enterprise seeking to maximize economic gains. It may have various objects of maximization. In one instance it may be security, in another power or prestige, in yet another the wage rate or the wage bill of the industry or dues payments. A trade union can and does have many ends, and its ends are from time to time quite separate and distinct from those of its members. The trade union is an institution and develops the means for its own perpetuation and advancement with some inevitable disregard for the accidental characteristics of its members at any given moment of time. It plans in terms of preservation and expansion of the institutional structure, and in this respect at least thinks beyond the immediate wants and demands of the membership. It seeks to "build the union." Substitution exists not only between wage and nonwage demands, but between benefits to the union as an institution and to its members as individuals. Union security might be evaluated in a cents per hour equivalent if the relative utilities were measured exclusively by the worker on the job. There is no monetary equivalent to union security for the trade union as an institution.

The employer is not the only threat to the security of a trade union. The trade union may be equally, and often more, threatened by a rival union. Here is clear evidence of the distinction between a trade union and its members. The threat of a competing union is essentially the danger that the membership or some part of it will prefer to be represented by a different union. The prudent trade union takes precautions against such defections. The problem of security involves the organization of a defense against shifts of sentiment on the part of the membership. In the light of this requirement, the master agreement is an effective device. It offers the trade union in its institutional aspect greater security than the single-plant contract.

The National Labor Relations Board is charged with the responsibility for determining the appropriate unit for bargaining purposes and this determines the universe within which the employees vote to select their agent. The history of collective bargaining is among the major determinants of the appropriate unit. A history of bargaining with an employers' association with authority to bind its members to the terms of its agreement is a virtual guarantee that the National Labor Relations Board will designate the multi-plant group as the appropriate unit. This is powerful protection against the incursion of a raiding competitor. When, as in a number of master agreements in the San Francisco area, the bargaining unit consists of more than one hundred plants, the task of organization for the rival union is virtually insuperable. It requires simultaneous organizing effort over an area much broader than the ordinary trade union can manage in order to show a majority of the employees of all the plant units voting for new representation. In this institutional security, during a period of intense rival unionism, lies one compelling reason for union support of master agreements in the San Francisco area. Defeats of organizational attempts by rival unions in the pulp and paper and cannery industries on the West Coast in recent years are notable evidences of this principle.

While the master agreement has this previously unsuspected advantage to the established union in a period of organizational competition, the new union, as well as the rival union, takes a different view. The new union prefers to organize and gain recognition one plant at a time and industrywide employer organization makes this more difficult. The dispute in 1946 between the Retail Merchants' Association of Oakland and Berkeley and the Retail Clerks is an illustration. The Merchants' Association contended that the union must get a majority of workers in thirty affiliated stores before it could negotiate for any employees. The association refused to deal individually with the union, pointed out that it had

master contracts with other unions, and organized support
for the two "victim" stores against whom the union was concentrating its attack.

Economic advantage for the union, regardless of its organizational position, would seem to lie with the individual contract which permits the application of full union force against
single employers. The rapid organization of employers' associations in San Francisco is evidence that the employers, at
least, hold this view. The occasional efforts of unions to split
off individual employers for separate treatment is further evidence. The strike and job action are more costly and less
constantly available weapons against the well-organized employers' association. At the same time, the standardization
which results from the master agreement satisfies certain common trade union notions of equity, although there are reasons
to believe that unions are at least as much interested in the
process of standardization as in the result. Standardization
is commonly a process of upward levelling and provides many
opportunities for the alert and aggressive union. Once
standardization has occurred in San Francisco through the
master agreement, several unions have turned their attention
to standardizing outlying areas at San Francisco levels, using
the master agreement there as the base of operations and the
basis of argument. Administrative convenience in negotiating and administering the over-all contract also recommends
the master agreement to union leadership.

The master agreement, aside from cutting out wage competition, may occasionally lend itself to jointly administered
price collusion with the spoils divided between the collaborat-
ing parties. The mutual advantage lies in higher profits and
wages, at the expense of the consumer. The master agreement
in San Francisco, as developed in the past decade, has not generally had this collusive action as its goal or its result. Collusive
arrangements apparently do exist in San Francisco but they
generally antedate the modern master agreement. Most frequently they have occurred in industries where a strong union
has faced relatively numerous and small employers and has

been instrumental in organizing these employers for the joint benefit of both groups.

Regardless of the balance of good and evil in the master agreement and employer organization from the union point of view, the San Francisco pattern owes so much to employer imitation of union tactics that the unions can hardly in good grace condemn it.[1] While in this case imitation may not be the sincerest form of flattery, the unions are not in a position to condemn employer unionization, the "buycott," the "standard rate," and other devices and policies, without casting doubt on their own pursuits. Although closer to the business union than the reformist union in motivations and tactics, the parallels are sufficiently easy to discern.

Originally opposed to the employer device of the master agreement and the multiple-employer unit because of the unfavorable shift in relative power, the established unions have made their peace with them. The administrative type of employers' association generally renounced the anti-union program of the precedent Industrial Association. The master agreement places a barrier in front of the rival union. On balance, from the union's point of view, these guarantees of institutional security offset the loss in prospect of economic gain.

AREA OF THE MASTER AGREEMENT

Each master agreement has an area over which it is effective. It is larger than the individual establishment but smaller than the sum of all enterprises which conceivably might be signatory. Great variation exists in the effective area of the various master agreements. The principles determining the boundaries of the contract area are not so easy to discern as

---

[1] Willoughby noted this same tendency forty years ago: "As regards methods, it is interesting to note to how large an extent the employers' associations have profited by the experience of the trade unions, and have copied the means of action developed by them. Almost every important feature of trade-union organization finds its counterpart in the employers' organizations." (W. F. Willoughby, "Employers' Associations for Dealing with Labor in the United States," *Quarterly Journal of Economics*, XX [November, 1905], p. 143.)

economic theory might suggest. Accident and union organizational necessities or opportunities have played their part, along with labor market and product market forces.

Geographically the contract area may be identified with the extent of the local labor market or the boundaries within which products or services are competitively produced, or it may exceed both of these. Occupationally the area may be craftwide, or it may be industrywide, including all or nearly all workers engaged in producing the same goods or services, or it may extend beyond both of these limits.

The working of these locational principles is perhaps more important than their identification. From the employer point of view certain arrangements have distinct advantages, so also with the various types of unions. In the San Francisco area, employers have evidenced a distinct preference for industrywide rather than craftwide bargaining. Craftwide bargaining results in jurisdictional disputes and frequently in lack of cohesion among employers. The latter arises because the craft is found in many otherwise unrelated industries and is of varying importance to the several employers. Lodge 68 of the Machinists' Union, for example, supplies machinists to machine shops where they constitute the largest labor cost and also to industrial establishments requiring the services of only one or a few machinists among numerous other workers. The willingness and ability to concede gains to the union varies enormously, and the solidarity of employers in the face of craftwide bargaining is difficult to assure. Similarly employers are opposed to bargaining areas going beyond the workers engaged in producing the same goods or services. Here again, cohesion is hard to attain because of the dissimilar problems and interests of the employers. The employers prefer the industrywide unit since the unifying forces are maximized under those circumstances.[1] The community of inter-

---

[1] Barnett in his study of the failure and survival of the many employers' associations established around 1900 concluded that homogeneity of membership was a prerequisite to survival. (G. E. Barnett, "National and District Systems of Collective Bargaining in the United States," *Quarterly Journal of Economics*, XXVI [May, 1912].)

ests among employers in an industry association is very much wider and the basis for cooperation broader. The industry association often acts as a trade association as well as a collective bargaining agency.

On geographical boundaries the employers have no single choice. Little resistance is met in extending the area to cover the local labor market, since this is recognized as an ideologically acceptable unit and a tendency exists for wages to achieve some uniformity within this area. Efforts to expand the contract area beyond the labor market meet with resistance. One prominent council of employers in Northern California views as its major task the confinement of contracts to labor market areas, and a representative has stated:

It is association policy to negotiate industry-wide contracts within given labor market areas. This is a very controversial point inasmuch as unions are now endeavoring to negotiate over wide areas, which is contrary to our policy. . . . Another objection from the employer's standpoint to this procedure is that it tends to level the rival areas to the highest wage rates in the industry and the metropolitan areas can afford higher wage rates due to their volume than rural areas. . . . The local unions would not have as much voice in the proposals advanced. . . . The different conditions prevailing in the local labor market areas have resulted in agreements more closely suited to the localities.

This resistance is encountered from employers in the lower wage areas, adjacent to San Francisco. The associations in San Francisco, where the higher wages are centered, normally do not strenuously resist, and some individual employers welcome, as a means of equalizing wage rates, the extension of a master agreement to outlying areas, if they are at all competitive in production. This conflict of interests among employers makes a contract area limited to the local labor market unstable where the product market is more extensive. Most, if not all employers, unite in opposing expansion beyond the product market area. Again, cohesion is lost with a reduction in homogeneity of interest. Employers are particularly bitter at the tendency toward nationwide bargaining. The results may not relate closely to the local necessities, and sovereignty is completely extracted from the local area. From the point of view of the employers' association, cohesion based on similarity of economic interest is the basic locational compulsion. The agreement for an industry on a labor-marketwide or a product-marketwide basis seems to meet this requirement best.

The contract area, however, is more determined by union preferences than by those of the employers. These union preferences are more diverse. The craft union is uniquely interested in job competition. The principle to which the craft union adheres in its wage demands, and for which it has gained acceptance among employers, is that of a uniform wage for the craftsman in whatever industrial context he may appear. The definition of a journeyman becomes a controlling consideration, and the individual who qualifies according to this definition receives the set wage regardless of what the product may be. Not even job evaluation systems alter the case. For the well-organized craft is as much outside the influence of a job evaluation system as it is outside the influence of the individual industries or enterprises within which its members work.

The craftwide form of collective agreement derives strength, on the union side, from several sources. The member of a craft union ordinarily is relatively skilled, and substantial control over entrance at the apprenticeship level places the union in a monopoly position. Further, the craft employees of an establishment frequently represent a small minority of the employees, and their wages comprise a small proportion of total costs. It will often appear more prudent for an employer to settle than it would if a larger wage bill were involved. It is also at the craft level that the withholding of function produces the maximum pressure with the minimum application of force. The withdrawal of the work of a handful of craftsmen from among a large working force will effectively close the plant. There is no smaller group, except management itself, whose abstention from productive effort will produce so complete a paralysis.

It is interest in the craft, rather than the product, which is the centralizing force. The craft must be protected within the competitive labor market area. Developments in places external to this area, except perhaps the learning of the craft skill, may be of little local concern. Job monopoly and preservation of bargaining strength are the key concerns of the union and its members. Craftwide, labor-marketwide bargaining and master agreements result.

The industrial union is more concerned with the product market. The members in the higher wage areas within the product market consider lower wages unfair competition and press for wage standardization. Members in the low wage areas consider it improper that they should receive less money for producing the same product to be sold at the same price. Employers in the higher wage areas likewise favor standardization of wages. Product competition becomes the primary force in drawing the lines around the contract area. Because of this comparative mutuality of interest, the industrywide product-marketwide master agreement is the most common type of labor agreement existing in the San Francisco Bay area.

The mutuality of interest in the area of the agreement may under these circumstances spread to other joint concerns. Labor and industry do not always and under all circumstances remain opponents at the bargaining table. Whenever it becomes a relatively simple matter to pass on increases in cost to the consumer, the advantages of resistance are not great. The advantages of cooperation are very much greater when employers bargain through an association with an industrial union and their contract area is coextensive with the area within which products are competitively produced. Joint action can be taken against the new firm, the nonunion firm, the price-cutting firm, the nonmember firm. The reasoning is simple and doubtless appealing. Labor is entitled to high wages. Industry is entitled to adequate profits. Excessive competition adversely affects both. Cooperation in legislative matters is another example of the kind of harmony that can readily develop. This is particularly suitable in industries subject to state or federal law.

It is quite clear that industrywide associations in San Francisco were not generally organized in recent times for this type of cooperative endeavor, and there is no evidence that they contemplate it on any significant scale. Collusive action, however, is intrinsically more possible in one kind of collective bargaining system than in another, and of the various types of collective bargaining, industrywide bargaining covering the product market is the most suitable environment for the development of collusive effort. The principal antitrust actions involving unions in the San Francisco area have arisen out of industry bargaining on a marketwide basis, but usually that has been where dominant unions have welcomed, and even supported, the organization of small and individually weak employers into associations, without which collusive action could not have been taken.

One of the essential guarantees of the National Labor Relations Act is the right of workers to have a union of their own choosing. The exercise of this right may lead to results which are independent of any logic of craft or industry, or of labor market or product market. An aggressive union, driven by a desire for expanded influence, organizing where it can and whom it can, may emerge from an organizing campaign with jurisdiction over a wide variety of enterprises in quite different industries. The employers then, although diverse with respect to product and to sources and types of labor, have one problem in common—defense against the single union with whom each must deal. If that problem seems important enough, the employers may enter into an association for common defense. The Distributors' Association of Northern California is such an association. It includes various types of wholesalers, mayonnaise manufacturing plants, soap and chemical manufacturers, flour mills, and many others. The products are noncompetitive. Labor is at least partially noncompetitive. The sole source of mutual interest is the union. The primary object of the association of the employers is to make the area of employer action subject to a single decision as wide as that of the union. The master agreement arising out of this relationship must of necessity be very general. Until 1944, it provided for only three wage rates—a minimum rate for men, a minimum rate for women, and a rate for foremen, plus a provision that all existing differentials should be maintained.

Three general patterns of contracts thus emerge:

(1) The craftwide, labor-marketwide agreement.
(2) The industrywide, product-marketwide agreement.
(3) The unionwide agreement, based on the area of jurisdiction of a union unlimited by customary boundaries.

Job competition is the keynote to the first, product competition to the second, and union power to the third. The second type is the most common in San Francisco. Some agreements cover coextensive labor and product markets, or industries where all or most workers are likewise members of the same craft. The area of coverage under such agreements seems most stable. The least stable area is that covered by the unionwide agreement, for no bounds exist except the extent and success of the power drive of the union. Economic influences alone are not sufficient to determine the boundaries. Political rather than economic considerations are controlling.

The area of a master agreement is a strategic consideration in the contest between the employers and the union. Where the balance of advantage lies with an area which is neither labor market nor product market, the economic influences emanating from the market will not determine the area. The object of organization is achieved by any area which tends to establish the most advantageous conditions for the more powerful party.

The trend in the San Francisco area has been for the master agreements to cover gradually larger and larger areas. This has political, as well as economic, repercussions. Democracy is more difficult to achieve as decisions are increasingly removed from the individual level. More formal techniques are

required for associating the individual with the final determination. Employer-employee relations become less and less
important. Final decisions may have little to do with a group
of employees and their employer. Problems become more
complex and the individual has greater difficulty and less
opportunity to grasp them.[1]

WAGE DETERMINATION UNDER MASTER AGREEMENTS

Master agreements in the San Francisco Bay area have not
yet had a long enough life to test empirically the kind of economic instruments they are. The majority of the agreements
are less than ten years old and, during the greater part of their
lives, times have been prosperous. How they will work economically in a period of depression has not yet been seen.

Wage bargaining under master agreements relates to the
circumstances of all the firms jointly bargaining, rather than of
the single firm. Reference to the firm's profits, prices, markets,
and prospects is replaced by reference to the prospects of all
the firms, each of them having different claims on its income,
different levels of efficiency, different labor costs per unit of
production, and perhaps different products and different markets. How the needs of the individual firm, particularly the
marginal firm, may be reconciled with the over-all wage possibilities of the industry has not yet been determined. The
problem arises, for the union and association, of where to set
the wage in the ascending scale of ability to pay. Particularly
is this the case in unionwide master agreements where the
member firms produce different articles or services, and labor
costs vary from a small to a substantial portion of total costs.

The alternatives are clear. The wage may be pitched to
the level of the marginal producer. In this case the union
accepts the lowest level that any employer can afford. It is to

[1] Robert J. Watt has observed: "Unless market-wide collective bargaining
is completely democratic in character, it is likely to weaken rather than
strengthen the democratic basis of trade unions. The further removed from
the individual members in the control of the wage for his service or even of
the choice of his negotiating agent, the greater the likelihood of 'top controls' of labor unions." (Trends in Collective Bargaining [New York,
Twentieth Century Fund, 1945], p. 233.)

be expected that powerful support of the marginal enterprise will be forthcoming from inframarginal firms, since the weak profit situation of the marginal establishments is a valuable asset to the inframarginal enterprise wherever a single wage is to be fixed. As a second alternative, the wage may be set above the capacity to pay of the marginal firm, and a number of producers may face extinction unless sufficient improvements in efficiency can be made. The third major alternative is alteration of the master agreement itself by offering special wage concessions to marginal firms. This alternative is the least likely because of the strong emphasis of both organized workers and organized employers on standardization.[1] The unions, largely for reasons of internal politics, favor standardization even though a policy of price discrimination would increase total wage income. The identical problem arises whether the issue is a wage increase demanded by the union or a wage decrease demanded by the association, although the problem may be more acute in the latter case. The member firms of an association are not homogeneous with respect to the wages they will endure, and out of this lack of homogeneity arises the dilemma. The real test will come when the business cycle is no longer on the upswing.

Rather than being concerned with the internal possibilities of the firm or industry, wage determination has depended more on external considerations such as the cost of living and, particularly, relationships with other wages. Relationships, however, are meaningless within the competitive labor market. A uniform wage is already paid within this area, since the contract sets both a floor and a ceiling to wages. This complete uniformity of wages for occupational groups in the community made the War Labor Board doctrine of raising stragglers to the "minimum sound and tested rates" difficult to administer in San Francisco. The stragglers had already been raised and instead of being a safety valve for upward

[1] Lester and Robie in their study of national and regional bargaining have found the same emphasis on wage uniformity. (Richard A. Lester and Edward A. Robie, *Wages Under National and Regional Collective Bargaining* [Industrial Relations Section, Princeton Univ., 1946], p. 91.)

wage pressures, the doctrine became a strait jacket, and the board was subjected to mass pressure to provide wage relief outside the established formulas.

Reference is made principally to wages of related or comparable, but not necessarily competing groups in the same labor market area, and to wages paid for the same occupations in other, noncompeting, labor market areas. The standard comparison in wage determination with the same type of workers in the same area is not available as a guide. The operation of the labor market, except within very broad limits, has little to do with wage-setting. The supply of and demand for the particular occupational group in the same labor market is of relatively little influence except as it sets lower and upper limits to the bargain. The firm and industry adjust to the wage rate, rather than the wage rate being adjusted to the situation of the firm and industry.

Formally defined concepts of "equity" replace market forces. It might be said that, through the system of comparisons, market forces once-removed do influence the wage. But these other markets, particularly for comparable or related workers in the same locality, may also be subject to the same noncompetitive influences. External, rather than internal factors, are particularly influential on wage rates in a master agreement such as that signed by the Distributors' Association of Northern California and the Longshoremen's and Warehousemen's Union, where internal considerations, due to the heterogeneity of the employees and employers, would yield quite inconclusive results.

Wage leadership on a national basis has in San Francisco, as elsewhere, been more important than any other factor since the end of World War II. The bargains made in steel, automobiles, and other large industries have mainly determined local bargains. Whether that will continue to be the case remains to be seen. Wage determination by leading industries on a national basis removes sovereignty from the individual employer and local union much more than the master agreement type of bargaining. Both the individual employer and local union have more control over their own wage destinies under the local master agreement than under national wage leadership. Yet many groups which condemn the former as reducing freedom of action readily accept the latter. Wage leadership, however, also exists on the local level through the system of comparisons described above. A "chain reaction" takes place, with the wage movement spread by formalized processes and in accordance with formal concepts, rather than through its effects on the distribution of the supply of labor. The contract repercussions are important rather than labor market repercussions.

The labor market, stripped of its wage-determining power, still exists as the area within which laborers with fixed residences seek work, and employers seek employees. With wage competition limited or abolished as a means of distributing labor among the firms competing for the labor supply, the question arises as to what takes its place. In some fashion labor must be allocated among the firms, and during periods of manpower shortage the problem is acute. Three means of distributing the labor supply in the absence of wage rate competition have been most used in San Francisco: (1) assignment from a hiring hall, (2) nonwage competition, and (3) variations in the take-home pay. The second means of distribution has given rise to union attempts to standardize the nonwage concessions, however informal they have been, and has aroused the employers' association to place limitations on such concessions.

The effect of the master agreement on flexibility of general wage movements can so far only be viewed during a period of general business improvement, and the effects even then are not clear. Wage rates in San Francisco did rise less rapidly than in almost any other major urban area in the United States during World War II.[1] The San Francisco Employers' Coun-

---

[1] U.S. Bureau of Labor Statistics, "Trends in Urban Wage Rates," *Monthly Labor Review*, LXI (September, 1945).

cil explains this retarded rise by the stabilizing influence of
the master agreement. The statistics, however, are not conclusive since San Francisco was a high wage area at the start
of the war and wages in such areas quite generally did not rise
as rapidly as in lower wage areas. On the other hand, San
Francisco was subject to an unusually great expansion in
manufacturing employment, which placed more than average
pressure on its wage structure. Regardless of the factual evidence, it seems likely that wage changes both upward and
downward would be delayed and reduced by the master
agreement, as compared with plant-by-plant bargaining or
situations where no bargaining exists at all. Collective bargaining interferes with what are considered to be natural
economic processes, and the master agreement, as a highly
developed form of collective bargaining, interferes more than
the less developed forms of bargaining.

The labor market, defined as the geographical area within
which persons with fixed residence seek employment, still
exists, but it has less and less effect on price. Supply and
demand adjust to price, rather than price to supply and demand. Nor does reference to related labor markets return
wage determination to an economic basis, because the relatedness of labor markets is increasingly the relatedness of organizations, policies, and ideas of equity.

One "seller" of labor faces one buyer of labor. Even if
bilateral monopoly were shown to have a determinate solution
for commodity markets, it would still be indeterminate in labor
markets because of the importance of noneconomic objectives.
In fact, reference to analysis of bilateral monopoly may only
serve to confuse the situation, since it assumes that the seller
is interested in both price and quantity but in little else,
whereas unions, in the short run at least, are generally little
concerned with quantity. It is more important to inquire
how a political body, subject to many pressures, only one of
them the volume of employment, fixes a price. This is almost
as much a problem in politics as in economics. In order to
use profitably the concept of bilateral monopoly, it is necessary

to assume, as Dunlop does,[1] that a trade union acts on the model of a profit rather than a nonprofit institution and endeavors to maximize the total wage bill, an assumption which is seldom valid. Its interests usually lie far more with rates than with aggregate sums.

EFFECT ON LABOR DISPUTES

The development of the master agreement in San Francisco has had a decided and determinable effect on labor disputes. The decline in strikes is attributed by the San Francisco Employers' Council to the widespread adoption of this system of collective bargaining:

As a result of strong organization on both sides and the recognition of the consequences of a strike, strikes in San Francisco are comparatively rare. We do not have any little strikes or quickie strikes. The only strikes we have today are products of the calculated, deliberate decision of both sides that the issues are sufficiently important to justify the punishment that all parties will have to take.[2]

Strike statistics do show a comparative decline in number of strikes in San Francisco relative to Los Angeles and the United States, beginning with 1934 when the associational system of collective bargaining began to emerge. For San Francisco the average length of strike, the persons involved per strike, and total man-days lost per strike have, during the same period, all risen. Total man-days lost per year as a result of strikes have remained relatively constant.

Because of the greater organizational strength on both sides, a strike or lockout once started is likely to last a long time and involve many people. Once the cost of such controversies is realized, the parties make greater efforts to settle without resort to strikes or lockouts. Increased cost leads to increased advance deliberation. Presumably the continued

[1] John T. Dunlop, *Wage Determination Under Trade Unions* (New York, Macmillan Co., 1944), Chapter 3.

[2] George O. Bahrs, President, San Francisco Employers' Council, in an address, Phoenix, Arizona, April 9, 1946.

realization of the expenses of conflict may, as has been true in
Sweden and Great Britain, work to reduce the resort to force
still further in the future, so that not only will the number of
strikes be reduced but also the over-all man-days lost annually.

Aside from the changing character of strikes, a further
effect on labor disputes has been the expanding use of voluntary arbitration. Considering the size of the area, probably
no other city in the United States compares in the constant
use of arbitration in primary disputes. The adjudication by
a third party of the terms of a new contract is more widely
accepted as standard procedure in San Francisco than in any
other part of the nation.

Under multiple-employer bargaining, strikes and lockouts
are particularly costly, and the "just price" is harder to ascertain through negotiation, since ready reference to market rates
is no longer possible. Likewise, the larger bargaining units of
workers and employers, with their diverse components, may
lead the executives to prefer adjudication by an outsider to
voluntary acceptance of what some of their clientele might
consider an unfavorable bargain. The arbitration process,
possibly because of the pattern of collective bargaining and
the importance of precedents, is highly legalistic and formalistic.

While from the point of view of organized industry and
organized labor the single large strike may be preferable to a
series of small strikes, this is not the reaction of the general
public. The single large strike is administratively easier to
handle for industry and labor than a constant stream of little
strikes. Both business and the unions compare favorably the
postwar experience of San Francisco with that of Detroit,
where production processes and employment continuity have
both been upset by the constant resort to minor strike actions.

The community, on the other hand, has greater capacity
to absorb a number of smaller stoppages than a single large
one.[1] Many single bakeries or meat markets may be shut

[1] Sumner H. Slichter has questioned the general advisability of industrywide bargaining on these very grounds. (*Trends in Collective Bargaining*,
pp. 232-33.)

down one at a time without too great public inconvenience, but the public is seriously concerned when all meat markets or all bakeries close simultaneously, as happened in 1946 in San Francisco. Public injury by strikes is likely to lead to public control of strikes. This fear of public control, however, may itself serve to reduce the number of large strikes, and thus make control less likely, just as fear of unfavorable repercussions from the bad strike reputation of San Francisco following 1934 encouraged both labor and industry to reduce their open strife for the sake of the economic expansion of the community. Whether the master agreement will reduce the immediate impact of strikes on the public as it has reduced the number of strikes, remains to be seen. If not, the day of public control of industrial relations is brought that much closer. The inability to reach agreement ceases to be a private disagreement and becomes increasingly civil conflict.

SAN FRANCISCO EMPLOYERS' COUNCIL
AND UNITED EMPLOYERS (OAKLAND)

The organization that most aggressively sponsors the administrative type of association and the master agreement is the San Francisco Employers' Council.[1] Organized in 1938, it united a number of pre-existing industry associations which had already evolved the general philosophy and strategy. It is comprised of member associations and individually affiliated firms. Altogether over two thousand enterprises are indirect or direct members.

The council is the chief spokesman for employers in San Francisco. It carries on over-all relations with its two opposites, the Central Labor Council (AFL) and the Industrial Union Council (CIO), and represents employers before governmental authorities and the public. It provides its members

[1] In the terminology of Hilbert, the council is a "general association." However, the council does not conform to Hilbert's conclusion that general associations "are not designed for collective bargaining, but for a reactionary destruction of the unions, and a return to the old system of individualism." (F. W. Hilbert, "Employers' Associations in the United States," *Studies in American Trade Unionism*, edited by Jacob H. Hollander and George E. Barnett [New York, Henry Holt & Co., 1906], p. 183.)

with legal, research, negotiating, arbitration, and informational services.   Through it the general strategy of the employers is planned.   A uniform areawide approach to concessions demanded by labor is attempted, with resistance encouraged wherever one industry or one firm contemplates concessions that the rest of industry in San Francisco is not prepared to grant.

The philosophy of the council on industrial relations was stated by its first president as follows:

Collective bargaining is primarily a pressure game.   Labor unions have been effectively organized into city-wide councils and national organizations.   By and large they are well staffed and financed. They have definite programs and objectives, and they are eternally on the job to secure concessions for their members and to strengthen their positions. . . . When one is engaged in a pressure game with a competitor who is well organized and financed and knows where he is going, it is simply good common sense to meet organization with organization, and this is exactly what we propose to do in San Francisco through the agency of the San Francisco Employers' Council.   In the vernacular of the waterfront, we expect to "Match Heat with Heat." [1]

The council was not intended to combat organization by labor, but to organize employers to bargain with organized labor:

Essentially, the new Council provides a means for city-wide mutual cooperation of employers and employer groups in employer-employee relations.   It seeks to promote sound industrial relations founded upon collective employers' strength comparable to the strength of organized labor. [2]

Group action was to replace individual action:

. . . the great majority of employers in San Francisco have abandoned any hope of dealing with labor unions on the basis of rugged individualists who do not require the aid of their fellow employers. Whether we like it or not we have reached the point where we are prepared to admit that the rugged individualist has largely passed from the San Francisco labor relations picture. [3]

[1] Almon E. Roth, *Objectives of the San Francisco Employers' Council* (New York, American Management Association, 1939.)

[2] *Ibid.*

[3] *Ibid.*

The United Employers is the comparable federation of employers on the Oakland side of the Bay. In 1938 an "Oakland Plan" was advanced which envisaged a mediatory association with representation from industry, labor, and the public. When it failed to develop, largely through lack of support by the unions, the United Employers was established. Six hundred firms are now members of the association. It states that it:

operates on the principle that any labor matter concerning even the smallest employer has community-wide significance. Like the fire department, United Employers functions, often without publicity, as a protective force—putting out the small flame before it becomes a conflagration. . . . A commitment made under pressure or through lack of knowledge of what other employers have done may establish a "prevailing practice" in future employer-employee relationships, not only in that business or industry but for the entire community. Such a risk is too great for one individual to assume.[1]

The United Employers serves as the employers' "business agent"[2] and performs the following functions, among others: (1) negotiating and drafting labor agreements, (2) handling grievances, (3) interpreting state and federal laws, (4) preparing job evaluation and incentive plans, (5) providing informational services, and (6) conducting research. "The organization does not indulge in labor-baiting tactics nor does it fight labor except in defense of its members."[3]

From San Francisco and Oakland the plan for areawide general associations of employers to bargain with unions has spread to adjacent areas in Northern California. A Northern California Council now unites nine similarly organized associations. More recently, councils patterned after the San Francisco experience have been established in Reno, Phoenix, and Los Angeles. A Pacific Coast Council has been established.

Increasing acceptance in the region has served to arouse opposition elsewhere. The administrative employers' association has been condemned by belligerent anti-union associations, and also by those groups in industry which oppose any

[1] United Employers, *United Employers,* 1947.
[2] *Ibid.*
[3] *Ibid.*

multiple-employer bargaining. A representative of the National Association of Manufacturers has stated: "To my mind, nothing is more damaging to good labor relations than industry-wide bargaining." [1] The master agreement, the administrative employers' association, and the areawide employers' council are viewed essentially as socializing and collectivizing influences. According to this philosophy, they facilitate government control, eliminate wage and possibly price competition, and can be used as instruments for destroying the small firm. [2] However, in a day when wage leadership by large firms and joint informal action by employers is so well developed, the more formal organization of the San Francisco type is perhaps no more distant from pure competition in fact, regardless of how it may appear in theory, than is so-called "free enterprise" in industrial relations. The strong predilection for "individualism" in labor relations may actually mean no more than a mere lack of formal organization.

Some local employers, members of associations, while convinced of the necessity of collective action, regret its effect on employer-employee relations. They no longer can deal directly with their own employees and consider that this reduces the morale of their working group. What is gained through lower money costs per hour is in part lost by lower production. Informal man-to-man, personal relations, according to these employers, are replaced by formalized group relations. Personnel managers in plants frequently oppose the system for this reason, and also because it tends to reduce their functions to those of an employment manager.

If the San Francisco pattern continues to expand its influence, the conflict between the opposing schools of thought may become more pronounced. The San Francisco Employers' Council patterned its program in part after the Swedish

[1] Ira Mosher, San Francisco Labor Relations Conference, October 10, 1946.
[2] A further, although unexpressed, reason for opposition to the master agreement may be the belief of some employers, noted by McCabe, "that an industry-wide agreement cements into the industry a union that might otherwise be got rid of." (David A. McCabe, "Problems of Industry-Wide or Regional Trade Agreements," *American Economic Review*, XXXIII, Supplement [March, 1943], 169.)

and British experience, where formal group action by employers, coupled with acceptance of trade unionism, is the accepted practice. The traditional pattern in the United States has been individual action by the employer, or, if group action, either by the belligerent association or by relatively informal group negotiation. Notable exceptions to this pattern have existed. The system spreading out from San Francisco is one of the exceptions, and places the difference in approach almost on the ideological level. The San Francisco Employers' Council has renounced individualism in industrial relations. This renunciation has been strongly condemned in favor of a continuation of the more traditional approaches.

SUMMARY AND CONCLUSIONS

1. Multiple-employer bargaining is now the standard pattern in San Francisco. Employers are organized in administrative associations, which manage as well as negotiate contracts. Master agreements are signed between these associations and the unions. Over-all confederations, the San Francisco Employers' Council and the United Employers (Oakland), unite the various industry associations.

2. This associational structure of collective bargaining has developed primarily since 1934 when dominant power shifted to the trade unions. The employers organized in defense, with the master agreement as one of their tactics.

3. The established trade unions have accepted the master agreement, partly because it gives them security from the attacks of rival unions, although their relative bargaining power against the employers has been reduced.

4. This associational type of collective bargaining has not generally resulted in collusive action against the consumer. Nor is there any evidence that small firms have suffered. Rather they are given greater consideration in final decisions than under the contract leadership form of bargaining.

5. The administrative form of employers' association does, however, reduce the sovereignty of the individual firm in industrial relations. For the sake of bargaining strength, the

individual employer sacrifices the right to determine labor policy in his own plant. The influence of the local unit of the union also is reduced.

6. The San Francisco pattern has been attacked, in part for these reasons, by the principal organization of industrialists in the United States. Two of the objections, at least, have not generally materialized in San Francisco—elimination of price competition and destruction of the small firm.

7. The area of the agreement tends to conform to the local labor market in the craftwide type, the product market area in the industrywide type, and the dominion over which the union exercises power in the unionwide type.

8. Strikes have been reduced in number but have increased in the severity of their direct public impact. Increasing maturity of relationships may later come to reduce strikes sufficiently so that the effect on the public is also lessened. Arbitration of primary disputes has been widely used.

9. Wages are relatively little influenced by the supply of and demand for competing groups of workers in the local labor market. The manipulation of power and formalized concepts of justice have replaced atomistic market forces in determining the price of labor. Wages have become less flexible, at least in the upward direction.

10. The bargains, made over a larger area, are based on more careful deliberation, and consideration is given to the effects on larger groups of workers and employers. Industrial relations become more a study in political economy and less one in pure economics, as the area of the bargain grows and unitary decisions replace market forces.

11. The San Francisco pattern has been spreading up and down the Pacific Coast and eastward. It has developed during a period of governmental protection of unions and rising prosperity, and in an area where unions are unusually strong and aggressive. Whether it will survive under the strain of a depression or during a period when unions do not have the active support of the federal administration, or can be extended to areas where unions are less influential, remains to

be determined. Experience in Great Britain and Sweden, at least, would indicate that the long-run future may be with the type of collective bargaining developed in San Francisco rather than with the more traditional, single-company pattern largely dominant elsewhere in the United States.

CHAPTER THREE

Grievance Proceedings and Collective Bargaining

by *Neil W. Chamberlain*

LITTLE attempt has been made in the literature that has poured forth on the subject of collective bargaining to explore systematically the structural niceties of industrial government. In no aspect of the subject has this been more true than in the determination of the relation of grievance proceedings to collective bargaining.

The lack of systematic exploration of the subject may be due to the fact that collective bargaining has only recently become a generally adopted method of settling industrial disputes in this country; or that its widespread imposition upon management has necessitated a fundamental revolution in managerial thinking; or that there have been so many other more pressing problems requiring immediate solution in the smoothing of industrial relations in the last ten years. Another important reason, however, is a distinct reluctance by many to consider the need for any formalization of the union-management relationship, in however slight a degree or for whatever purpose. This reluctance is at the same time understandable and unfortunate. It is understandable in so far as it is based upon a desire to keep the relationship flexible and devoid of rigidities, to emphasize that it is essentially a system of mutual accommodation in the day-to-day process of living together in the working world. It is unfortunate to the extent that it precludes careful thinking of the requirements for achieving that harmonious working relationship which is the objective.

DIFFICULTIES OF DEFINITION

Let us plunge into the problem with a glimpse at the grievance procedure. The grievance procedure is commonly established by the collective labor agreement. Through it are funneled most disputes arising subsequent to the signing of the agreement. The usual grievance machinery provides for submission of a worker's grievance first by a shop steward to the shop foreman, then, in the event of an unsatisfactory settlement, by the local union grievance committee to the general foreman or department head, perhaps next by the local committee to the personnel manager, and if still the disputants are dissatisfied, by the national union officials to the company management. Increasingly, disputes unsettled at this stage are referred to an "impartial chairman" or arbiter who makes final disposition of the case. Where does this scheme of disposing of controversial issues fit into the union-employer relationship?

The basic question concerning grievance proceedings is whether this relationship is to be considered as part of the collective bargaining process, or whether it shall be considered as a relationship to be distinguished from the bargaining process. Stated in these terms the question appears largely one of definition, smacking of the formalism to which such strenuous objection is frequently raised in the area of industrial relations. Much more than definition is involved, however. At issue is the broader problem of functional powers and responsibilities.

A reluctance clearly to define terms in the field of industrial government was initially displayed in the National Labor Relations Act itself when the term "collective bargaining" did not appear among the eleven definitions of the act requiring it. In the case of collective bargaining, the more vocal element among those concerned with industrial relations has contended either that everyone knows what is meant by the term, or that the proper procedure is to hammer out a definition on the anvil of experience, bit by bit. These same viewpoints hold true with respect to the definition of grievance proceedings. Despite such assertions, it is simply not true that general agreement exists as to the relation of grievances to the collective bargaining process unless one picks his authorities. Nor is it true that an attitude of "let developments take their course" is necessarily the most desirable in an effort to establish the framework of industrial order.

A proper definition of grievance proceedings necessarily requires a prior definition of collective bargaining. Here, at the outset, we encounter major difficulties in achieving a generally acceptable understanding of terms. For one thing, the concept "collective bargaining" has lost all literal meaning. It has been used to embrace situations involving a single workman and his employer, as well as systems of arbitration involving judicial determination rather than horse-trading by the parties.

Without doubt one reason that it has been difficult to arrive at a generally acceptable and significant definition of collective bargaining is the lack of agreement and understanding as to the nature of the process. Competent students of labor problems have referred to bargaining as a treaty-making process between sovereign powers, apparently unmindful of the fact that neither party is sovereign since each exercises jurisdiction, concurrently with the other, over at least one identical constituency, and since each is functionally impotent without the other.

A more tenable position has been assumed by some of the foremost labor economists who see collective bargaining as a system of industrial government: contract negotiations form the legislative branch, the grievance procedure supplies the judicial process, while the official families of the respective parties provide the administrative and executive functions. This conception of collective bargaining is scarcely that premised by the National Labor Relations Board, however. For such a view of the meaning of collective bargaining necessitates the existence of an agreement or contract establishing the industrial government, and the board has specifically denied that the process of collective bargaining obligates agreement.

We may accept these two points as being something in the nature of polar definitions. On the one hand, collective bargaining is conceived as simply laying down the terms of relationship. On the other hand, collective bargaining is considered as the whole system of devising those terms, administering them, and adjudicating differences arising under them—in short, the union-management relationship in whatever form it appears. The conclusion which will be reached in this analysis is that it is not really material which point of view is adopted so long as there is a full and complete recognition of the implications flowing from the definition.

THE NATURE OF INDUSTRIAL DISPUTES

Perhaps the simplest way of approaching the problem is to isolate the various types of disputes which may develop between the union and the management. These are basically four, which may be differentiated as follows:

(1) Disputes as to the terms of relationship.
(2) Disputes as to who shall apply the terms of relationship.
(3) Disputes as to the correctness or justice of the application of the terms of relationship.
(4) Disputes as to whether a term of relationship exists which may be applied.

If a working harmony is to be established between the organized employees and the management, some machinery for resolving all four of these types of disputes must exist. Whether such machinery shall be *called* collective bargaining, grievance procedure, contract negotiations, arbitration, or any other name is immaterial, so long as the function and purpose of the machinery are clearly established. The use of such names does become important, however, if one person uses, to identify a functional process, some term which to another person stands for a process with a completely different function. Unfortunately, we find ourselves in just such a situation at the present time. It is essential, therefore, that we examine these various types of disputes to determine what functional process is required to dissolve them. Terminology we may worry about later.

Disputes as to what shall constitute the terms of relationship are disputes over matters of interest. These are issues arising between the union and the management which can be resolved by no appeal to mutually accepted standards, to law, or to prior agreements. It is the very absence of mutual standards and agreement which evokes the dispute. Any arbiter who has worried over the size of a wage increase which he shall award is only too well aware of this absence of any such agreement as to the basis for decisions. To what extent shall the profit position of the company be considered, or the cost of living, or the hazards or physical demands of the job, or the competitive position of the company, or the scale of wages paid elsewhere in the industry for similar types of work, or the level of wages in the community, or the manpower requirements of the company? There is no common determinant. If this is true of wages, it is equally true of all the other terms of relationship which may be found in any collective agreement. The terms are accepted only after a process of compromise, economic coercion, and persuasion. In the field of government, this process is known as legislative. The result is law governing conduct. In business, it is more commonly referred to as policy formulation or decision-making. The result is exactly the same.

Disputes as to who shall apply the terms of relationship are concerned with the administration or execution of the agreement. Some terms may be executed by managerial representatives; for example, dismissals on the basis of seniority standards as laid down in the agreement. Other terms may be executed by union representatives; for example, the supply of workers under a closed shop provision. Still other terms may be mutually carried out; for example, the effectuation of safety standards by a joint committee. In order that terms agreed upon shall be put into practice, and that authority and responsibility for their execution be clearly granted and accepted, there must be an understanding between the union and management as to where such authority and responsibility have been placed. Without this location of the administrative or executory functions the terms of relationship become virtually meaningless. With confusion as to their location, friction and disagreements are certain to arise. Decisions as to where administrative and executive authority and responsibility shall be lodged are part of the policy-making process. No policy statement is complete unless it carries provisions for its application. Decisions as to placement of administrative or executive power are therefore only one aspect of the general process of establishing the terms of relationship. Disputes concerning such decisions may be resolved by that same functional process. They too are legislative or policy-formulating in nature.

Disputes as to the correctness or justice of the application of the terms of relationship involve an appraisal as to whether the persons designated to administer or execute the agreement are performing those functions in accordance with its terms and spirit. One party may feel that actions taken by the other are not protected or sanctioned by the agreement reached, and may indeed be violative of the agreement. The other party may claim privilege or right by its own—variant—construction of a contract provision. Here the question is one of interpretation and of measurement of the action complained of against the standard established in the agreement. This standard, it is to be noted, is one which has been mutually accepted. The action disputed may therefore be judged on the basis of commonly established rights, privileges, and powers. In government this function is called judicial. In business it is frequently known as compliance. The purpose in both cases is the same: to determine whether in practice there has been adherence to the law or policies prescribed.

Disputes as to whether a term of relationship exists which may be applied are frequent in the field of industrial relations. Essentially, they involve a determination of whether actions taken are within the scope of the agreement. In this respect they cannot be distinguished from those problems which are resolved by the judicial function. The determination, however, may establish that the dispute is in fact covered by the terms of the agreement, in which event there is the additional judicial question of whether the action conforms to the provisions of the contract. On the other hand, the decision may establish that no terms exist by which the action may be judged. In this event the dispute can be resolved only by the agreement-making process. Disputes as to whether a term of relationship exists which may be applied are therefore judicial questions as to jurisdiction, and ultimately are either judicial or legislative questions in substance.

The four types of disputes arising between unions and management may thus be resolved by two functional processes —legislative (or policy-making) and judicial (or compliance). The former is used to resolve disagreements as to the terms of relationship, including questions as to who shall apply those terms. The latter operates to settle differences as to whether the terms have been complied with, or whether terms exist by which compliance may be judged.

If this analysis seems too formalistic and forbidding for application in the field of industrial relations, that objection may be countered by asking just what purpose the collective agreement serves. If it is intended to establish terms to which both parties mutually consent to conform, that purpose can be achieved only by making the above distinctions. If compliance is confused with policy formulation, no stable contractual relationship exists. No rights would be established by the contract, no executive authority bestowed, that could not be altered by a noncompliance conceived of as a right of policy-making. Without law and the enforcement of law, or policy and the application of policy, anarchy would result in the industrial as in the political world. We shall revert in more detail to this proposition later. It is brought up at this point only to establish the importance of distinguishing between these two functional processes in industrial relations.

CONFUSION ON THE TERMINOLOGICAL FRONT

The question may now be faced as to where collective bargaining and grievance proceedings fit into the picture as processes performing one or both of these functions. Here we run head-on into confusion and disagreement. There is in fact no broad acceptance of the functional content of these terms. Collective bargaining has been used as the symbol to identify one of these processes (the legislative or policy-formulating) and has also been employed as the symbol to identify them both. In the latter use, it has often been considered as an "umbrella" covering both the legislative and judicial functions though the distinction between those functions has been understood. On the other hand, grievance proceedings have sometimes been accepted as the term for one of the two functions (the judicial or compliance), while at other times it has been used to cover them both—many times without an appreciation as to their distinction. Moreover, grievance proceedings have been identified with collective bargaining—in some cases as constituting a form of collective bargaining, in other instances as simply a synonym.

Let us then dispose of the notion that there exists among the "authorities" any uniformity of opinion as to the relation of grievance proceedings to collective bargaining. It is more nearly correct to say that a sharp disagreement prevails on this question. Of forty-two representatives of companies and labor unions questioned on this point, twenty-four maintained that grievance proceedings were a form of collective bargaining; twelve thought they were, rather, a method of adjudication to be distinguished from collective bargaining as a method of policy-making, and the remaining six considered that such proceedings involved collective bargaining in the sense of policy-making, as well as adjudication. These answers simply illustrate the existing confusion.

It is interesting to note that more union agents than company representatives lumped collective bargaining and grievance proceedings together, while more company than union officials sought to differentiate them. Such a divergence in views between company and union representatives does not lead to the conclusion that a distinction between bargaining and grievance functions is a "union-busting" device, however. It seems probable that the more prevalent union view is a result of a traditional approach coming down from the period when the signed agreement was rare and acceptance of the union even rarer. The company attitude, on the other hand, probably stems from a desire "to know where we stand" and hence a desire to preserve the contractual boundaries of union and management rights for the period specified in the agreement.

It is instructive to examine some of the expressions of opinion of these negotiators.

Collective bargaining is a question of taking up the grievance on the job. It is the day-to-day relationship. The two weeks or so of contract negotiations are only to determine how you are to bargain collectively during the other fifty weeks. (Member of the executive board, Amalgamated Clothing Workers.)

It is my experience that you do more bargaining in grievance proceedings than in negotiations for a contract. (Industrial relations director for a "Little Steel" company.)

As far as grievances are concerned in regard to a contract, I feel these are more a matter of adjudication than collective bargaining. Where grievances are committed in a certain department by a certain person, or certain circumstances, and a complaint is made by an employee through the proper parties, according to the contract, I feel that the final outcome of the grievance is purely a matter of adjudication, in regards to the terms of the labor contract involved. (President of a food processing company.)

Collective bargaining, in my opinion, is the procedure of having the representatives of the Union membership bargain on behalf of the membership for wages and conditions relative to their work. Grievance procedure, rather, is the enforcement of the provisions of the Working Agreement and when matters arise which are not covered by the Agreement other courses are followed—one of arbitration and the other a strike to enforce the economic demands of the Union. (Secretary-treasurer of a teamsters' local union.)

Grievance procedure is a form of collective bargaining, but distinguished from contract negotiations as a form of collective bargaining. (International president of a craft union.)

I would say that grievance procedure should be a form of adjudication although in practice it is frequently more closely related to collective bargaining. (President of a cement company.)

This same confusion is evident in the administration of the National Labor Relations Act. The board has moved toward the position that grievance proceedings are not only a part of collective bargaining but in fact they are identical and indistinguishable. The clearest expression of this view is perhaps to be found in *Matter of Hughes Tool Company*.[1] After weighing the respondent company's action in dealing with individuals and a minority group on particular applications of an existing collective agreement (grievances), the board ruled: "We are convinced, upon a consideration of all the facts, that the appropriate remedy in the circumstances of this case is to order the respondent to bargain collectively with the union."

In this case, the board adopted the intermediate report of the trial examiner with only minor qualifications. Because of the significance of the issues raised, it is worth citing from that report:

It is not questioned that the Union, having been designated by a majority of the employees in an appropriate unit, is the exclusive representative for the purpose of collective bargaining of all the employees in that unit. It is contended, however, that the grievances settled by the respondent without consulting the Union are something separate and apart from collective bargaining. This contention, in the undersigned's view, is without merit. There is no distinct cleavage between collective bargaining and the settlement of grievances whether individual or group. . . . Since, as already noted, *there is no real distinction between collective bargaining and the settlement of grievances,* the respondent's practice of settling grievances with individual employees, groups of employees and the representatives of minority groups constitutes conduct

---

[1] 56 NLRB 981 (1944). See also *Matter of U.S. Automatic Corp.,* 57 NLRB 124 (1944).

proscribed by the language of the Act and the above-cited judicial
pronouncements concerning the Act.[1]

This view of the board as to the inseparability of collective
bargaining and grievance proceedings did not withstand court
examination. The Hughes case came up before the Fifth Cir-
cuit Court of Appeals which, while confirming the board's
cease and desist order, did so only upon condition of its modification to order the company to cease and desist *from adjusting grievances* without calling in the majority representative.
In its opinion, the court took pains to deny the board's doctrine
of the identity of collective bargaining and grievance proceedings and to chide the trial examiner for having misconstrued a
previous ruling of the same court on the same question. For
its contrast with the board's doctrine, the court's opinion is
condensed below:

Taking the quoted provisions [of Section 9(a) of the Act] together,
it is plain that collective bargaining in respect to rates of pay,
wages, hours of employment and other conditions of employment
which will fix for the future the rules of the employment for everyone in the unit, is distinguished from 'grievances,' which are usually
the claims of individuals or small groups that their rights under the
collective bargain have not been respected.[2] These claims may

[1] 56 NLRB 992, 993. Italics added.
[2] The following footnote of the court appeared at this point: "To support
the idea that grievance and collective bargaining are the same thing, the
Board quotes this court, *Humble Oil and Refining Co.* v. *National Labor
Relations Board,* 113 F. 2d 85, 87, as saying: 'So long as a majority of the
employees in each plant freely choose to belong to or be represented by the
Federations they are the bargaining representatives and the contracts they
make cannot be ignored. Minority groups may separately present their
grievances, but must submit to bargain through the majority representatives.'
Grievances were not confused with bargaining, but contrasted. This court
very plainly indicated in its view that the collective bargain was one thing,
and the personal grievance arising under it another thing, in *Moore* v. *Illinois
Central R.R. Co.,* 5 Cir., 112 F 2d 959. The cases cited by the Board from
the Supreme Court, *J.I. Case* v. *National Labor Relations Board,* 321 U.S.
332, 64 S. Ct 576; *Railroad Telegraphers* v. *Railway Express Co.,* 321 U.S.
342; and *Medo-Photo Supply Corporation* v. *National Labor Relations Board,*
321 U.S. 678, 64 S. Ct. 830; all deal with making contracts, not with adjusting grievances. They hold there can be no contracts made except through
the bargaining representative. They say nothing on the subject of personal
grievances. In *Steele* v. *Louisville and Nashville R.R. Co.,* 65 S. Ct. 226, the

involve no question of the meaning and scope of the bargain, but only some question of fact or conduct peculiar to the employee, not affecting the unit. They may, however, raise a question of the meaning of the contract, or present a situation not covered by the contract touching which an agreement ought to be made. In the latter cases it is plain that the representative ought to participate, for bargaining, rather than the mere decision of a case according to the contract, is involved. . . .

Permitting the rival union to present grievances of its members we have held to be not intended by the Act, but it can hardly be called a refusal to bargain, unless the representative in a grievance which really called for bargaining rather than mere decision, had offered to bargain but was refused. It is only by a great strain that the mere omission to notify the representative of the pendency of grievances of sorts which the employer considers, and so far as is shown correctly considers, to involve no interpretation or change of the collective contract, can be called a refusal to bargain. The order ought to be merely that the Company cease and desist from adjusting grievances not presented through the representative without notifying the representative, except the informal adjustments with the foreman provided for in the contract.[1]

It thus appears that those who would avoid any academic discussions of the terminology of industrial relations will be forced to retreat from their position. For terminological difficulties are now getting in the way of understanding. Are grievance proceedings the same as collective bargaining? The board says yes. The court says no. Let us examine one of the sources of confusion that may develop from this official disagreement as to meanings.

The board is in the position of saying that disputes over interpretation and application of the agreement (involving the judicial or compliance function) are no different from disputes over the terms of relationship (involving the legislative or policy-making function). The board has called both "collective bargaining." Now, over a period of years the NLRB has evolved certain standards by which to measure the good faith

Supreme Court twice likened the collective bargain to legislation. Grievances similarly resemble cases to be decided according to the law."
[1] *Hughes Tool Co.* v. *N.L.R.B.*, 147 F (2d) 72, 74 (1945).

of an employer in fulfilling his duty to bargain. Certain of
these standards have meaning only when applied to collective
bargaining in the sense of contract negotiations, but lose their
significance if applied to a collective bargaining that also comprehends grievance proceedings. For example, the board has
held that good-faith bargaining requires a counterproposal.
But need an employer who believes, in good faith, that he is
living up to the terms of an agreement make a counterproposal
to the presentation of the union's grievance? If so, his contractual rights are being denied him.[1] Such a construction of
the employer's obligation would sweep away the very intent
of the signed agreement which the board has said, and right-
fully, is the object of negotiations. Such an interpretation
would make the agreement not much more than a springboard
for the obtaining of further concessions.

Again, the board has held that good-faith bargaining precludes unilateral action while negotiations are in progress on
the subject matter under discussion. For example, an increase
in wage rates while wage rates are being discussed has been
held to constitute refusal to bargain. If grievance proceedings
are collective bargaining, does this mean that employers are
barred from applying a specific term of the agreement while
that application is under discussion? If so, this form of injunc-
tive process could hamstring managerial action and stall the
machinery of production. Grievance proceedings have generally been understood as permitting union objection to managerial action *after* that action has been taken. If management
is proved in the wrong, restitution for the wrong is customarily
provided for. As one umpire has said, "When a controversy
arises, production cannot wait for exhaustion of the grievance
procedure. While that procedure is being pursued, production must go on."

It is thus readily evident that at least some of the board's
criteria for bargaining in good faith may be fully accepted in
the field of contract negotiations, to establish the terms of

[1] This is obviously the Court's view in *N.L.R.B.* v. *Sands Mfg. Co.*, 306
U.S. 332 (1939).

relationship, but when applied to grievance proceedings, to test the interpretation or application of the terms, the result may be confusion. *Some* terminological order is clearly needed to clarify the union-management relationship. It is essential that those who normally shy away from any sort of formalism in this field hide their reluctance sufficiently to assist in this clarification.

As has been suggested before, there are three possible approaches: (1) grievance proceedings may be considered as one aspect of collective bargaining; (2) grievance proceedings may be considered as totally different from collective bargaining; (3) collective bargaining and grievance proceedings may be considered as one and the same thing. If the last view is accepted, there seems little point in perpetuating both terms. One is sufficient, since they are synonymous. This would, however, permit no differentiation between the policy-making and compliance functions, a vital weakness. Fortunately, we need concern ourselves little with this point of view. Despite the support of the board (carried, perhaps, to an extent it does not realize nor intend), this view has little currency. Only six of the forty-two union and management representatives interviewed in the survey mentioned above gave it any consideration.

The opinions that (1) grievance proceedings must be considered as one aspect of collective bargaining, or (2) that they must be considered as totally different from collective bargaining, are those most widely held. It matters not which of these views is accepted, so long as the underlying implications are understood. The results of using each of the above approaches are illustrated in the diagram on the next page.

Either one of these approaches thus leads to the same desired result—the distinction between the legislative or policy-making function and the judicial or compliance function. In neither case are grievance proceedings considered the same as collective bargaining. Though this may seem elementary, the distinction is far from established or accepted, even though logical consistency would seem so to demand.

The Relationship	How designated under approach (1)	How designated under approach (2)
The over-all union-management relationship	Collective bargaining	No commonly used term; sometimes referred to as industrial relations or industrial government
The legislative or policy-making function	No commonly used term; sometimes referred to as contract negotiations	Collective bargaining
The judicial or compliance function	Grievance proceedings	Grievance proceedings

The point requiring emphasis is that regardless of how one views "collective bargaining," under either of the above commonly accepted outlines of industrial relations, grievance proceedings are designed to play a judicial or compliance function, not one of legislation or policy-making.

CAUSES OF CONFUSION [1]

Several reasons may be adduced for a persisting reluctance to identify grievance proceedings as a judicial function. The first of these is a belief in the indistinguishability of grievance proceedings from the legislative function in fact if not in theory. The president of one manufacturing company thus stated: "If a certain demand has been made and rejected or compromised, and a collective bargaining agreement has been entered into for a term with that demand definitely disposed of for the term of the agreement, I would assume that it was improper to bring the question up again until the term of the agreement is ended. But some other item may well come up, come up in the form of a grievance which will require further negotiation and a grievance procedure merges so easily into a collective bargaining procedure that it is, as I say for a company the size of ours, one and the same thing."

[1] Much of the material in this section has been drawn from my article on "The Nature and Scope of Collective Bargaining," *Quarterly Journal of Economics*, LVIII (May, 1944), with the permission of the editors.

Nevertheless, negotiations for a contract can be distinguished from settlement of grievances under the contract in the same manner that legislation can be distinguished from judicial proceedings in government generally. The former, as we have noted, are concerned with decisions of interests. The purpose of grievance proceedings, on the other hand, is to interpret and apply, rather than establish, the conditions of employment. They involve decisions of rights defined by the agreement. This distinction has been frequently made in bargaining practice and in labor legislation. In the New York State Labor Relations Act, refusal to discuss grievances has been made an unfair labor practice, distinct from refusal to bargain. The National Labor Relations Act safeguards to minority groups and individuals the right to plead cases of inequitable action or of unlawful action under the contract at the same time that it bars them from bargaining with respect to the terms of general agreement. Legislation both in the United States and abroad has distinguished disputes between employers and organized employees over interests (subject to negotiation and voluntary mediation or arbitration) from disputes over rights (subject to judicial consideration, sometimes compulsory even in countries not given to compulsory arbitration of employer-employee conflicts over interests). Thus the National Railway Labor Act, as amended in 1934, established the National Railroad Adjustment Board, which may upon petition of either or both parties, make compulsory awards binding upon the disputants, in cases arising out of the interpretation or application of a trade agreement.

The language and procedure of the grievance machinery customarily is the language and procedure of the courts. *How to Win for the Union,* a UAW (CIO) handbook, advises: "The steward's greatest difficulty will come on grievances which do not appear to be covered by the terms of the contract. . . . In practically all cases where a worker has a legitimate complaint it will be possible to find some clause of the contract which, with a little pulling and hauling, can be made to cover the situation. Lawyers have been able to use a

Constitution written over 150 years ago to cover the complex issues of modern life. A bright steward should be able to do just about as well with his contract." Some grievances not expressly covered by an agreement, and perhaps difficult to cover by any general formula, have been handled as proceedings in equity (as in certain decisions of the impartial chairman in the full-fashioned hosiery industry), or have been decided on the basis of "industrial common law" where union-management relations are of long standing (as in the men's clothing and women's garment industries). In some cases the rule of *stare decisis* is becoming established; as F. Nathan Wolf has pointed out in *Industrial Control in the Coat and Suit Industry,* a Ladies' Garment Workers' pamphlet of 1941: "Over the course of years, decisions have been written in disputed cases which have in effect become the law of the industry, despite the rule that no decision is to be a precedent for any other."

In many instances a separation of the legislative and judicial powers has been consciously made. The agreement between General Motors and the UAW (CIO) provides that "the Umpire shall have no power to add to or subtract from or modify any of the terms of this Agreement or any agreements made supplementary hereto." So in a decision on hiring rates for new employees the umpire refused to pass upon a new scale of hiring rates, referring the issue back to the parties without decision and adding: "The Umpire strongly recommends, however, that the problem discussed herewith be carefully considered by the parties by collective bargaining procedure." In *Handling Grievances,* a Steelworkers' handbook, a grievance committee's decision is given which concludes: "After considering all the facts in this case giving due consideration to Section 11 of the contract, found that no inequality existed and the matter of request for an increase in wages was a question of future negotiations; therefore, it was agreed that the Company's denial for an increase in wages was proper and in line with the contract and, therefore, held accordingly." The agreement and working rules of the Employers Operating Automatic Feeding and Flowing Processes and the Glass Bottle Blowers Association rest the function of interpreting the agreement in the hands of the president of the union, while in the New York City trucking industry a similar power was held for a time by one of the employers, in both cases necessitating a sharp distinction between negotiations for a contract and grievance proceedings.

Such developments in the law and practice of labor relations undermine the statement that no tenable distinction can be made between negotiation and adjudication. It is undeniably true that at times the line of demarcation between disputes over interest and disputes over rights becomes tenuous, but that such a line can be drawn, as a matter of general practice, has been demonstrated.[1] That it should be drawn in the interest of efficient and satisfactory resolution of industrial disputes will be made more evident later.

A second cause for identifying grievance proceedings with the legislative function lies in the failure to distinguish the mechanics of the procedure from the nature of the issues brought up via the procedure. This confusion is perhaps inescapable when the same machinery is employed for adjusting differences under the contract as well as for negotiating on issues not covered by the contract. Agreements which establish procedures for the settlement of "any grievance which may arise" lend themselves to such double duty. The vice-president of one large manufacturing company reports, "It has been our experience that the grievance procedure is used by the union to attempt to obtain matters which were not obtained during negotiations. Accordingly, the procedure is used for collective bargaining in some cases." Professors

[1] Note James Bryce, *The American Commonwealth* (2nd ed., 1891), New York, Macmillan, Vol. I, p. 235: "The legislature makes the law, the judiciary applies it to particular cases by investigating the facts and, when they have been ascertained, by declaring what rule of law governs them. Nevertheless there are certain points in which the functions of the two departments touch, certain ground which is debatable between the judiciary on the one hand and the legislature on the other." Despite the existence of these disputed areas of political competency, we have not sought to merge Congress and the judiciary!

Leiserson and McCabe have both noted this use of the grievance procedure for dual purposes, the former writing, "New questions and new problems frequently arise, however, which have to be settled before the agreements expire. . . . Under trade union agreement these are usually settled by the joint grievance or arbitration committees . . ."[1]; while the latter notes that "what is called a 'grievance' is often in reality the raising of an issue that requires supplementary collective bargaining, rather than a protest against a patent invasion of a generally acknowledged right of the worker."[2]

At the same time, it is important to realize that, granting the distinguishability of grievance proceedings from negotiations for the amendment or extension of the contract, a point which has been argued immediately above, this use of the same machinery is in itself insufficient cause for identifying grievance proceedings with the legislative or policy-making functions. It would be difficult to maintain, for example, that grievances handled through legislative machinery were legislation, while those handled through special procedures were not; or that new issues funneling through the grievance procedure were grievances concerning compliance, but when presented in contract negotiations they were not. It seems clear that it is the nature of the issue, not the mechanics for disposing of it, which is determinative. Until this is made plain the appropriate procedures consistent with the type of issue cannot be devised or work efficiently.

Another cause for considering grievance proceedings as simply a form of agreement-making is the fact that in some employer-union relationships both types of proceedings are conducted by the same personnel. The same committees which negotiate the contract in such cases are also called upon to settle grievances. This arrangement may constitute a temptation for the parties to seek concessions in the course of applying the agreement which they were unable to obtain in

---

[1] "Constitutional Government in American Industries," *American Economic Review*, XII, Supplement (March, 1922), 63.

[2] *Notes on Collective Bargaining* (mimeographed, 1939), p. 71.

the determination of the agreement, but to which they feel entitled. It constitutes as well another source of confusion, but scarcely provides a justification for refusal or failure to recognize the different functional roles which these representatives perform.

DISTINCTION FOR A PURPOSE

Assuming, then, that grievance proceedings as a judicial or compliance procedure can be distinguished from contract negotiations as a legislative or policy-making process, what value lies in insisting upon that distinction? Aside from some intellectual pleasure in understanding the functioning of the employer-union relationship, what utilitarian end may be served by holding to this differentiation? The value of the distinction has already been suggested, but we may examine it in greater detail now.

For one thing, such a distinction should lead to greater stability in the day-to-day working arrangements between the parties to the agreement. If the employer seeks to whittle away the area of contractual responsibility to the union by renegotiating the agreement in each case presented under the grievance procedure, or if the union makes every grievance case an occasion for rebargaining the contract to obtain what it could not obtain before, an unstable relationship will result. The atmosphere of the bargaining table will prevail, with the strike power of the union and the strategic position of managerial authority feeling each other out. The terms of the agreement will provide only an uneasy equilibrium around which the received benefits of the contract will oscillate. To the extent that efficient union negotiators are successful in obtaining in grievance cases advantages not specified in the contract, there will be continuing membership pressure on their representatives to expand the boundaries of the agreement. In the political framework of union organization, such pressure may compel a belligerency in settling grievances hardly conducive to the maintenance of a cooperative working relationship.

On the other hand, if both union and company representatives come to appreciate that the agreement represents in fact the *terms and conditions of employment* and seek only their fair and just application, each party to the agreement will have a reasonable expectation of the continuity of a known relationship.

This is not to deny either union or employer the opportunity to press for modification of the agreement. It does anticipate, however, that such legislative or policy-making proceedings shall be clearly understood as negotiations for a change in the terms of relationship, and that failure to obtain the desired change shall not be ground for charging a breach of contract or a violation of the agreement.

By far the most overwhelming reason for making a clear-cut demarcation of grievance proceedings from the legislative function consists in its greater potentialities for the development of the machinery for industrial peace. Precisely because grievance proceedings are disputes over rights, a judicial method of settlement is possible which would frequently be quite unacceptable in the disputes over interests which characterize contract negotiations.

One needs only a passing familiarity with the labor difficulties of the day to appreciate the reluctance if not outright refusal of employers to submit to arbitration many of the issues over which conflicts of interests arise. This attitude has likewise been found in certain labor leaders. At the same time that arbitration of interests has been refused, however, arbitration of rights has found acceptance. In fact two different kinds of arbitration are involved. One, which has sometimes been designated as appraisal, corresponds to the legislative function in that it involves determination of terms. The other is similar to grievance procedure in that it is concerned with application of terms. The General Motors Corporation is an outstanding example of a management group which has refused arbitration of issues of the bargaining table—indeed, in such strong language as at times to generate increased friction and tension between the parties [1]—but has, on the other hand, cooperated with the union in the establishment of the office of impartial umpire to render final determination of issues arising under the agreement.

The persistence of the view that grievance proceedings cannot be distinguished from the legislative or policy-making function—which is to say that disputes over rights are not to be differentiated from disputes over interests—is hardly conducive to the spread of arbitration. For if rights and interests are to be lumped together indistinguishably, negotiators, to avoid arbitration of interests, may be forced to refuse the adoption of permanent arbitration machinery.

Two distinct procedures evidently are called for. One, the negotiations for the contract or for changes in the contract, should be continuously available for the settlement of disputes of interests, as these may arise. The other, grievance procedure, desirably and almost necessarily culminating in an office of arbitration, should be continuously available for the disposition of disputes of rights arising under the contract. If issues presented via the grievance procedure are found in the course of their presentation to involve matters of interests, they may and should be referred to the negotiation procedure, for settlement without delay.

It is true that the distinction for which a plea is here raised may have an unfortunate tendency of reducing a living relationship to a legalistic form. There is no denying that danger. One of the most successful of industrial umpires has underscored it by a warning to the parties he serves:

[1] "Actually your proposal means that an arbitration board would assume the responsibilities of management; that it would assume responsibility for determining what is a sound financial and economic policy for General Motors; that the presently constituted management would relinquish functions which have been assigned to it by the owners of the business—the stockholders; that the duly elected officers of General Motors would surrender their functions and responsibilities to outsiders including a representative of the union.

"The union's proposal would require that General Motors management transfer to outsiders unlimited discretion over all the essential affairs of General Motors. This would be a surrender of the vital and essential functions of management." (The *New York Times*, Nov. 24, 1945.)

Unlike litigants in a court, the parties in a collective labor agreement must continue to live with each other both during the dispute and thereafter. While they are antagonists in some respects, they are also participants in a joint enterprise with mutual problems and mutual interests. The smooth and successful operation of the enterprise is important to the welfare of both. A labor dispute submitted to arbitration is not a controversy as to a past transaction, like the typical law suit in which each litigant desires to win, and, win or lose, to wind up the litigation and have nothing more to do with the matter. A labor dispute submitted to arbitration is a mutual problem which affects the future relations of the parties and the smooth operation of their enterprise. The objective of the parties, notwithstanding their contentions in advocacy, must be, not to win the immediate contentions, but to achieve the best solution of the problem under the circumstances. An apparent victory, if it does not achieve such a solution, may boomerang into an actual defeat. An award which does not solve the problem and with which the parties must nevertheless live, may become an additional irritant rather than a cure.

This means that the parties' approach must be radically different from that of litigants. A litigant does not care whether he wins his law suit because the tribunal understood the problem and made a wise judgment or because the tribunal was actually confused or was influenced by wooden technicality, or irrelevant or emotional considerations. But the parties in a labor dispute submitted to arbitration, seeking an award with which they must both live harmoniously in the future, must seek not merely a victory but a wise and enlightened award based on relevant factors and full understanding of the problem. And they must, therefore, seek to have the arbitrator know as much as possible about their enterprise, their interests in it, and the problem involved. . . .

And, so long as the parties continue to use the same arbitrator, having confidence in his integrity and wisdom, he should be free of the normal restrictions which adhere to court procedures. He should be free to mediate whenever a mutual settlement, rather than a decision, seems the wisest course.[1]

Such pointed advice, the fruit of rich experience, cannot be shrugged aside. Nevertheless, it seems clear that if arbitration of disputes arising under the contract is to be fostered,

---

[1] Harry Shulman, in his Preface to *Opinions of the Umpire,* privately printed for the Ford Motor Company and the United Automobile Workers (February, 1946).

awards which "solve the problem" must adhere to the terms of the agreement unless the parties specifically consent to a decision on other grounds. Unless management is assured of such a judicial-like approach, it will be reluctant to consent to arbitration of grievances. Disillusion will otherwise be sure and swift, as in the case of the New York City master painters who in 1940 agreed to an arbitration arrangement which they subsequently found—by court action—to invest the umpire with broader powers than they intended.

Obviously what is called for is the *development* of a union-management relationship in which both parties have confidence in each other and also in their umpire. With such a relationship, flexibility of grievance determination may easily follow, permitting adjustment where strict application is unsuitable. This type of relationship does not grow overnight, however. It may represent the desired fruition, but it is attained only by slow maturing under wise cultivation. Until it develops quite naturally, premature forcing carries the danger envisaged by one arbitrator, Clark Kerr, in a grievance case involving seniority rights:

The Arbitrator fully agrees that his powers are judicial, and not legislative, and that a strict approach has its advantages. A loose construction permits modification by interpretation. Certainly when the contract is relegislated once a year, such loose construction is not necessary to keep it in line with changing circumstances. A strict interpretation also leads to certainty and consistency. If a loose approach is used, then the question becomes how loose and in what direction. This approach would lead to a greater use of arbitration than desirable, as each party might seek to gain an advantage not obtained through the collective bargaining process itself.

The wave of postwar strikes brought with it a wave of proposals for the prevention of strikes. Among the recommendations made were a number looking to establishment of labor courts where industrial disputes must be taken for settlement. Proponents did not always specify *what* disputes were to be so referred, but the emphasis upon avoidance of strikes sometimes prompted the conclusion that all disputes were to be subject to the jurisdiction of the proposed labor courts. Here we have the logical outcome of the confusion of the policy-making and compliance functions in the union-management relationship. Courts to settle contract issues would be courts in name only—they would perform the function of industrial legislatures. But courts to settle grievances arising from the application and interpretation of contracts would be courts in function as well as name. In one case there would be the radical departure of an imposition of terms of relationship. In the other would be involved only the acceptance— now routine in virtually all areas except industrial relations— of an independent determination of the meaning of a contract.

Regardless of whether arbitration comes through private office or public court, however, or through both, we are entitled to the hope for its continued spread. In that direction lies the narrowing of areas of conflict and the enlarging of the areas of industrial order. To distinguish the judicial function from the legislative function, grievance proceedings from the establishment of the terms of relationship, is to contribute to that result. This is *not* mere verbalism, it is *not* an intellectual toying with terminology. It is distinction for a purpose.

CHAPTER FOUR

Union-Management Cooperation: An Analysis

by *Joseph Shister*

FOR THE purposes of this paper, union-management co-operation will be said to exist when the union and the management in question, through joint action, attempt to reduce the unit costs of production. Union-management cooperation, as here defined, should not be confused with industrial peace, for it is more than that. Cooperation cannot be practiced without peace, to be sure; but industrial peace can obviously exist without any joint efforts on the part of labor and management to reduce unit costs significantly.

How do economic conditions influence union-management cooperation? Which union objectives contribute to cooperation? Which objectives deter cooperation? What roles do management and union leadership play in cooperative plans? Why is union-management cooperation practiced in some firms and not in others? Will union-management cooperation grow in the future?

THE ECONOMIC SETTING

To the author's knowledge, there are on record in the United States and Canada only three cases of union-management cooperation having been introduced when the bargaining unit was in a relatively "prosperous" condition.[1] Aside

[1] One case occurred in a steel plant in Canada. (See Golden and Ruttenberg, *The Dynamics of Industrial Democracy* [New York, Harper and Brothers, 1942], pp. 283-84.) The S. Buchsbaum and Company case offers another illustration. (See *Applied Anthropology*, No. 4 [Fall, 1946].) The Adamson Company is the third case in question. (See *Life*, XXI [December 23, 1946], 93-94.)

from these cases, however, all union-management cooperation plans that have been introduced to diminish unit costs of
production during a peacetime period [1] arose only because the
bargaining unit was in an adverse economic situation. The
adversity referred to has taken on a variety of forms, separately classified below, but actually interrelated in practice.

The impact of nonunion competition on organized plants
has often generated union-management cooperation schemes
designed to reduce unit costs. The men's clothing industry
is the classical case in point; in the 1920's costs were reduced
by wage concessions, introduction of payment by results,
elimination of restrictive rules, etc.[2] The full-fashioned
hosiery industry offers another illustration of cost reduction
through joint cooperation of the parties in order to meet the
adverse impact of nonunion competition. In 1938 the union
(American Federation of Hosiery Workers) agreed to accept
wage reductions from the northern manufacturers, with the
understanding that the manufacturers, in turn, were to introduce more modern equipment; all this was done to meet the
lower costs of the unorganized mills of the South.[3] The use
of a special technical department by the Printing Pressmen's

[1] The cooperation plans introduced during the war to accelerate production, which were greatly encouraged by the WPB, were obviously an out-
growth of the war period with the (relatively) unique conditions attendant
upon it and are not likely to reappear in a peacetime era. It should also be
noted that the publicity afforded the wartime plans was far greater than
their actual performance.

One plan inaugurated during the war in Canada is worthy of note. It
occurred at the Lever Brothers plant at Toronto and was a bona fide union-
management cooperative venture. It is interesting to note the "adverse" circumstances under which the plan was introduced. "It is the feeling of
management that while Joint Committee procedure was an expedient means
of introducing the forty-hour week under wartime conditions of manpower
shortages, stable costs, and fixed volumes of production, that the plan cannot
be considered as a sound basis for measuring and sharing all kinds of increases in productive efficiency. For the present both union and management
have been content to allow union-management cooperation on productive
efficiency to lapse." (W. R. Dymond, "Union-Management Cooperation at
the Toronto Factory of Lever Bros., Ltd.," *Canadian Journal of Economics
and Political Science*, XIII [February, 1947], 65.)

[2] See S. H. Slichter, *Union Policies and Industrial Management* (Washington, The Brookings Institution, 1941), chapter 17.

[3] *Monthly Labor Review*, LII (1941), 1356.

Union designed to cut down costs in commercial and newspaper printing was introduced originally in the commercial field, where nonunion competition was pressing heavily on the union shops.

The depressed state of business activity resulting from cyclical fluctuations in the economy has been partly, although not exclusively, responsible for union-management cooperation in some instances. The steel industry offers quite a few illustrations in this context. Harold Ruttenberg, formerly of the United Steelworkers, has described the situation in the following terms: "As a rule, union-management cooperation in the steel and allied industries has been inaugurated because of the force of economic circumstances, not as a result of an intellectual acceptance of its principles."[1] The drastic wage cut taken by the hosiery workers in 1931 was agreed to partially (although not exclusively) because of the depressed state of trade.[2] An interesting illustration of wage reduction during the great depression occurred in an agreement between the International Brotherhood of Electrical Workers (Local 38) and the Electrical Contractors' Association of Cleveland. The union members agreed "to a reduction in their wage scale in order that salesmen might be hired to develop a market for their labor, through the improvement or modernization of old buildings, residences, or industrial plants. . . . The employer, in order to be eligible for the benefits of the lower wage rates, agreed to employ not less than one full-time salesman who would have knowledge of the work covered by the agreement and whose sole duty was to be to solicit work specified to be performed at the lower rates. . . . [3]

Union-management cooperation has found its way into bargaining units which were undergoing secular declines because of the advent of competition from entirely new products or services. The union-management cooperation plans on certain railroads were introduced when the competition from

---

[1] "The Fruits of Industrial Peace," *Harvard Business Review*, XVIII (Spring, 1940), 287.

[2] In addition, there was the question of nonunion competition.

[3] *Monthly Labor Review*, XXXVI (1933), 146.

new transportation media (trucks, buses, automobiles, airplanes) was growing in intensity. And the Naumkeag cooperative experiment [1] was generated, partially at least, by the long-term shift in demand from cotton to silk and rayon.

The inception of production standards in the Cleveland ladies' garment industry resulted from the fact that the absence of such standards would have impaired the ability of the employers to compete with New York plants ". . . and [would have] reduced the employment opportunities of Cleveland workers. The union leaders realized that the city, not being a style center, was at a disadvantage in competition with New York and less able than New York to stand higher costs. In addition, they knew that the prevalence of production in sub-manufacturing or contract shops in New York would prevent time-work from affecting production costs as much in that market as in Cleveland, where most of the work was done in the so-called inside shops." [2]

It is not surprising to find that union-management cooperation has appeared mainly, although not exclusively, when the bargaining unit was in an adverse economic situation. A decrease in unit costs to the firm may well spell the difference between profits and losses in many instances; and an improvement in the firm's situation will often reflect itself in "substantial" improvement in the (relative and/or absolute) employment and income opportunities for the union members. [3] The latter point needs some comment. If the cost reductions involve hourly wage rate reductions, then it is necessary that the employer's demand for labor be elastic over the relevant range. A union would not be apt to agree to reduce wage rates, under union-management cooperation, if it did not see a possibility of gaining more than proportionately in employ-

[1] See Slichter, *op. cit.*, chap. 18.
[2] *Ibid.*, pp. 396-97.
[3] It goes without saying, of course, that a sufficient decline in income and/or employment opportunities for the membership can spell complete destruction of the union. Furthermore, where there is a rival union in the field, the decline need not be too great to entail a mass exodus of the membership to the rival organization.

ment and/or income from the wage reduction. On the other hand, if the cost reductions do not directly involve hourly wage rates (e.g., improvement in the flow of materials, introduction of better technical equipment, etc.), then the union would not need to consider whether the employer's demand for labor was elastic or inelastic over the relevant range. This follows from the fact that a cost reduction not involving a cut in wage scales will increase the productivity of labor and increase the demand for the labor, which means a shift of the demand curve to the right.

Although union-management cooperation may arise where the business unit is faced with an adverse economic situation, it does not necessarily follow that an adverse business situation *always* generates cooperation between management and organized labor. In many instances, union-management cooperation has failed to arise even where an adverse situation prevailed. To put it differently: an adverse business situation is usually a necessary, but never sufficient, condition for the emergence of union-management cooperation. What then are these other conditions that must prevail? We shall consider them under several headings: union objectives, worker psychology, union leadership, and employers' attitudes. Obviously, there are numerous interrelationships between these elements in practice.

UNION OBJECTIVES

It has been frequently asserted that there is inevitably a conflict between unions and management simply because the former want to get as much as possible and the latter want to give as little as possible. While such a statement may well be true as far as it goes, it does not go far enough. To understand whether there is really an organic conflict of objectives between unions and management, one must interpret these objectives in the context of the *concrete* elements attendant upon the daily relationships between the two groups in question. When such an interpretation is attempted, it is found that in many instances there is a similarity of objectives *within the framework of the concrete immediate environment impinging on the parties.* Certainly some of the union-management cooperation plans briefly alluded to in the previous section could not have arisen had there been no community of objectives between the unions and managements in question. In fact, one of the requisite conditions for union-management cooperation is that the union objectives *in regard to the bargaining unit environment* do not conflict with those of management. (The question of management objectives is discussed below.)

It should be noted that we are concerned here with *basic* union objectives. The problem of secondary objectives or tactics, such as supervision of the incentive system, participation in marketing policy, etc., is analyzed in the section on employers' attitudes.

In the light of the above comments, it is not surprising to find that in some instances where the company was in adverse economic circumstances, union-management cooperation failed to arise because of the basic objectives of the unions in question. The United Mine Workers are an excellent case in point. There never has been cooperation between the miners and the operators, even though such cooperation was badly needed during the twenties, when the unionized mines were losing business to the unorganized mines with substantially lower labor costs. And the reason for this failure of the union to cooperate by reducing labor costs lies mainly in the basic objective of the United Mine Workers, which was designed to get a high wage rate for those who would succeed in retaining employment, even if this did mean the layoff of a considerable number of union men. The rationale of this objective was put by John L. Lewis in the following terms:

In insisting on the maintenance of an American wage standard in the coal fields, the United Mine Workers is doing its part . . . to force a reorganization of the basic industry of the country upon scientific and efficient lines. The maintenance of these rates will accelerate the operation of natural economic laws, which will in time eliminate uneconomic mines, obsolete equipment and incompetent management.[1]

Obviously then, if the basic objective of the union is the maintenance of a high wage rate even though this does result in unemployment for union men, it follows that the union's objective must necessarily be at odds with those of the employer. Such an objective has not been uncommon to certain trade unions in this country,[2] and that helps to explain, in part at least, the failure of union-management cooperation to arise in situations involving these unions.

Several observations are pertinent with regard to a union objective of high wages despite curtailed employment. (1) There presumably is a "critical" point of unemployment (different for each organization) beyond which the union becomes willing to make cost concessions to management. (2) Trade union objectives of any kind are not a static matter; they undergo changes over time.[3] Consequently, a union pursuing such an objective in one period will not necessarily pursue it in another. (3) The union objective must be interpreted with regard to the organization involved in the negotiations with the management in question. The necessity for such interpretation becomes obvious when one realizes that different locals of the same national union may display different objectives in bargaining with their respective employers.

Another union objective frequently obstructing the genesis of union-management cooperation relates to basic union philosophy. A union with "left-wing" or "revolutionary" objectives, assiduously intent on developing "class consciousness" among its constituents, would consider it undesirable to cooperate with the "capitalist" class. It should be noted, however, that left-wing unions may sometimes cooperate with management when such cooperation becomes an absolute ne-

---

[1] *The Miners' Fight for American Standards* (Bell Publishing Co., Indianapolis, 1925), p. 41.

[2] See J. Shister, "The Theory of Union Wage Rigidity," *Quarterly Journal of Economics*, LVII (August, 1943).

[3] The Amalgamated Clothing Workers are a case in point. As this union developed, its original "revolutionary" objectives gradually disappeared.

cessity in the light of the existing political events—witness the
cooperation practiced by left-wing unions in this country after
Russia entered World War II. Furthermore, the reference to
a union being "left-wing" or "revolutionary" does not necessarily mean that all (or even a majority) of the members
have revolutionary ambitions. In many instances, only a faction within the union may be so inclined, but this faction
may be powerful enough to guide the policies of the organization.[1] The case of the Ladies' Garment Workers' Union during the twenties, when it was riddled with factional strife, is
illustrative. Thus, the general executive board of this organization reported to the membership as follows: ". . . the administration [of the union label] depends mainly upon the
Union. The Communist administration of the Joint Board
[New York] in 1926, even prior to the strike, completely
sabotaged the Prosanis Label as an instrument of 'class collaboration,' and the strike itself with its complete breakdown
of standards, hampered, in fact almost destroyed, the work of
the label division."[2]

An objective which can sometimes obstruct union-management cooperation resides in the union's need for recruitment of
new members, not to mention the retention of the current
ones. It is difficult, although not impossible, for a union to
cooperate with management in cost reductions when it is trying to convince prospective members to join the organization.
The use of a high wage rate as an inducement for members to
join a union is present even when the alternatives open to the
worker are only to join the one union in the industry or to
remain a nonunion man. The wage inducement becomes particularly important where competition for the same workers
prevails between two or more rival unions.[3] With only one
union in the industry, the organizing objective as an obstacle

---

[1] Such a possibility becomes easy enough to understand when one realizes
that the average union member is quite indifferent to the affairs of his union,
while the left-wing members take a very active interest in its operation.

[2] *Report of the general executive board to the 18th convention,* p. 280.

[3] The competition can be just as intense in the case of two AFL unions,
for example, as in the case of an AFL versus a CIO organization.

to union-management cooperation is only a temporary one; once the area in question is organized, attention can be turned to union-management cooperation. Not so, however, where there are two or more rival unions in the field. In that case, each of the rival organizations must constantly take into account the competitive pressure of the other group and act accordingly.

Worker Psychology

While it is true that when a worker becomes a union member he takes on new contacts and new allegiances, with corresponding differences in his behavior, it is equally true that many of his attitudes as an unorganized worked are carried over into his attitudes toward management qua union member. Some of these attitudes have frequently obstructed union-management cooperation.

The introduction of incentive wage systems (piece-rates, bonus payments, etc.,) is often a means of reducing unit costs in the plant. But many workers still refuse to accept an incentive system [1] simply because of opposition to such a system "in principle." This attitude of the workers has nothing to do with any fear of a decline in monetary return (either per unit of effort or absolutely). Instead, it represents a fundamental attitude firmly imbedded in the worker's psychology because of some past experience. [2] The following situation illustrates this point most vividly:

At a large rubber plant a group of maintenance men were put on measured day work so that they could participate in incentive earnings. Their bonus was given to them in separate checks. These

[1] It goes without saying that incentive systems cannot be introduced in some types of work. What we are concerned with at this juncture is opposition to incentive systems where the *technical* conditions of production *do* permit their installation.

[2] By contrast, "workers are hard to rouse against incentive methods in some cases simply because they have known nothing else and an alternative system of payment is difficult for them to visualize; thus tonnage rates and various bonus plans seem unalterable fixtures to many workers in the primary steel industry." (Van Dusen Kennedy, *Union Policy and Incentive Wage Methods* [New York, Columbia University Press, 1945], p. 58.)

were returned and the men continued to refuse bonus although their work was still measured and they were earning it.[1]

In the case of some unions, opposition to incentive systems stems from the fear of "rate chiseling" by employers. This fear is generated by the experience with "rate chiseling" which many members underwent as unorganized workers.[2]

The mitigation of output restriction under incentive systems, which would obviously contribute much to cost reduction, is beset with serious obstacles. And these obstacles must be traced largely, although not exclusively, to worker psychology. Restriction of output among *unorganized* workers because of fear of rate chiseling or unemployment has been common knowledge for some time.[3] Similarly, non-pecuniary motivations leading to output restriction among unorganized workers [4] have also been responsible for the attitude of certain unions toward this problem.

Union Leadership

Since a trade union is a body politic, the question of leadership within the group becomes of cardinal importance. The membership must look to the leaders for guidance, particularly in matters of collective bargaining, if for no other reason

[1] *Ibid.*, p. 62.

[2] Writing in 1917, Hoxie stated: ". . . there is an essential incompatibility between the basic ideals of scientific management and those of the dominant type of trade unionism. . . . It is, I believe, this. Scientfiic management can function successfully only on the basis of constant and indefinite change of industrial conditions . . . on the other hand, trade unionism of the dominant type can function successfully only through the maintenance of a fixed industrial situation and conditions." (*Quarterly Journal of Economics*, XXXI [November, 1916], 77-78.)

The implication of this statement is that mere frequency of change, as such, is opposed by the unions. The truth of the matter is, however (and Hoxie's own analysis points in this direction), that it is not the mere frequency of change as such, but rather the *consequences* of the change that the unions dislike—if these consequences are antagonistic to the interests of the unions. As a result, the focal point of analysis must be centered on the consequences (e.g., loss of employment, undercutting of rates by employers, etc.) that the change entails.

[3] Cf. S. B. Mathewson, *Restriction of Output Among Unorganized Workers* (New York, Viking Press, 1931), chap. 5.

[4] Collins, Dalton, and Roy, "Restriction of Output and Social Cleavage in Industry" (*Applied Anthropology*, V, Summer 1946).

than that the leaders have so much more opportunity to gain a thorough insight into the problems of the business unit. Imperfection of knowledge on the part of the rank and file, resulting in an inaccurate evaluation of the environment impinging on the union, has frequently been responsible for the failure of union-management cooperation.

The inability of the rank and file to gauge accurately the importance of the encroachment of nonunion competition on the volume of business of the unionized plants has occurred in numerous instances and has obstructed the development of union-management cooperation. The Philadelphia upholstery workers are an excellent case in point. Although the Philadelphia mills were losing business to outside nonunion plants quite rapidly after 1925, "the union membership did not recognize that this decline involved a more serious situation than earlier declines which were the result of style changes or general business depression. . . . In addition to lack of knowledge of the basic trends in the trade . . . many union members, too, had a definite belief that the skill of the workers in Philadelphia could not be matched in other areas and that, sooner or later, superior skill would demonstrate its value in the market. This position overlooked the fact that, in time, less skilled workers in outside centers would acquire greater skill as they worked in the trade. It also overlooked the fact that recent trends in the industry had lessened the demand for the expensive novelty fabrics which were difficult to make and increased the demand for cheaper goods which could be made with less skilled labor."[1]

Further illustrations of the inability of the rank and file to recognize the potency of nonunion competition are available among the Philadelphia carpet workers,[2] the lamp chimney (glass) workers,[3] and the Brockton shoe workers.[4]

[1] Palmer, *Union Tactics and Economic Change* (Philadelphia, University of Pennsylvania, 1932), pp. 63, 65.
[2] *Ibid.*, p. 43.
[3] Slichter, *op. cit.*, p. 349.
[4] *Ibid.*, p. 364.

It was pointed out in a previous section that the onslaught of a cyclical depression has sometimes been, at least in part, responsible for the inception of union-management coopera- tion plans. It is equally true, however, that in some instances a cyclical depression has resulted in the abandonment of cooperative action. The contradiction between these two statements is more apparent than real. The truth of the mat- ter is that one of the variables in the problem—state of knowl- edge of the rank and file—is different in the two cases. In the former instance, the rank and file (either themselves or through proper leadership guidance) had an adequate under- standing of the situation in hand; while in the latter, this knowledge was lacking.

The failure of the rank and file to discern between the results flowing from cooperative action and those resulting from the impact of a cyclical depression leads to confusion of the two in the minds of the workers. They can recognize only the immediate facts—layoffs, for example—which they find completely unsatisfactory. The results do not at all corre- spond to the gains they expected to reap from union-manage- ment cooperation. Under such circumstances, it is not at all surprising that they should oppose the continuation of the cooperative venture. True, without cooperation the workers would have been worse off than they actually were with it, but the lack of adequate insight into the situation results in the failure of the workers to make this important distinction. Cases to illustrate this pattern can be found in the Naumkeag cooperative experiment,[1] in the Cleveland garment industry,[2] and, to some extent, on the railroads.[3]

Under certain circumstances, the proper type of union leadership can alter even basic union objectives and worker psychology. But it is with regard to *informing* the member- ship on the significance and implications of each bargaining

---

[1] Slichter, *op. cit.*, pp. 544 ff.
[2] *Ibid.*, pp. 430 ff.
[3] *Ibid.*, pp. 480 ff.

situation that leadership can play its most important role.[1] The importance of the leadership function is illustrated very vividly by the following case:

At one of the plants of a large concern the workers, although on hourly rates, were maintaining production performance as good as, or better than, that of plants on bonus and were thus entitled to additional earnings. Nevertheless, they refused to accept the bonus system which would have increased their earnings without extra effort largely because the local president, an influential lay preacher, was so vigorously opposed to all incentive plans. Later, with a change in the union presidency, the plant went on bonus.[2]

The function of leadership in educating the rank and file to union-management cooperation—particularly insofar as union-management cooperation is obstructed by the imperfection of knowledge of the members with regard to the impact of particular bargaining situations—involves two elements: (1) insight into the situation on the part of the leader, and (2) ability of the leader to convince the rank and file of the desirability of a given course of action. Each of these points needs some elucidation.

The insight of union leadership into a given economic situation will vary between national and local leaders, new and old leaders, militant and nonmilitant leaders. As a result of a lengthier, and particularly more intimate, association with the management group, national leaders usually have more insight and show a better understanding of the economic problems of the bargaining unit than local leaders. Through such association, in negotiations and otherwise, they grow to learn about many of the problems that management has to face, and can ascertain quite readily an adverse situation when one arises. The local leaders do not have the opportunity to acquire such experience. In many instances, the

---

[1] It goes without saying that the leaders' role of serving as informants can, in practice, be intimately tied in with the leaders' role in altering basic union objectives and worker psychology.

[2] Kennedy, *op. cit.*, p. 58.

local officer is not even a full-time official, but consents to guide the union in his spare time. Under such circumstances, the local leader does not have much more opportunity to learn about the economic problems of the industry than does the rank and file. Furthermore, the local leader is under the influence of the same emotional predilections as the rank and file, for he is just as closely identified with any local situation as they are. The national leader, on the other hand, being removed from the local scene of strife between the parties, can view any situation far more objectively. In the light of all this, it is not surprising to find instances where union-management coöperation was obstructed because of the lack of insight by local union leadership. The Brockton shoe workers are a case in point,[1] and there are others.

The insight of leadership will also depend on whether it is an old or a new organization, regardless of whether local or national leadership is involved. In a new organization the union leaders will not have had time to become acquainted with the economics of the firm, as they would have had in an older union.

In order for union leaders, at any administrative level, to gain an insight into the economic conditions of the firm, they must first have the confidence of employers; for only when such confidence obtains, can the leaders gain the necessary information on the status of the company—how serious non-union competition is, the financial standing of the firm, the variations of labor costs, etc. It follows, therefore, that when employers show a bitter hostility toward the union in question, they will want little to do with the union leaders. This employer attitude will generate a militant union leadership,[2] and this militancy will deter the leaders from showing enough interest in employers' economic problems, so that even when

[1] See Slichter, op. cit., p. 364.
[2] Thus, in the case of the Philadelphia carpet weavers, "discrimination against union officers by employers brought the fighters into power of necessity. . . . Fighting the manufacturers was therefore the major activity of the union leadership and if they occasionally fought an employer into bankruptcy, well and good." (Palmer, op. cit., p. 48.)

an adverse situation arises and the employers are actually willing to explain the condition to the union leaders, the latter will show very little interest.

The understanding by union leadership of a given adverse situation is a necessary, but not sufficient, condition for leadership to convince the rank and file of the desirability for cooperation. A "stronghold" on the membership is also necessary. Thus, for example, the leaders of the flint glass workers [1] saw the need for union-management cooperation just as vividly as did the leaders of the men's clothing workers, but the latter were able to convince the rank and file of this need while the former were unable to do so.

Where the union affairs are highly centralized, with a great deal of control (formal and otherwise) vested in the officers, the leaders can often convince the rank and file of the necessity for cooperation in the case of an adverse situation impinging on the firm.[2]   In organizations where the existence of factions prevents the development of great control by the leaders, the task of the latter to convince the rank and file of the necessity for union-management cooperation becomes very difficult, if not impossible. The faction in opposition to the group in power usually obstructs the efforts of the leaders to "sell" the rank and file on cooperation. This is essentially a political necessity, which becomes particularly evident where one of the factions is left-wing, although it is present even if there is no left-wing element in the union. Thus, in the case of the Philadelphia upholstery weavers, "political factionalism, which had been characteristic of the local for some years, broke up the discipline of the union in the crisis. It is probable that the rejection of the action of the local's accredited representatives . . . was primarily the result of political factionalism in the union. . . ." [3]

It should be noted, of course, that even where no factionalism prevails in the union, the lack of adequate power in the

---

[1] Slichter, op. cit., p. 349.

[2] This assumes, of course, that there are no union objectives present which can obstruct the genesis of union-management cooperation.

[3] Palmer, op. cit., p. 72.

hands of the officers may make it impossible for them to "sell" the rank and file on union-management cooperation.

The preceding paragraphs point up a rather significant relationship between the politics and economics of the collective bargaining process. If the lack of adequate centralized control within the union can often obstruct union-management cooperation, it follows that there is frequently a direct conflict between sound collective bargaining and the degree of democracy within the labor organization in question.

A further comment is necessary before we leave this section. Given the "degree of democracy" in the union, national leaders are usually (although not always) more successful in persuading the rank and file to follow a given course of action than the local leaders. This difference stems from two sources. First, the rank and file usually has more respect for the opinion of the national leader than for that of the local man. The reasons for this are obvious enough and need no elaboration here. Secondly, the local may find that it has to rely on the national office for various types of services and policy approval —statistical information, strike approval and strike funds, etc. Under such circumstances, it would be unwise for the local membership to antagonize the national officer or his representative by refusing to go along with his policy recommendations.

EMPLOYERS' ATTITUDES

Union-management cooperation is obviously a two-way affair, involving management as much as unions. Hence, if we assume that adverse conditions impinge on the given company and that the union attitude is conducive to union-management cooperation in every respect, it may still be impossible to inaugurate a cooperative plan because of management's attitude. What must the attitude of management be, therefore, to enable union-management cooperation to flourish? Before answering this question, it is necessary to analyze the basic approaches of different management groups to the question of collective bargaining. And in this context, one can classify American management into four rather broad groups. Needless to say, this classification is an analytic one, which means that over time a given employer may shift from one group to the other.

In the first group one can include all those employers who are bitterly opposed to trade unionism in the labor market "as a matter of principle." These employers are accustomed to dealing with an unorganized labor force in their plants. They have become habituated to individual bargaining, and cannot reconcile themselves to collective bargaining. Their opposition to collective bargaining does not stem from any rational calculus pertaining to the impact on profits or managerial salaries, but represents instead a basic psychological attitude which has nothing to do with any monetary calculus as such. Even if it were possible to demonstrate to these employers that collective bargaining may actually represent a net monetary gain for them, they would still be opposed to it because of nonpecuniary motives.[1] The employers in this group deal with unions only because the law of the land compels them to do so. And in dealing with the unions, within the scope of the legal framework, they are certain to show nothing more than the minimum amount of "cooperation" which the law requires.

A second group would include employers whose opposition stems from the belief that, as a result of unionism, their net monetary gains are reduced. In some cases this belief may very well be justified in the light of objective data, while in others it may not. But even if it is not, it still remains the compelling force that motivates the employer's behavior. This is not meant to imply that nonpecuniary motivations are absent here.[2] But these motivations are not the exclusive or predominant forces that they are for the employers in the first group. However, like the employers in the first group, they deal with unions only because the circumstances compel it.

In the third group, one can include employers who have come to recognize that the unions can improve personnel

[1] The desire for absolute retention of control is one of these.
[2] This point becomes clear enough when one recognizes that in our society power is so frequently a function of economic status.

relations in the plant by improving the morale of the workers, reducing labor turnover, etc. Furthermore, some employers in this group have found the union a useful indirect instrument for controlling "undesirable" conditions in the product market.[1] The employers in this group are, therefore, willing to accept trade unions as a medium through which they can learn about the workers' job demands. But they are not willing to accept trade unionism as anything more than this. They believe that there are certain prerogatives which are the exclusive property of management and with which the unions should not meddle. These prerogatives include a host of matters which have been discussed elsewhere,[2] and so need no repetition here.

In the fourth group are those employers who, in their dealings with unions, can be labeled "mature." These employers not only find that unionization leads to certain economic benefits,[3] but are also willing to allow the unions to participate in managerial functions *when this becomes necessary*. This does not mean, of course, that these employers have no concept of "exclusive management prerogatives." But it does mean that they have adjusted their views on this matter to meet the impact of the stubborn facts of reality. As one mature management representative has put it, "Limitations on management prerogatives create definite problems, but these problems are not insoluble and they are minimized if management is willing to treat them on their merits and does not regard them as issues in themselves." [4]

Given that union-management cooperation requires the participation of the trade union representatives in certain managerial functions, it follows that, *even in adverse circum-*

[1] For example, when uniform minimum wage rates for all employers (where labor costs are a substantial proportion of total costs) set a floor to price-cutting in the product market.

[2] L. H. Hill and C. R. Hook, Jr., *Management at the Bargaining Table* (New York, McGraw-Hill Book Co., 1945); also see E. W. Bakke, *Mutual Survival* (Labor and Management Center, Yale Univ., 1946).

[3] In the needle trades, e.g., the employers have found the unions a boon to mitigating cutthroat competition in the product market.

[4] M. Kestnbaum, "A Study in Management Prerogatives," *Harvard Business Review*, XIX (Autumn, 1940), 98.

stances, only the mature management group will show a willingness to cooperate. It is not surprising, therefore, to find that in many instances the failure of union-management cooperation to arise has been attributable to the attitude of management.[1]

It has not been the purpose of these paragraphs to decide whether management people falling into the first three groups analyzed above are right or wrong in their attitude. The important point, for the purposes of this paper, is that only where management is mature can union-management cooperation prevail. Another point to note is that management which is mature today has not always been so—witness the employers in the needle trades. Consequently, it is possible that there may be more mature employers in the future than at present, but this is a point pertaining to the entire future of union-management cooperation in this country, which will be taken up in the next section.

A final comment is necessary before leaving this section. In many cases when we speak of "management" we are actually referring to an entire administrative hierarchy ranging all the way from the foreman to the president of the corporation, not to mention the board of directors. Consequently, it is important that all those who have control over dealings with the union maintain a mature attitude if union-management cooperation is to succeed.

THE FUTURE OF UNION-MANAGEMENT COOPERATION

The preceding sections have shown what conditions have been necessary and sufficient to generate union-management cooperation in the past. These are: adverse economic circumstances (usually, though not always), coupled with the "required" structure of the demand for labor; union objectives and workers' psychology which are not at odds with the basic

[1] See H. Ruttenberg, "The Fruits of Industrial Peace," *op. cit.,* pp. 290-91; W. Gomberg, "Union Interest in Engineering Techniques," *Harvard Business Review,* XXIV (Spring, 1946), 356 ff.; E. C. Robbins, "Management-Labor Cooperation," *Harvard Business Review,* XXI (Summer, 1943), 420-21; Kennedy, *op. cit.,* chap. 5.

pursuits of management; an understanding of the situation by the rank and file, mainly through the influence of leadership; and mature management. On the basis of this analysis, what can be said about the future of union-management cooperation in the United States? Will it grow or decline? If it grows, will it change the institutional structure of our society? What other effects can it have?

The growth of union-management cooperation in the future will depend, of course, on the significance of the variables which, together, have given rise to cooperation in the past. The future role of each of these variables will now be examined in turn.

Adverse Situations. Given the rapid spread of unionism in recent years, the importance of nonunion competition as a source of adversity for unionized employers is bound to decline. Many industries are now completely unionized and will, in all likelihood, stay so. And even in those industries where there is still some nonunion competition, the unorganized plants base their policies regarding wages and other conditions of employment largely (although not exclusively) on those prevailing in the unionized plants. That practice stems not only from a desire to forestall unionization, but also from the desire to prevent the loss of the better workers to the union plants. Therefore, nonunion competition as a source of union-management cooperation is bound to decline in importance.

Whether cyclical depressions or so-called secular stagnation will again ravage the economy in the future is impossible to predict at this juncture. To a large extent, the answer depends on policies adopted by the federal government. For the purposes of this analysis it is enough to point out that both cyclical depression and secular stagnation can generate the kind of adverse situation which leads to union-management cooperation (if other factors do not obstruct it), and that it is possible for either of these conditions to arise in the future.

The economic facet of society is always undergoing change, and one of the manifestations of this change is the genesis of new industries and the decline of old ones. The rapidity of change obviously varies from period to period, but that it occurs is clear enough. Therefore, we can expect to have declining industries in the future. And a declining industry has often served in the past as a stimulus to union-management cooperation.

It is also reasonable to assume that we may expect shifts in demand from one unionized center to another. That also results from the dynamic character of economic society, and again we have a condition favorable to union-management cooperation.

It follows from the above that an adverse situation impinging on the business unit, which is usually one of the necessary and sufficient conditions for the emergence of union-management cooperation, will not be lacking in the future.

The historical conclusion that adverse economic circumstances are usually (although not always) necessary for the emergence of union-management cooperation can be buttressed by deductive analysis. When the bargaining unit is in a prosperous condition, management is not nearly as much preoccupied with costs as it is during an adverse situation. It is during a depressed condition that management becomes very conscious of the cost factor because of the relentless pressure flowing from the operation of the product market, and under this pressure management makes very serious efforts to reduce unit costs. If management becomes really interested in cost reduction during an adverse situation only, how much truer is this of the unions?

Union Objectives. The purpose here is to examine the degree to which union objectives, which have obstructed union-management cooperation in the past, will be prevalent in the future.

Intra-union exploitation [1] as an objective of labor groups will doubtless prevail in many an organization in the future. On the other hand, it is not out of the question to expect some

---

[1] By intra-union exploitation is meant a union objective designed to maximize the *income* of the employed at the expense of the unemployed. See above pp. 92-93.

unions to shift away from exploitation to income maximization of all the union members indiscriminately, inasmuch as union objectives are not static. The significant point is that, at present, there are no characteristics of the socio-economic environment which point definitely in the direction of either an increase or decrease in the prevalence of intra-union exploitation.

Left-wing unionism or, more specifically, unions under left-wing control, seem to be growing. Recent developments in the labor field point to the conclusion that there is a good deal of "boring from within" by the left-wingers. Even in such a conservative union as the Painters, for example, left-wing factions are beginning to assert their importance. Now, left-wing unionism does not necessarily rule out union-management cooperation, as was shown above. But it does make cooperation hinge on issues not necesarily involving the economics of the firm.

The future of left-wing unionism is not unrelated to the future of economic conditions in this country. A serious depression involving considerable unemployment may well create an environment conducive to left-wing ideology. If this be true, it points up an interesting conflict: a severe depression would, on the one hand, generate a condition favorable for union-management cooperation (adverse circumstances), and, on the other, foster a union objective obstructing cooperation.

In those bargaining units where two or more rival unions are competing for membership, the competitive struggle between the two unions will continue to foster policies which are not always compatible with union-management cooperation.[1] Since, in many cases, the rivalry is a function of the split in the labor movement, the future role which this organizing objective will play will depend on the chances of unity between the two federations. At this writing there seems to be little likelihood of such unity in the near future. Power

---

[1] The rationale of competition between unions operating in the same bargaining unit is explained in J. Shister, "Trade-Union Government: A Formal Analysis," *Quarterly Journal of Economics*, LX (November, 1945), 93ff.

drives and conflicting labor and political philosophies are the significant obstacles. It would seem that only under the most serious threat to the existence of organized labor in this country (say an administration bent on destroying unionism) can one hope for unity in labor.

Mention should also be made of the fact that the split in the labor movement has created a serious rivalry between leaders of unions that do *not* compete for membership in the same bargaining unit. Today, more than ever before, the rank and file judges its leaders by comparison with other leaders. And in this comparison, immediate monetary gains are the common denominator. It is not difficult to visualize how such a condition can generate union policies obstructing cooperation with management.

Rank and File and Leadership. Some of the basic attitudes of workers which have obstructed union-management cooperation in the past may well continue in the future. The opposition "in principle" to incentive wage systems will doubtless continue to prevail among those workers who have held such a view in the past. On the other hand, as these workers leave the active labor force, there is a possibility that the newcomers to the labor market—or at least a portion of them—will not necessarily hold those views.

To the extent that we can succeed in avoiding depressions, we should be able gradually to eliminate the workman's fear of insecurity. Under such circumstances, the opposition to incentive rates stemming from the fear of insecurity would eventually disappear. On the other hand, it must be noted that the mitigation or elimination of cyclical depression would eradicate from the labor market one of the adverse situations which, in the past, has contributed to union-management cooperation.

Should we expect the rank-and-file union members to show a greater insight into the economics of the firm in the future? Some of the trends seem to point to the possibility of an affirmative answer. The composition of the American labor force in general is changing in many ways, not the least important of which is the growing proportion of high school graduates in its make-up. And in the case of the unionized portion of the market, we are witnessing the growth of organization for the first time among white collar and professional workers. These two facts taken together spell a more "intelligent" group of unionized workers. But will this greater intelligence be utilized for a more thorough understanding of the problems faced by management? To a large extent, the answer depends on the type of leadership in the union.

Two forces now seem at play in American trade unions which point to the growing importance of national officers in the union governmental hierarchy. First is the spread of industrywide agreements. Secondly, even where agreements are local or companywide, structural conditions are compelling the local members to turn more and more to the national officers for counsel and guidance in collective bargaining.[1] Since national leaders have more insight into given bargaining situations than local leaders and since national leaders usually have greater control over the rank and file than the local leaders, it follows that this centralization trend in union affairs may well improve the chances for the development of union-management cooperation.

Management Attitudes. Given that mature management is a prerequisite for union-management cooperation, the significant question becomes, will mature management grow in numbers and influence in the future? It should be remembered that those employers who would be classified as mature today were not always so. The employers in the needle trades are an excellent case in point. While the unions in these trades participate actively in many managerial functions today, it was not always thus. This historical perspective must be kept in mind at all times if one is to make any worthwhile prognostications about managerial attitudes toward unions.

Employers who are opposed to collective bargaining basic-

---

[1] Cf. J. Shister, "The Locus of Union Control in Collective Bargaining," *Quarterly Journal of Economics*, LIX (August, 1946).

ally because of nonpecuniary motives are not likely to change their attitudes in the future. But most of these employers are older men, who will retire from active positions before long, and their places will be taken by younger men who have become much more inured to the collective bargaining process. In fact, some of their successors will have known only collective bargaining as a pattern of industrial relations. The attitude of these younger men is bound to be substantially different from that of their older predecessors. It does not follow from this, however, that they will necessarily be of the mature management type when they take office. The only point here is that they will probably not belong to the first group in our classification.[1] Which of the other groups they will fall into, it is impossible to predict without a detailed analysis of the concrete situation in each instance.

As regards employers who insist on the retention by management *exclusively* of certain business prerogatives, it is not at all out of the question to expect them to alter their attitude on this question and thus gradually drift into the mature management group. It may well be that in many cases management will be forced to alter its attitude on the question of prerogatives as a result of the impact of union bargaining power. But in such instances, management may well realize, after a time, that the sharing of certain management functions with the union does not raise havoc with the firm.[2] Indications that this transmutation is already in its embryonic stage are not lacking.[3]

One of the recent trends in union wage policies may well serve to induce many employers to renounce their allegiance to the concept of "exclusive management prerogatives." The

[1] See above, pp. 103-104.

[2] Speaking about the acceptance of the seniority principle by the railroads in the nineteenth century, one observer has stated: "Doubtless railroad managements finally came to realize that, while seniority would entail a partial surrender of their prerogatives of job allocation, the loss therefrom might be compensated by a decrease in the extremely high rate of labor turnover." (D. H. Mater, "The Development and Operation of the Railroad Seniority System," *Journal of Business*, XIII [October, 1940], 403.) Also see "From Conflict to Cooperation," *Applied Anthropology*, V (Fall, 1946), 5.

[3] See Bakke, *op. cit.*, pp. 20-21.

allusion here is to the tendency for uniform wage concessions to be obtained from employers in any given industry (and to some degree, also between industries), even where bargaining is on a local or companywide basis. To the extent that this continues to prevail, future differentials in labor costs will develop mainly as a result of the nonwage elements in cost. Consequently, if some employer in the industry is desirous of getting a jump on his competitors, he may well accept the union's participation in certain managerial functions if, by doing so, he can cut his unit labor costs below those of his rivals. It does not require any great imagination to realize that once such a move is started by one employer others will follow, and in this manner the enforcement of "exclusive managerial prerogatives" will be impossible.

The analysis in the preceding paragraph does not hold indiscriminately in every industry. Two limiting conditions must be observed. First, there must be no substantial "degree of monopoly" in the sale of the product. Secondly, labor costs must constitute an appreciable portion of total costs.

It should be noted that the prediction in the above paragraphs is premised on the assumption that the sharing of managerial functions does not lead to a reduction of the employer's net monetary gain. In other words, it was assumed that the socio-economic conditions prevailing in the bargaining unit were of such a nature as to enable the management to maintain its economic position despite the sharing of management functions. But what if the bargaining unit is not of such a type? This brings us to the analysis of the future role of management falling into the second group in our classification.[1]

The employers whom it will be most difficult to convert to mature management will be those who have nothing to gain from unionism, economically speaking. The rather hostile

[1] More specifically, that portion of the second group which interprets the objective data in an accurate fashion. As for those employers in this group who are quite erroneous in their belief that unionization reduces their net monetary gains, there is ample opportunity for them to correct this misinterpretation over time.

attitude of employers in this group stems from a calculus which interprets the actual data in an accurate fashion. And because the interpretation is accurate, there is no way of refuting it by allusion to reality. So long as this hostility prevails—and it will continue to do so unless the objective data change—management will certainly not inspire cooperative effort on the part of the unions. As a result, therefore, even when the bargaining unit is in an adverse situation, there may be no cooperation forthcoming from the union because the employer will have alienated the goodwill of the union.

On the whole, it would seem that management attitudes will not be a uniform obstacle to union-management cooperation in the future. In the long run, the real obstacle will reside in those areas where management happens to be correct in its belief that the impact of unionization on the firms spells a reduction in net monetary gains.[1] These circumstances will generate a hostility of management toward the union. This hostility will alienate the union, create militant leadership, and thus obstruct cooperation even when the firm is under the influence of an adverse economic situation.

Miscellaneous Elements. In our analysis of the necessary and sufficient conditions required to generate union-management cooperation, the question of union structure was not discussed. This was essentially because the historical data disclose that union-management cooperation plans have been instituted in areas of both craft and industrial unionism. Despite that fact, however, there are deductive grounds on which to suppose that, other things being equal, cooperation on cost reduction will be fostered more easily in the case of industrial unionism than in the case of craft organizations. Where several crafts bargain independently with the same employer, each craft is likely to concentrate on the fact that its cost to the employer is only a "negligible" part of total costs. Any cooperation on its part to reduce costs, therefore,

---

[1] One of the important gaps in labor market economics is the lack of information regarding the effect of unionization on the firm's unit costs in both the short and long run.

may have very little effect on the improvement of the economic situation of the firm as a whole. Since there is no
assurance that the complementary crafts will also cooperate,
the efforts of any one craft may well be discouraged.[1] It is
obvious that such a situation could not arise were there only
one union representing all the employees in the plant.

If the above comment is accurate, then the growth of
industrial unionism in recent years should be a favorable factor
for the development of union-management cooperation in the
future.

CONCLUDING REMARKS

The preceding analysis of the future of union-management cooperation in this country does not lead to any categorical conclusions regarding the growth of this aspect of labor-
management relations. There are factors pointing to its
development and factors pointing to its decline. What the net
result will be is impossible to say at this juncture. We should,
therefore, beware of rather facile, categorical predictions
about this problem. One should remember, however, that
union-management cooperation is something more than just
"industrial peace," although not unrelated to it. This means
that even if union-management cooperation were to decline in

---

[1] An illustration of the above point is afforded by the commercial printing
unions in New York City. The New York commercial printing plants were
losing business to other centers during the twenties and the thirties, largely
(although not exclusively) because of the high labor costs prevailing in New
York. One of the obstructions to a reduction of these costs by means of
union-management cooperation was the existence of several craft unions
bargaining independently with the employers. In the words of a vice-president of the Typographical Union: "There are elements entering into the
cost of printing in metropolitan centers . . . over which we would have no
control if we adopted laws from now until the middle of next month. We
have few restrictive working conditions; we have few make-work rules. However, we are only one of the component parts of the printing industry.
Without mentioning names and in an endeavor not to accentuate the feeling
which might and does exist as between crafts, permit me to say that in a
particular jurisdiction I know of a requirement wherein seven men are necessary to man a certain machine, but within five or six miles of that jurisdiction it requires only two men to man the same machine, producing the
same volume." (Typographical Union, *Convention Proceedings* [1936].
p. 62.)

the future, industrial peace might still become more prevalent. The need for "mutual survival" [1] may well reduce the amount of industrial warfare in the future, but whether the same motivating force will also generate union-management cooperation is quite another question.

The emergence of an era of full employment has some very significant implications for union-management cooperation. With complete utilization of resources, increasing wage rates will eventually be translated into increasing prices unless productivity can be raised to compensate for the higher wage scales. Since union-management cooperation is designed to increase productivity, it would seem that we have here an ideal solution for the problem of inflation. Such is not, however, the case.

The analysis in the preceding pages has stressed the fact that union-management cooperation in the past has required (in most cases) the existence of an adverse economic situation in the relevant bargaining unit. But in a period of full employment most firms are likely to be in a fairly prosperous position. This conflict may well mean that we shall have to accept inflation together with full employment. Or it may mean that government control of prices will prevail even in peacetime. In such a case, it would become imperative to control wages also, and free collective bargaining would become a thing of the past.

There is, of course, a way out of this dilemma. It involves a radical change in attitude on the part of both management and organized labor toward the problem of cost reduction. Both parties will have to become far more cost conscious in prosperous periods. While such a transmutation in basic philosophy is not at all impossible, the historical evidence and current signposts certainly do not point unequivocally in that direction.

[1] Cf. Bakke, *op. cit.*, chap. 6.

CHAPTER FIVE

New Patterns of Collective Bargaining

by *Everett M. Kassalow*

THE GROWTH of labor unions and the extension of collective bargaining to millions of "new" workers and "new" industries has moved so swiftly in the past ten or twelve years that it is difficult to grasp the magnitude of this change. As World War II ended, all parties—labor, management, and government—took up the plea for a return to the old forms, the kind of bargaining that preceded the war. Actually, too many of the props had changed to permit a return to the old setting.

Naturally, some relaxation of the kinds of public control that were exercised over labor and management during the war was inevitable. Turning back the clock entirely, however, was impossible. Today, collective bargaining operates in a new social and economic framework. Its ramifications impinge far more sharply upon the entire economy than ever before, and it seems likely that the public's stake in collective bargaining must inevitably influence the conduct of management and labor, in one way or another.

We shall examine some of the main outlines of these developments and try to indicate some of the emerging trends. Although the greater part of this analysis will be devoted to the union side of the picture, somewhat similar developments are observable on the management side of the table.

COLLECTIVE BARGAINING AND THE PUBLIC

In less than a dozen years collective bargaining has been transformed from a process involving only a small sector of

116

our economy into a major institutional force in American life. As late as 1934, union-management contracts fixed the wages and working conditions for some three or four million workers and were confined, to a great extent, to the so-called sheltered trades such as printing, construction, or bakeries, or to regulated industries like railroads. Today, collective bargaining agreements cover nearly fourteen million workers. They set the pace, so far as wages and working conditions are concerned, in almost every important manufacturing industry, in mining, in transportation, in important segments of the lumber industry, and in other trades and services.[1]

Sheer numbers have blown up the importance of labor-management relations into national concern. What goes on between fourteen million workers and their employers affects the entire nation. Perhaps even more significant has been the type of bargaining that has developed during the past five or six years in the mass production industries. In the steel, automobile, electrical machinery, and other basic industries, bargaining now proceeds on an industrywide, or at least corporation-wide basis.[2] Corporate and market organization in these industries has, of course, long been established on a national basis. For this reason the development of collective bargaining in these industries almost inevitably took the line it followed.

The importance of this development stands out. When wage negotiations at one sitting *directly* involve a quarter or a half million workers (and the wage levels of many millions more, indirectly, as will be pointed out below), the old notion that the parties can go off into a corner and bargain merely unto themselves runs into difficulties. These negotiations affect the aggregates of total national income and the general

---

[1] See *Monthly Labor Review*, LXII (April, 1946), 567, and Leo Wolman, *Ebb and Flow in Trade Unionism* (New York, 1936), National Bureau of Economic Research, p. 193.

[2] Industrywide or corporation-wide bargaining is not, of course, anything new in American labor history. The "new" industries covered by this kind of bargaining magnify its importance today.

price level, and they naturally become a matter of public concern.[1]

It is true that even before the late thirties the outcome of negotiations between labor and management did have important consequences for the public. Still, the situation was not quite the same. The wage agreements, for example, between the building trades' unions and employers in New York, Chicago, San Francisco, and in all the other major cities did, in the long run, seriously influence the construction industry as a whole. But obviously, since these agreements were not negotiated simultaneously or in the same place, they did not make an immediate, combined impact upon the national economy, and they might proceed relatively unnoticed. Such is not the case in negotiations between, to take an example, the United Steelworkers of America (CIO) and the United States Steel Corporation.

The nearest pre-World War II analogue to the current labor-management situation in the mass production industries is the bituminous coal industry. For several reasons, however, the economic questions involved in the coal negotiations are not comparable to those in steel and in other mass production industries. To select one important difference, the coal industry for some years before the war was highly regulated by the federal government. Pricing, marketing, and other important phases of this industry, as a consequence, were not comparable with the manufacturing industries.[2] In addition, the rather isolated geographical nature of the industry made it less likely that the decisions reached between the coal operators and the union would affect other industries.

The isolated character of collective bargaining in coal

[1] On the other hand, the notion that we can outlaw these virtually, and inevitably, nationwide bargaining agreements flies in the face of existing economic institutional arrangements.

[2] Curiously enough, the United Mine Workers' leaders, whose power renascence dates in no small measure from the passage of the NRA and the Guffey Coal Act, in recent years have been the most vociferous proponents of a government hands-off policy in almost all economic and labor relations questions.

should not, however, be overstressed. Anyone familiar with the development of collective bargaining in the steel industry is aware of the manner in which it has been entwined with coal. It is not accidental that the United Mine Workers of America was a prime mover in the formation of the CIO and the organization of workers in the mass production industry.

Aside from the national-income effects of collective bargaining already mentioned, industrywide bargaining and corporation-wide bargaining with large firms have other serious implications for the entire country. Here the analogy with coal is clearest. In the years immediately preceding the war and also during the war the recurring threat of a stoppage in the coal industry was a matter of national concern. Obviously a stoppage in steel has similar overtones, and to a lesser degree, the same can be said of the automobile industry. Then, too, whole sets of communities and large numbers of workers are directly involved in the corporation-wide type of bargaining that exists in the electrical equipment, rubber, meat packing, and farm equipment industries.

The great public interest in the negotiations in steel, automobiles, and other industries has found reflection in the tactics employed by the parties. To a considerable extent, for example, the negotiations in steel and automobiles are conducted in the public press. Leaders call press conferences to state their cases, the correspondence between the parties is frequently made public, the briefs are distributed, etc.

The 1946 strike conducted by the United Steelworkers, in particular, marked a new departure. A careful public relations campaign was undertaken to help the union tell the "facts" about the steel strike to the country. This campaign included a series of radio broadcasts over a national hookup. Speakers who broadcast on behalf of the union included prominent religious leaders and a university professor. Lower-rung steel union leaders were instructed to tell the story in community meetings. Even the printed material that was issued differed from the usual union pamphlets. Most effective of these was a so-called picture-written [1] pamphlet which explained the steelworkers' need for a two dollar a day increase.

NEW ECONOMIC APPROACHES

An examination of the economic arguments used in some of the major labor disputes after V-J Day further enforces the view that new ground is being broken. The General Motors case in 1946 particularly pointed this up. Recognizing that the problem of long-deferred wage adjustments in the mass production industries would have far-reaching economic implications, the General Motors Department of the United Automobile Workers (CIO) "attacked" on a broad front.

This UAW-GM issue raised a number of important and interesting problems and is worthy of careful consideration. We can here indicate only some of the main features.

Significantly enough, the first gun in the UAW campaign was an open memorandum entitled *How to Raise Wages Without Increasing Prices*, by UAW Vice-President Walter P. Reuther,[2] addressed to William H. Davis, then Director of Economic Stabilization.[3] This document is immediately distinguished by the fact that although it was issued by one union, indeed by only one section of one union (the GM department of the UAW, which has bargaining relationships only with the General Motors Corporation), it was concerned with the general problem of national wage policy to underwrite full employment in peacetime.

Much of the memorandum dealt with the price and profit phases of the case, but its real significance was not understood in most quarters. While unions, in bargaining situations, have frequently contended that existing profits were large enough

---

[1] This method of visual presentation is known, technically, in the advertising business as the "rebus method."

[2] Mr. Reuther was later elected to the presidency of this union.

[3] In original form this was a mimeograpned document addressed to Mr. Davis. It was later modified somewhat, and issued as a general pamphlet on the question *How to Raise Wages Without Increasing Prices* (Detroit, Mich., no date). The references here are to the original mimeographed memorandum to William H. Davis.

to raise wages without raising prices, the UAW stated the issue somewhat differently. The union argued that unless prices were held constant, and wages were raised (to increase purchasing power [1]), with a resulting cut in profit margins, the nation was doomed to slip back into the prewar policy of high prices and low output, which spelled unemployment in the thirties. The UAW memorandum cited a U.S. government study of sixty-five important manufacturing industries which indicated that American industry could, on the average, break even when operating at only 52 per cent of full capacity.[2] The study showed, the union argued, "that most manufacturing industries look forward to a profit base so high as to permit them to break even at output levels well below capacity." The union added,

Going into the postwar period with a wide gap between prices and wages, industry will not need to find markets for the products of full employment. It can produce at half or three-quarters of capacity and break even, or slightly more and make a profit. . . . It can sit down comfortably in the expectation of selling a lot for a little. It does not intend to adopt a new pattern just because we have passed through a war which has demonstrated—to its embarrassment—the tremendous, but strenuous, profit potential of capacity operations. It wants to get back to normalcy.[3]

To prevent industry from reverting to a pattern of high profit rate and low volume, the union insisted on the necessity for wage increases within the existing price structure. To quote again,

It is *desirable* to raise wage rates without raising prices, because a stabilization program that aims to stabilize the economy must be geared to a plan for achieving capacity operation at the earliest possible moment, and must refrain from making low-level opera-

[1] With the loss of overtime pay after the end of the war, the union contended a large wage increase was necessary to offset the loss in purchasing power and to maintain living standards. This objective, of course, was more in keeping with the traditional collective bargaining framework and with the tactic pursued by many other unions after V-J Day.

[2] See *War Production Board Release No. 7996* (May 16, 1945). The figures were based on management's own estimates.

[3] *How to Raise Wages Without Increasing Prices*, p. 21.

tions profitable by holding wages too low in relation to prices, as they now are.[1]

In a real sense, the campaign represented an attack on some of the monopolistic practices in American industry. For the union was contending that the existing general price patterns in manufacturing industries established high profit rates, which, in turn, would encourage low volume operations.

The question of looking at the corporation's books, about which a great deal of erroneous information was written, and of its ability to pay wage increases can now be seen in better perspective. In the brief which it presented to the corporation (entitled, significantly enough, *Purchasing Power for Prosperity, The Case for Maintaining Take-Home Pay Without Increasing Prices*), the union asked for a 30 per cent wage increase. The increase was needed in order to offset the loss of overtime pay after the war's end and to boost mass purchasing power. Shifting to the price side, the union insisted that the increase could be granted without raising prices and without injuring the company's prewar profit position, if the corporation would aim at a full-capacity operation. To do otherwise, that is, to raise prices, would perpetuate the low break-even point referred to above and would eventually undermine the hope for full employment.

So sure was it of its own position that the UAW went on to indicate that, if the corporation would demonstrate its inability to pay a 30 per cent wage increase without raising prices, the union would reduce its wage demands. The issue of ability to pay and opening the company's books enters here, for patently, before the union would trim its demands, it was insisting on a clear demonstration of inability to pay by the company. It was for this reason that the union insisted the company's books might have to be opened for examination.

The rigid insistence on the price question reflects the union's recognition of the public stake in the bargaining. Indeed, the entire UAW-GM case is a curious combination of

[1] *Ibid.*, p. 6.

a broad public argument for full employment and mass purchasing power on the one hand, and of an ordinary labor-
management dispute on the other hand. The UAW brief, for
example, which includes a careful analysis of the past, present,
and future profit-making capacity of one company, the General Motors Corporation, occasionally shifts off to considerations such as the following:

The country looks to the durable goods industries to provide a
sound basis for postwar prosperity, and it is up to these industries
—and particularly to the automobile industry—to convert the present pent-up demand into a large and permanent reservoir of demand through wider distribution of purchasing power.[1]

The tendency for unions to project their own immediate
collective bargaining problems on to the national economic
level, has been noted in a recent survey by E. W. Bakke of the
Yale University Labor and Management Center. Indeed, he
finds that to be one of management's major criticisms of
organized labor. Typically, management asserts:

The union's economic arguments involve living costs in general,
the general distribution of wealth, and like matters. Management
of a particular firm doesn't have any control over that. When we
say their [the unions'] economics are unsound, it doesn't mean
really that their reasoning isn't proper for the country as a whole.
But we in this company aren't managing the country as a whole.
We're responsible for showing a profit to *our* stockholders.[2]

It is not surprising, of course, that the unions, representing large numbers of workers in different geographical regions,
should be more immediately concerned with the welfare of
the entire economy than are the executives of individual corporations, who naturally tend to concentrate on their own
special problems.

The General Motors case is only an example of the new
paths being taken by labor-management bargaining. During

[1] *Purchasing Power for Prosperity, The Case for Maintaining Take-Home
Pay Without Increasing Prices* (October, 1945), pp. 16-17.

[2] E. Wight Bakke, *Mutual Survival, The Goal of Unions and Management*
(Labor and Management Center, Yale Univ., 1946), p. 42.

the wage drive in the fall of 1945 and winter of 1946, for instance, the Congress of Industrial Organizations established a top, over-all Wage Research Committee, composed of representatives of the three largest unions in the CIO. This committee functioned as a general adviser and policy-maker for all the CIO unions. While such a development might seem to be perfectly logical, it apparently marked a new departure in American trade union history. In the past, it has been the practice for some unions to consult with one another informally on wage policy questions, either on a local or national basis. The AFL building and printing trades' unions are a good example. This type of relationship has never been formalized, however, as in the case of the CIO Wage Research Committee. The committee issued a series of twenty-eight memoranda dealing with the economic issues in the wage drive and finally summed up the entire wage case for the CIO in one separate pamphlet.[1]

The range of subjects covered in the publications issued by the Wage Research Committee during the 1945-46 wage campaign are of considerable interest. While traditional collective bargaining subjects such as labor costs, profits, the rise in the cost of living, etc. were covered by the committee, some of the memoranda are a far cry from the old pattern of labor relations.

Among the twenty-eight were three surveys of "the national pay envelope," which analyzed the general problem of purchasing power and continued prosperity in the light of organized labor's needs. Several others dealt with different groups in the community and their stake in substantial wage increases for labor. In *The Farmer's Stake in Substantial Wage-Salary Increases,* the committee explained,

Farmers have a big stake in labor's efforts to see that wages and salaries are raised substantially. There can be no farm prosperity when city dwellers are underconsuming. But to buy what they

---

[1] These memoranda will be referred to as CIO Wage Research Committee Memorandum No. 1, 2, 3, etc. The summary pamphlet will be cited by its title, *The CIO Case for Substantial Pay Increases.*

need takes adequate pay envelopes. If only small wage and salary boosts are made, the farmer is going to feel it in lower prices and in unprofitable acreage. There can be no farm prosperity without substantial increases in the pay envelopes of the city wage earners and salaried employees who buy the farmers' products, because farm income is directly related to how much purchasing power is in the hands of urban wage earners and salaried employees.[1]

The report also included a summary of a series of Department of Agriculture studies which showed the probable level of farm income if the nation maintained a full employment economy, as well as what would happen to food consumption and prices if the nation reverted to prewar conditions, etc.

Again, the point to be noted is not the mere appeal to other groups in the community, since this is done regularly in labor-management controversies. The significance lies in the fact that these relationships are spelled out in some detail as an integral part of the CIO wage program.

In summarizing the CIO wage case, the general-public note was struck resoundingly. Wage increases were needed, Philip Murray stated, "to lay the groundwork for an era of full employment." On prices, the summary insisted that industry could pay a 31 per cent wage increase without raising prices. Accumulated reserves and high profits would more than make up the increase in the wage bill.

If, in the face of reserves and earnings on this scale, prices nevertheless rise, it will be not because of any economic necessity. It will be simply because the political pressure of industry is too great for the government to resist. . . . [Industry's] position is economically indefensible. It stems from a desire to receive higher than wartime profits during peacetime, at levels which defraud the workers, threaten the economy. For industry to plead poverty, inability to pay, and the danger of inflation, as answers to the CIO's pay demands, displays an arrogance and a lack of concern for the country's welfare which is profoundly shocking.[2]

The kind of public-interest wage campaign which was carried on by the United Automobile Workers, the United Steel-

---

[1] *CIO Wage Research Committee Memorandum No. 16,* pp. 6-7.
[2] *The CIO Case for Substantial Pay Increases,* p. 12.

workers, and the CIO Wage Research Committee is not, of course, being followed by all unions. What does seem important, however, is the emergence of a trend which probably has considerable portent for both labor and management in the future.

That this type of development is not transitory is indicated by the fact that the Wage Research Committee was reconstituted by CIO President Philip Murray in the summer of 1946 in order to prepare the ground for the negotiations in 1947. Its membership was broadened to include the five largest CIO unions,[1] as well as a representative from the CIO Committee for Maritime Unity. The Education and Research Department of the national CIO office coordinated the committee's work.

In the fall of 1946, the CIO pushed its public, economic attack on an even broader front. Mr. Robert Nathan, prominent economist, was commissioned to prepare an analysis of the wage-price-profit outlook, with a view toward helping to formulate wage policy for 1947. The report that Mr. Nathan and his associates issued was entirely their own, and "the research, analysis, and conclusions" rested "solely with the authors" and was "not to be imputed to the CIO."[2] The Nathan report and its conclusions, it might be noted in passing, were different in many important respects from the report of the CIO Wage Research Committee.[3]

The national character of the type of bargaining negotiations described above tends to impose the results upon other industries. As we have already observed, a great deal of publicity attends negotiations with the large steel, automobile, or electrical companies. This, plus the fact that other industries

[1] The United Steelworkers of America, The United Automobile Workers, the Textile Workers Union of America, The Amalgamated Clothing Workers of America, and the United Electrical Radio and Machine Workers of America.

[2] *A National Wage Policy for 1947* (Washington, D. C., Robert R. Nathan and Associates, Inc., 1946).

[3] *The Case for Substantial Wage Increases in 1947*, CIO Wage Research Committee, 1946 (mimeo.).

are linked with them by financial and organizational ties, all but makes it incumbent upon leaders in other unions and companies to press for settlements similar to those consummated in the major industries. This can have some grim results, as the ordinary give and take of collective bargaining is subordinated to aping a pattern arrived at in some other industry whose cost, price, and profit picture may be quite different.

THE NEW ROLE OF THE SPECIALIST

The new framework of collective bargaining, which we have been outlining, has naturally affected the techniques employed, as well as the personnel involved in bargaining. In many instances, rhetoric has given way to, or at least, is supplemented by the written brief bristling with facts and figures. The union or management seeks to enforce its position by economic logic, which may sway the public and/or government officials. As a consequence, the table-pounder's place is, to some extent, usurped by the "professional"—the research expert and the lawyer. Where the traditional forms of pressure, such as threats of discontent and of work stoppages, are retained, they now are frequently applied against new "opponents," namely, government officials. Lest it be imagined that this applies only to unions, we can recall the steel industry's delay in accepting President Truman's recommendation for settlement of the wage dispute between the steel companies and the United Steelworkers in the winter of 1946, or the General Motors Corporation's rejection of the recommendations of the federal government's fact-finding board in 1946. It is the widespread importance of negotiations, as in steel or coal, that sometimes brings the government into the picture.

The influence of the National War Labor Board during World War II was very significant. Presenting a labor dispute before that body was a relatively difficult technical exercise. It demanded a kind of formal statement, and in the major cases, at least, involved detailed briefs and testimony. All that, naturally, strengthened the role of the professional technician.

The effects of these developments upon traditional unionism are indicated in the following editorial, which appeared in the monthly organ of one of the oldest unions in America. The editorial was written at the time the organization had finally, albeit reluctantly, decided to establish a research department.

In recent years the task confronting your international officers has become increasingly difficult because of the remarkable changes made in the field of organized labor and the processes of collective bargaining. . . . In present day negotiations we are required to meet our employers who have their lawyers and statisticians to present truck loads of factual information to bolster their claims of inability to meet our demands so that unless we are prepared to substantiate our claims with counter statistics and data our case is lost at its very inception. With the result that we are often required to utilize the services of men with university degrees, as well as statisticians, economists and attorneys, to prepare our cases. . . . It is not sufficient for us to say that we do not like the trend that collective bargaining is taking. These things are facing us every day and we must be prepared to meet them. . . . With this thought in mind it is the purpose of the International, immediately after the first of the year, to establish a research department at headquarters. . . .[1]

While the number of economists employed by unions is still surprisingly small, their importance has grown considerably in the past decade. The kinds of work they now undertake have also shifted somewhat. In the preparation of the United Steelworkers' case in 1945, for example, the union's research department conducted a study of the earnings, expenditures, and savings of workers in a typical steel community. The study involved sampling and the usual techniques applied in interview research. It was conducted in the best scientific tradition, following consultation with various

[1] *The Boilermakers Journal,* December, 1944, p. 273. While this action was taken during wartime when government controls pressed even more tightly upon collective bargaining, the need is clearly not limited to the war period.

public agencies, including the U.S. Bureau of Labor Statistics.[1] That is a far cry from the "old days."

While there is little danger that the professional economist will steal the center of the union stage in the future, one can look to an expansion of this type of service in the labor movement. Even on the day-to-day level of labor-management relations, such as the routine adjustment of grievances, the professionalization of the personnel involved is proceeding rapidly. The unions have probably held an edge on employers in the skill of their "bargainers." Naturally their negotiators deal with many companies, and are in labor relations full-time, which gives them an advantage over their counterparts in any one company. That is changing, however, with many corporations employing labor relations specialists.

Even more interesting is the widespread development of industrial relations programs in various universities of the country. While these programs have many and varying objectives, it seems safe to predict that one of their important by-products will, eventually, be the training of a corps of young college graduates, schooled in industrial relations. Although some of the graduates will undoubtedly be employed by labor unions, the bulk of them will probably enter management where the level of remuneration is higher, so that industry will probably come up with the lion's share of the catch. In any event, the professionalization of labor relations will continue.

Professionalization or, more aptly, bureaucratization [2] of collective bargaining has also been accelerated by the widespread adoption of arbitration clauses in union agreements. These clauses provide that any dispute arising out of the interpretation and application of a union-management contract is to be referred to arbitration for final and binding decision. Both parties, consequently, forswear resort to a

---

[1] *The Braddock Steelworker, An Income and Expenditure Study for January, 1945, of Steelworkers in Braddock, Rankin and North Braddock, Pa.* (1945).

[2] Bureaucratizing in the sense of impersonalizing and "legalizing" what has been a very human and personal process.

strike or lockout as long as the agreement is in effect. Such arbitration clauses were found by the U.S. Department of Labor to be included in three-fourths of all union agreements in fourteen important industries.[1]

Clauses of this type tend to impart a kind of judicial coloration to labor-management relationships. Key disputes arising out of the day-to-day grievance problems are often prepared and argued by specialists versed in tricks and maneuvers and in the legalistic interpretations of union agreements.

In corporation-wide contracts in heavy industry, provisions for such arbitration are especially prevalent. Often the arbitration of unsettled disputes is performed by one individual, a permanent umpire, who is chosen by the parties at the time the agreement is signed. A kind of pyramid effect seems to result from this setup. Grievances begin at the shop steward and foreman level, work up to the committeeman and the department superintendent, and then may be carried to the plant committee and the top plant management.[2] Failing settlement by this stage, the grievance is referred to the international union office and the central office of the corporation. The whole procedure has the appearance of a sort of judicial hierarchy, with the arbitrator sitting as a kind of supreme court for grievances which the top union and company officials fail to settle.

All this goes a long way toward "judicializing" labor relations. Grievance procedure at the local plant level is all too often cramped and restricted. Important policy cases almost invariably make their way to the top level of the union and the corporation, where the case is argued before the umpire with full use of precedents, tortuous interpretations of clauses, etc.

Several union officials have complained to this writer that

[1] U. S. Bureau of Labor Statistics, *Arbitration Provisions in Union Agreements*, Bulletin No. 780 (1944), p. 1. The number is probably greater today.
[2] Of course these titles and the levels vary somewhat from union to union and from company to company, but the main steps are substantially similar.

the acceptance in an agreement of a so-called no-strike clause, with automatic arbitration of unsettled disputes, may invite management abuse.[1]   Management may "sit down" on many grievances and force them either into arbitration or the scrap pile.   Lack of time, money, and manpower make it inevitable that only a small number of grievances can be carried to arbitration.   As a result many justifiable (in the eyes of the union, at least) grievances are simply lost, by default, along the way.

The following complaint, made by a local of the International Association of Machinists, is typical of the protests being made by a number of other unions:

Consolidated Vultee Aircraft Corporation has repeatedly resorted to stalling tactics in an effort to defeat genuine collective bargaining. . . . It has been forcing all manner of minor grievances to arbitration in the hope thereby of depleting the local union of its funds and make it difficult for the lodge [local] to function.[2]

Other labor-management trends in recent years have also served to reduce real bargaining to formulas and technical criteria.   Under the influence of the National War Labor Board and a sales campaign by a number of industrial engineering firms, so-called "systematic wage-setting" has made considerable progress.   Scores of companies (in many cases with the willing cooperation of the unions) have called in industrial engineers to "redo" their wage structures and install job evaluation plans.   Again an essential element of collective bargaining is being taken out of the hands of the parties directly involved (labor and management) and turned over to a supposedly "impartial" expert and his slide rule.

As Solomon Barkin, Research Director of the Textile Work-

[1] Of course, union officials may use arbitration as a means of placing the burden of refusal of a grievance upon an arbitrator.

[2] *Aircraft Bulletin,* March 20, 1944.   Naturally this tendency to abuse the no-strike clause may have been more pronounced during the war, but the nature of the contract with the arbitration clause encourages it in any period. It is true that arbitration clauses and umpire systems have a long and seemingly "unabused" history in several industries, notably the needle trades.   It can be demonstrated, however, that the number and character of grievances in most other organized manufacturing industries are quite different from those in the needle trades.

ers Union has pointed out, "These job evaluation programs attempt to establish rigid formulae for establishing job rates and therefore reduce the area for collective bargaining." He notes that nearly all job evaluation systems "rest on the selection of an arbitrary list of job factors" and a schedule of values based upon them. Against these arbitrary factors and values, jobs are measured and rated. In contrast with this method of wage-setting, Barkin points out that under genuine collective bargaining,

Job rates are normally developed through mutual agreements. Many factors play their part in this determination. There is not a limited number of factors or a fixed graduation of values for each factor. Tradition, customary job relationships, productivity, supply and demand for specific skills, bargaining strength and job qualifications are constantly interplaying in the final determination of a rate structure under collective bargaining. Pressures change with time, new job values develop, and new rates are requested. Unions do not want a stratified method of appraising job values.[1]

As this professionalizing and "expertising" of collective bargaining has proceeded, numerous commercial services designed to "assist" management or labor have sprung up. Weekly and in some instances daily reports keep union or management officials posted on the latest trends in contract clauses, arbitration awards, NLRB rulings, etc.[2] The logical culmination of this process might be the codification of arbitration awards to serve as a kind of industrial jurisprudence binding on labor and management throughout the country. Indeed, some arbitrators have begun to cite the decisions of fellow-arbitrators (in cases involving entirely different companies and unions) as precedent for their own awards. This, in spite of the fact that a union agreement is obviously an instrument unique to the signatory parties, with its own origin, history, nuances, and intent!

---

[1] Solomon Barkin, "Wage Determination: Trick or Technique," *Labor and Nation*, I (June-July, 1946), 24.

[2] Some of the leading services are those published by the Bureau of National Affairs, Prentice-Hall, and the Research Institute of America.

A NEW ERA IN COLLECTIVE BARGAINING

Such developments seem far removed from the environment of personal give and take which, in the past, has been looked upon as essential for "healthy" collective bargaining. These new tendencies, however, appear to be inevitable. Superficially, they are probably a penalty for "bigness." More broadly, collective bargaining appears to be undergoing the kind of transformation that has occurred in so many institutions in modern society. In labor relations in many key industries a sort of formalization is setting in, and the older forms are giving way to more mechanical procedures and attitudes.

Although the future is unpredictable, it would seem, willy-nilly, that a movement involving fourteen million members and their families cannot pursue exactly the same sort of pressure-group tactics that were possible when it included only three or four million workers, largely concentrated in a small number of industries and skilled occupations. Increased social and political considerations on the part of the labor movement seem inevitable. And in the presentation of labor's economic demands this transition is already underway.

CHAPTER SIX

Collective Bargaining by Professional Societies

by *Herbert R. Northrup*

THE LONG depression of the thirties, the rapid growth of labor unions, and the failure of salaried groups to maintain their living standards as a result of inflationary prices have encouraged the expansion of unionism among professional employees. This in turn has precipitated a conflict within professional societies over (1) whether unionization is consistent with "professional ethics," and (2) whether it would be preferable to substitute "collective bargaining groups" controlled by professional societies for unions in areas where organization is deemed necessary. This chapter discusses the attempts of professional societies in the engineering, chemical, teaching, and nursing fields to establish themselves as collective bargaining agents, and develops certain implications of the organization of professional persons in the concluding section. To place the discussion in proper perspective, the union movement and its impact in these four fields is briefly surveyed and the question of "professional ethics versus unionism" is analyzed.[1]

UNIONS AND THEIR IMPACT ON THE PROFESSIONS

In none of the four professions is the union movement large, but rather in each instance derives its significance from the importance of the group. Thus according to available

[1] Some of the factual material in this paper relating to engineers and chemists is drawn from H. R. Northrup, *Unionization of Professional Engineers and Chemists*, Industrial Relations Monograph No. 12 (New York, Industrial Relations Counselors, Inc., 1946), by permission of the publisher.

occupational census data there are approximately 275,000 engineers (including chemical, mining, and metallurgical engineers) in the United States. Of these, no more than 150,000 can properly be classified as professionals; probably not more than 15,000 at most are members of affiliated or independent unions.[1]

Most professional engineers and chemists who are members of unions belong to the Federation of Technical Engineers, Architects, and Draftsmen's Unions (AFL) which dates back to 1918, or the Engineering and Technical Division (formerly the Federation of Architects, Engineers, Chemists and Technicians) of the United Office and Professional Workers (CIO), which was founded in 1934 and affiliated with the CIO in 1939.[2] In addition others are found along with rank-and-file workers in various American Federation of Labor and Congress of Industrial Organizations unions, and in several independent local and regional organizations composed of professional employees only, or in some cases, including also technical and/or white collar employees.[3]

The teaching field boasts the oldest and largest union in the professional groups studied—the American Federation of Teachers (AFL), founded in 1916, and today claiming a membership of 30,600.[4] In addition, there are numerous other teacher organizations varying in ideology from the New York City Teachers Union of the United Public Workers

---

[1] Estimates of number of engineers are from U.S. Bureau of Census *Statistical Abstract of the United States, 1944–45*, p. 133. The estimates of union members are by the author, as are those of the number of professionals among the engineers. The last were derived in part from Andrew Frasser, Jr., and A. F. Hinrichs, *Employment and Earnings in the Engineering Profession, 1929 to 1934*, Bulletin No. 682 (U.S. Bureau of Labor Statistics, 1941). Since chemical engineers are included with engineers it has not been possible to make a separate estimate as to number of union members among professional chemists.

[2] The A.F.L. union claims 6,200 members; the CIO, 10,000, but probably not more than 10 per cent of these are professional employees, the remainder being subprofessional technicians.

[3] See Northrup, *op. cit.*, pp. 10-12, 39-48 for details.

[4] *Report of the Executive Council of the American Federation of Labor to the Sixty-fifth Convention*, Chicago, 1946, p. 13. More recently AFL has claimed 50,000 members.

(CIO), which was expelled from the American Federation of Teachers because of Communist domination, to extremely conservative state and local associations, all of which may have a total membership many times that of the AFT, but many of which do not engage in collective bargaining. In view of the fact that there are approximately one million teachers in the country, the degree of unionization is thus still quite small.

The nursing profession is the only one of the four which does not have unions with special jurisdiction for its group and it has also had the least union organization of any. Probably not more than 3,000 to 5,000 at most of the more than 300,000 nurses are union members. They are mainly found in locals of the United Public Workers (CIO), the State, County, and Municipal Workers (AFL), the Building Service Employees' Union (AFL), and in locals directly affiliated with the AFL and the CIO.

Almost without exception unions in these professions have concerned themselves with the professional life of their members as well as with salaries and conditions of work. In part, this may be attributed to attempts of unions to prove that their activities are not "unprofessional." In part, it is also the result of the close relation of professional ethics and economics (e.g., the refusal to reduce fees or to charge less than the accepted rate is good ethics, but it certainly is not unrelated to economic standards). Whatever the cause, however, unions have thus invaded the areas of professional society operations. Hence, despite the small degree of unionization in the professions under discussion here, their effect on professional societies has been considerable. Since the early thirties the pros and cons of unionism for professional persons and the desirability of professional society participation in collective bargaining have been debated. The professional societies whose policies are examined here—the American Society of Civil Engineers, the American Chemical Society, the National Education Association, and the American Nurses' Association— have participated in collective bargaining to a degree hitherto never considered within a professional society's sphere. The reasons for this development can be understood best by an examination of the "professional ethics versus unionism" discussion.

PROFESSIONAL ETHICS AND UNIONISM

Engineers and Chemists. The controversy within professional groups over whether unionism is consistent with "professional ethics" is well illustrated by the debate which has been carried on since 1935 in the professional engineering and chemical journals. Initially, most of the leaders of these professions advised against entering unions. Such action, they argued, was unworthy of a professional man, and an engineer or chemist who joined a union was in effect giving up his chance to become a professional. The underlying assumptions of this point of view were that (1) most engineers and chemists would have an opportunity to become independent consultants, (2) this opportunity would be lost once an engineer or chemist became a union man, and (3) unions were necessarily destructive in approach and operation. As late as 1941, the dean of the College of Engineering of the University of Detroit advised engineers that they had to make a choice between unionism and a professional career. He stated: "There is a vast gulf between the professional man's personal work and responsibility and collective bargaining by labor union agents on behalf of multitudes of unknown and unidentified workers. No young engineer can straddle the gulf." [1]

This opinion has never been unanimous. In January, 1938, a committee on unionization, which had been appointed the previous summer by the Board of Direction of the American Society of Civil Engineers, concluded that "membership in a trade union is primarily an economic matter" which should have no bearing on a man's qualification for membership in the society; that it would be most unwise to seek exclusion of engineers from coverage of the National Labor Relations Act, but that the society might support efforts to "clarify the posi-

[1] C. J. Freund, "Unionism—An Issue in Engineering," *Personnel Journal,* XX (December, 1941), 222.

tion of professional and sub-professional men under the act, should that appear necessary"; that, since existing unions of engineers were "far from ideal," the society should stand ready to help its members form collective bargaining agencies if and when they desired; and that "to minimize the need for collective action by engineers," the society should publish a schedule of minimum rates, "seek actively to have such a schedule widely accepted," and be prepared to cite a member for unethical practice who paid less.[1]

Similar views were voiced in other societies. In 1939 a past president of the American Society of Mechanical Engineers declared that "enough engineers have become union members to force the leaders of certain important American engineering societies to recognize and discuss unionization as a serious problem in the profession. . . ." [2] This statement, made during the progress of a spirited discussion which lasted for over a year in *Mechanical Engineering*, was followed a few months later by the comment of another writer reminding those who looked longingly on the American Medical Association as a model, and who rejected as unprofessional the "coercive, restrictive and leveling" character of trade unions, that "there are closed professions which are so similar to unions that only skill in hair splitting will reveal a difference." [3] Some professional society members have voiced the complaint that the societies are employer-dominated. In 1934 the Detroit section of the American Chemical Society declared employee members of its chapter felt that "in the past, the ACS has been notably employer-minded as well as employer-dominated, and that, because of the dual nature of its employer and employee membership, the society has not in the past been able to serve them to advantage." [4]

[1] "Special Committee on Unionization Reports," *Civil Engineering*, VIII (March, 1938), 216-17.
[2] J. H. Herron, "Unionization of Engineers," *Mechanical Engineering*, LXI (November, 1939), 788.
[3] Letter to the editor by William Snaith, *Mechanical Engineering*, LXII (January, 1940), 67.
[4] *Register of Phi Lambda Upsilon*, XXX (January, 1945), 4, from *Detroit Chemist*, June, 1944.

More recently, there have been some careful and scholarly attempts on the part of professional engineers and chemists to explore possible conflicts between unionism and professional ethics in order to ascertain whether the two are inherently incompatible. Basic to any such discussion is a definition of what is meant by professional "ethics." Z. G. Deutsch, in one of the most constructive articles of this series, defined ethics as "a set of the rules-of-the-game" under which engineers conduct their activities and earn their incomes.[1] He then examined the possible points of conflict between such a code and unionism. Much stress in codes of ethics is laid on the confidential relationship of the professional man to his client or his employer. Although what Deutsch has termed "probably a narrow majority" of professional engineers and chemists do not now regard union affiliation as necessarily in conflict with professionalism, many feel that the nature of their "confidential relations" places them in direct opposition to unions. "Extremists among professional people (of which they are many) feel that joining a union is incompatible with holding membership in a professional society; that submitting to unionization constitutes surrender in the battle to secure recognition of engineering as a profession."[2]

Another consideration which professional people believe sets them apart from unionists is their "conservatism and professional dignity." As the Deutsch article points out:

Most codes of ethics of professional societies admonish the membership to avoid association with questionable enterprises, avoid sensationalism in advertising, be conservative in the promoting of schemes, and in all other ways, maintain professional dignity. Collective bargaining can, and on occasion is, conducted without conflict with this concept, although probably a large majority of professional people consider that the bulk of the efforts and statements of union organizers violate or at least ignore it. For this reason, perhaps as much as for any other, unions and unionization

[1] Z. G. Deutsch, "Collective Bargaining: Does It Conflict With Engineering Ethics?," *Chemical and Metallurgical Engineering*, LI (August, 1944), 96-99. This article is a good summary of the "ethics" discussion as it relates to engineers and chemists.

[2] *Ibid.*, pp. 97-98.

are distasteful to professional people, among whom are many who consider the difference between a profession and a trade to be like that between white and black . . . .

Those who believe that unionism is in fundamental conflict with the ethics of their profession find themselves in a dilemma when their positions are improved through the organized effort of other employees. For example, many companies follow a policy of adjusting the salaries of white collar and professional personnel to conform with raises gained for their factory workers by unions in collective bargaining. Professional people in such or like instances have questioned the ethics of accepting these gains while remaining aloof from participation in their acquisition. It has even been suggested that the combination of ability and education possessed by professional people could well be utilized in collective bargaining and that the true professional attitude in these situations would be to participate and to attempt to have the bargaining conducted on a high ethical plane.

Professional ethics, like unionism, does not condone low pay for professional work. It is regarded as bad professional ethics to pay low salaries, to "undercut," or to accept work at a fee or salary which is considered beneath the status or worth of a job. The committee on unionization of the American Society of Civil Engineers recognized this. Its forthright recommendation did much to strengthen the move within that society for the publication of a schedule of classifications and salaries, which was ultimately approved by the board of direction. Commenting on the relation of ethics and salary levels, a long-time member of the society wrote:

The worst offenders in the matter of paying low salaries to engineering employees have been the engineers themselves, both the consultants and the engineers at the head of engineering departments in . . . corporations. Some of the men who talked most about ethics in the ASCE were notorious for the low salaries they paid their employees. They capitalized on the idea that a young man must not just consider what was in his pay envelope, he must look ahead to the time when the job might lead to being a member of the firm.[1]

The preponderant view in this discussion is that unionism is not incompatible with the professional ethics of engineers and chemists. Many, however, who share this position would themselves be reluctant to join a union. To be sure, they recognize in principle that a professional person who joins a union to improve his economic standing by collective action should not lose or be considered to have lost any degree of his professional standing so long as he does not engage in, or condone, conduct considered unethical in the profession. They appear, however, apprehensive that in practice unionization will lead to such action, and that their profession and its members, whether approving or dissenting, will suffer loss of prestige.

Teachers and Nurses. Despite the long history of trade unionism in the teaching field, the debate over "professional ethics vs. unionism" is no less intense. Although both the proportion of union members and of those who do not oppose unionism is undoubtedly larger than in the engineering and chemical professions, most teachers have hesitated to initiate collective action. This is particularly true of college teachers. In the case of elementary and high school instructors, the shockingly low level of salaries in the face of inflationary living costs has induced an ever increasing number to unionize, and in several cases, to resort to strikes.

The large number of such stoppages since September, 1946, may prove a boomerang to the unionization of teachers. For it tends to associate strikes as the inevitable result of collective bargaining and to saddle the latter with all the distaste for the former that is common to professional and middle class groups in the United States. Although striking teachers have been treated sympathetically by the public, the Buffalo strike of February, 1947, marked the commencement of a reaction against such tactics which may prove seriously detrimental to

[1] Statement in a letter to the author.

peaceful efforts to improve teachers' salaries by collective action. On the other hand, it is true that teachers' strikes have dramatically called attention not only to the economic difficulties of those in the profession but also to the terrible effects of this condition on the caliber of the teaching force and the character of the public school system. To that extent these strikes have served a noteworthy purpose.

Of the four professions under consideration here, nursing has undoubtedly been least receptive to unionism. As late as 1938 a serious student declared: "As far as I know, no one has yet suggested the organization of mothers' unions, with standard scale of hours, wages, and other safeguards. In a sense, modern nursing is a specialization of certain functions formerly performed by mothers. The nurse serves others. A nurses' union would be almost, if not quite, as absurd as a Mothers' Union." [1] Inherent in such remarks is the belief that unionism might mean strikes and inferior service to patients—neither of which is, of course, compatible with professional nursing ethics.

Today, it is probable that the great majority of nurses regard unionization as unprofessional. Like teachers, however, they have been victims of high living costs, low wages, and especially of long hours and onerous working conditions. As a result, nurse membership in unions has climbed to its present figure, which, although an all-time high, still represents only a fraction of those in the profession.

PROFESSIONAL SOCIETIES AS BARGAINING AGENTS

The depression and unemployment of the thirties turned the energies of many professional societies towards means of alleviating the economic hardships of their members. Thus the American Society of Civil Engineers and the American Nurses' Association established employment reference lists. Other societies advocated sharing work, published salary

---

[1] J. K. Hart, "Economic Security for Nurses," *American Journal of Nursing*, XXXVIII (April, 1938), 393.

schedules, sought government relief and work for their members, or, as in the case of the medical and legal societies as well as several others, exhibited tremendous interest in means and methods of preventing "overcrowding" in their profession.

These developments were a natural result of the times. Professional people thus became accustomed to using their societies as avenues of economic improvement. Reluctant to turn to unions as did ordinary workers during this period, the professional man attempted to work out his economic problems with the aid of employment exchanges, personnel programs, and minimum schedules published by his professional society and urged on his employer by it.

With wartime inflation demanding stronger economic action, it was thus quite natural that professional societies should be urged to go one step further by inaugurating collective bargaining programs. Some society leaderships were quite hesitant to do this, especially in view of divided opinion among their membership. Others, particularly the leaders of the American Society of Civil Engineers and the American Nurses' Association felt decisive action was necessary if the societies were to maintain their position in the face of increasing trade union action. They believed that collective action was necessary and that the profession would be better served in collective bargaining by professional society leadership than by trade union leadership. It was for that reason that they inaugurated their collective bargaining programs.

Teachers. In the teaching profession, the situation is somewhat different. Having been in existence since 1916, the American Federation of Teachers was no newcomer to the field. During all this period, it has been competing with the National Education Association as well as with many local and state associations which reject affiliation with, or a community of interest in, the organized labor movement. Until recently, the National Education Association has not purported to act as a collective bargaining agent but has contented itself with issuing fair salary scales, fair personnel practices, and making representations to official bodies in behalf of teachers' salaries, etc. More recently, however, it has suggested that it could act directly as a bargaining agent. Moreover, several state and local organizations which heretofore had not been thought of as "unions" urged their local groups to act as collective bargaining agents, and many have done so. NEA affiliates have been involved in more strikes than have local unions of the American Federation of Teachers.[1] Despite the aggressiveness of many of the NEA bargaining groups, the AFT has termed them "company unions" and has urged teachers to affiliate with a "bona fide" union, which unlike NEA, has always opposed yellow-dog contracts or other restrictions on the right of teachers to unionize.

Teachers' bargaining organizations, whether union- or society-led, have many interesting problems, two of which may be discussed here. The first involves tactics. Because they deal with public bodies, their "bargaining" is likely to take the form of pressure tactics. That draws them close to the political field and political action. So far they have avoided, except in rare instances, any mass PAC-like political action, but have rather concentrated on legislative lobbying or local doorbell-ringing in order to impress government and voters with their needs and demands. Presumably, many teachers thus acquire valuable practical experience in how the politics of the country are generated. It is doubtful, however, if the necessity for them to engage in such activities increases their respect for the system of government which has not seen fit to compensate them more reasonably.

Since so much depends on public support, teacher strikes are desperate ventures produced by desperate situations. Unfortunately, however good the teachers' case or even their short-run gain, it is difficult to believe that strikes will aid their cause. Certainly, for the public welfare, there is immediate need to remove the source of their grievances. Otherwise

---

[1] Technically, NEA denies its affiliates have ever struck. Members, it claims, have merely refused to work without contracts. Practically speaking, however, as John L. Lewis has so forcefully demonstrated, NEA is making a distinction without a difference.

future generations will receive instruction from embittered and cynical participants in an economic warfare between government bodies and professional personnel.

The other problem of teacher bargaining groups deserving discussion here involves their operations. The typical group includes both supervisors and regular teachers. The effect is to restrain the latter from completely free expression and thus to lessen the effectiveness of collective bargaining for those of the group who are undoubtedly most in need of its economic benefits.

Despite common problems, lines are firmly drawn between NEA groups and teachers' unions. Teachers anxious for collective bargaining can take their choice between an experienced union and a professional society which has long eschewed a collective bargaining role. It is interesting to observe that competition between AFT and NEA is being transferred from the grounds of the latter to those of the former— i.e., instead of a union attempting to expand its activities into a professional society's field, a professional society is now striving to include collective bargaining within its domain.

Engineers. Active interest by professional engineering societies in collective bargaining, although relatively new, has occurred before. The American Association of Engineers was organized in 1915 "to raise the standard of ethics and to promote the economic and social welfare of the engineering profession," and it received its main impetus from professional engineers employed by railroads who desired representation before governmental wage boards during World War I in order to achieve salaries and raises already won by the railroad unions for their constituents. The AAE performed this service, whereupon most of its members dropped out. After a similar experience with state highway engineers, the AAE, greatly reduced in size and influence, henceforth confined its collective bargaining activities to publicity.[1]

---

[1] The AAE journal, *Professional Engineer*, and its publication, *Technologists Stake in the Wagner Act* (Chicago, 1944), by M. E. McIver *et al.*, are among the leading sources of information concerning engineers in collective bargaining.

It has remained for the much older American Society of Civil Engineers to be the first professional engineers' society to adopt a complete collective bargaining program. After much study and discussion the ASCE Board of Direction authorized the society's sections in October, 1943, to establish committees to act as bargaining agents for professional engineers. The following year this program was amended to minimize the possibility of employer domination of collective bargaining. The actual work of forming collective bargaining associations was divorced from the sections of the society and delegated to section committees composed solely of employee members. Since then, approximately one-half of the society's sixty-four sections have thus amended their constitutions but only a few have established active bargaining agencies.

The program of the ASCE is predicated on the assumption that professional engineers sooner or later would find it advantageous to engage in collective bargaining and that it would be preferable for leaders of the engineering profession, rather than leaders of organized labor, to control the bargaining agencies. The success of the ASCE organizations will determine to a considerable extent the future of professional society participation in collective bargaining. Unfortunately for those interested in further development of such activity, the ASCE bargaining agencies appear to be hindered by a number of factors.

First among these is the inherent defensive character of the organizations. Very often the bargaining groups have been established to ward off unionization by organized labor, to prevent professional engineers from being included with nonprofessionals in bargaining units established by the National Labor Relations Board, or to gain salary increases. Once the immediate cause of organizing has been removed, interest has often declined or even disappeared.

The civil engineers' organizations are also hindered by unrealistic rules and regulations. Thus the Board of Direction proposed annual dues of five dollars, prohibition on the use of strikes, boycotts, checkoffs, or union security provisions, and prohibition on any attempt to establish rules for preferential employment or for grievance machinery in behalf of those discharged for alleged incompetency.[1]

It can well be questioned whether dues of five dollars per annum are sufficient to maintain an organization even though all officers are volunteers and some assistance can be counted on from national representatives appointed to assist bargaining groups. This is especially true because the civil engineers' organizations are hampered by lack of personnel experienced in matters of organization and bargaining. Collective bargaining for even a small unit often requires not only experience but also full-time personnel, and to this the ASCE Board of Direction appears to have given too little thought.

Moreover, collective bargaining under the rules prescribed by the ASCE differs widely from the form in which it has been most successfully practiced. Although many unions have operated successfully without the aid of union security provisions or resort to the boycott, their main strength lies in their right to strike when they feel that fair conditions cannot otherwise be secured. Most unions would also insist on the right to submit grievances to employers on behalf of members alleged to be incompetent by the management or who might be discharged for no apparent good reason. The suggested rules of the ASCE, which would proscribe any such action, make collective bargaining exceedingly difficult. Indeed, although most of the society's bargaining groups had adopted the suggested regulations, at least one has not, because in the words of its leader, "Most professional men believe that the social problems associated with their work can be resolved around conference tables, but common sense dictates that the right to strike be retained by employees."[2]

Of considerable importance in the future of the ASCE bargaining groups has been the compatibility of their programs with the policies of the National Labor Relations Board. At first glance it appeared that the NLRB would pose no problems

---

[1] See *Civil Engineering*, XIV (May, 1944), 217.
[2] In correspondence, dated January 3, 1947.

for engineering groups who desire separate representation for professional personnel. Under the Wagner Act, the board consistently excluded professional employees from bargaining units composed of rank-and-file employees and just as consistently permitted professional employees to determine for themselves whether or not they desired to be included in the same units with white collar or nonprofessional technical groups.[1] The few instances to the contrary were largely traceable to instances in which the professional employees were performing nonprofessional functions or in which no request was made for exclusion from the bargaining unit by professional employees until considerably after the case was determined.

Nevertheless, there was a considerable amount of criticism of NLRB policies not only by the ASCE, but by several other engineering societies.[2] Most of this criticism was based on a misunderstanding of NLRB policies. The criticism of the American Society of Civil Engineers stemmed from the ASCE's proposal that bargaining units be based upon a model

[1] This is the NLRB's "Globe" doctrine, first enunciated in August, 1937, in a case involving *Globe Machine and Stamping Company*, 3 NLRB 294 (1937), whereby the bargaining unit is determined by permitting members of a homogeneous group within a plant to decide for themselves whether they desire to be represented by a union limited to their own group or by an industrial union in a larger unit. For its application to cases involving professional engineers and chemists, see *Matter of Shell Developing Co.*, 38 NLRB 196 (1942), and *Matter of Radio Corp. of America*, 57 NLRB 1731 (1944). For the NLRB's general policy of excluding professional personnel from bargaining units composed of general employees, see *Matter of Northrop Corporation*, 3 NLRB 237 (1937) and *Matter of Tennessee Copper Co.*, 5 NLRB 773 (1938). For a general discussion of NLRB policies affecting professional engineers and chemists, see Northrup, *op. cit.*, pp. 21-30.

[2] The five "founder" societies—American Society of Civil Engineers, American Society of Mechanical Engineers, American Institute of Electrical Engineers, American Institute of Mining and Metallurgical Engineers, and American Institute of Chemical Engineers—established a Joint Committee on the Economic Status of the Engineer which adopted a common policy in regard to the Wagner Act. Later, the National Society of Professional Engineers, an organization founded in 1934 to promote the economic welfare of licensed engineers, announced its support of any move to "clarify" the Wagner Act. See V. T. Boughton, "Where We Stand on Collective Bargaining for Engineers," *Engineering News-Record*, CXXXIV (February 8, 1945), 144; and "NSPE Convention Seeks Clarification of Labor Laws Affecting Professionals," *Engineering News-Record*, CXXXVII (December 19, 1946), 11. For the program of the American Association of Engineers, see *Professional Engineers*, XXXI (March, 1946), 304; and Northrup, *op. cit.*, pp. 25-26.

definition of the professional engineering employee. This the NLRB rejected and, in the opinion of this writer, rightly so. For what the ASCE proposed was to permit its committees to determine, on the basis of individual qualification, whom they should represent and therefore what employees should be placed in a given bargaining unit. Besides the fact that the Wagner Act gave the NLRB no authority to grant unions or associations the right to determine the bargaining unit, the ASCE proposal was thoroughly impractical. Under its program, each new employee's professional qualifications would have to be scrutinized before it could be determined whether he fitted into a bargaining unit. On the other hand, the National Labor Relations Board defined the bargaining unit in terms of job functions. Where professional employees can readily be delineated from sub-professional groups on functional grounds, the Board permitted the professionals to establish a separate bargaining group if they so desired and this proved a workable, satisfactory, and fair arrangement to most participants in elections.

Despite the NLRB's favorable policy, the ASCE spearheaded a drive to amend the Wagner Act, and in so doing, had general support not only from the other engineering societies, but also from the American Chemical Society, the American Institute of Architects, and the American Nurses' Association.[1] Congress rejected the ASCE proposal to define bargaining units on the basis of individual qualification, (as well as the ASCE demand to exempt professional employees from closed or union shop contracts), but it did include in the Taft-Hartley Act, the following proviso:

That the Board shall not (1) decide that any unit is appropriate for such purposes if such unit includes both professional employees and employees who are not professional employees unless a majority of such professional employees vote for inclusion in the unit.[2]

[1] U.S. Senate, Eightieth Cong., First Sess., Committee on Labor and Public Welfare, *Hearings on S.55 and S.J. Res.22, et al;* 1947, Part 3, pp. 1664-1669, 1702-1715.

[2] Public Law 801, Eightieth Cong., Section 8(b)(1).

The remarks of Senator Taft,[1] combined with the definitions of "professional employee" given in Section 2(12) of the Taft-Hartley Act, as one "engaged in" work defined as professional or engaged in work preparatory thereto, indicate quite conclusively that the intent of Congress was to codify existing NLRB policy. Thus, the ASCE must still reorient its thinking on bargaining units if it expects to win controversies on that subject.

Chemists. The American Chemical Society has not engaged in collective bargaining to the same extent as the American Society of Civil Engineers. The chemical society has, however, been very much concerned with the subject. Its intervention in a case decided in 1942 convinced the NLRB to apply the "Globe" doctrine to professional engineers, thus assuring professional employees of the opportunity to determine for themselves the character of their bargaining agent,[2] and it supported the recent amendments making this policy a matter of law. Following its experience in this case, the American Chemical Society sought advice of counsel as to whether it could engage in collective bargaining. The counsel's report pointed out that since the society was composed of employers (including corporations) as well as employees, it could not go beyond advising its members as to their rights and obligations under labor laws and offering them assistance as had already been done. The report of the counsel also urged the society to encourage the formation of unions composed entirely of professional men in instances in which collective bargaining was desired. One of the results of this report has been the formation of a number of such independent organizations. ACS is not likely to push collective bargaining to any great extent in the future, however, in view of the results of a poll recently conducted by Opinion Research Corporation, which found

[1] Reading the NLRB's decision in the key *Shell Development Co.* case (38 NLRB 196), Mr. Taft asked the ASCE representative "if that decision were made law, then that would satisfy most of your needs?" The latter replied affirmatively, apparently continuing the previous ASCE confusion which earlier had called the *Shell* case a victory for its way of thinking. (U.S. Senate, *op. cit.*, p. 1712.)

[2] This was the *Shell Development Company* case, 38 NLRB 196 (1942).

73 per cent of the ACS members unqualifiedly opposed to unionization and only 6 per cent in favor of it. The remainder were undecided or without opinion.[1]

Nurses. In line with sentiment in the nursing profession, the American Nurses' Association has never been favorably disposed toward unionization of nurses. In 1937, ANA announced that it did not "recommend nurses' membership in unions" because of its conviction that "in their professional organizations nurses had the instruments best fitted and equipped to improve every phase of their working and professional lives."[2] This negative policy was strengthened by a program urging state affiliates to "assume their responsibility for . . . standards of nursing care and employment conditions for nurses." At the same time the ANA urged coverage of private and public hospitals by social security legislation and acceptance of minimum wage and hour standards which it published.[3]

As early as 1941, however, nurses in the booming industrial centers of California demanded a stronger program. Faced with rising living costs, shortages of personnel, and long hours, they found hospitals unwilling to raise salaries in conformance with their scales. As a result, some nurses turned to unionization for relief. Meanwhile, the freezing of wages in October, 1942, added to the difficulty of obtaining salary adjustments. After fruitlessly inviting the state hospital association to join with it, the California State Nurses' Association (California branch of ANA) went before the National

[1] *Chemical and Engineering News,* XXV (February 17, 1947), 25-30; *Collective Bargaining for Professional Employees* (Washington, The American Chemical Society, 1944). See also Northrup, *op. cit.,* pp. 14-15, 23-25, 45-46. Recently, a proposal has been made to amalgamate the American Institute of Chemists with the American Chemical Society. Under this program, the former, which was founded in 1923 "to serve the professional interests of chemists" including "business problems, public relations, and civic responsibility," would take over all economic and collective bargaining matters as a branch of the chemical society. (See *The Chemist,* XXIV (January, 1947), 7-9.) The Institute of Chemists has favored "strong professional group or groups . . . to represent employed professional chemists." (See McIver *et al., op. cit.,* pp. 227-30.) The proposed amalgamation failed to materialize.

[2] *American Journal of Nursing,* XXXVII (July, 1937), 766.

[3] *American Journal of Nursing,* XXXVIII (February, 1938), 221-22.

War Labor Board and secured the full 15 per cent Little Steel increase.[1]

Having successfully represented nurses before the NWLB, the California State Nurses' Association requested its members in January, 1943, to vote whether they wished it to act as their collective bargaining agent. After an overwhelming affirmative response, the state association commenced signing collective agreements with hospitals and with a few industrial plants employing nurses.

The California experience and the subsequent entrance into the collective bargaining field by the American Society of Civil Engineers,[2] aroused the ANA to the possibility of recommending collective bargaining activities to its other state affiliates. After a favorable committee report had been adopted by the Board of Directors, the 1946 ANA convention unanimously approved the program. A number of state affiliates have since established collective bargaining agencies as ANA has recommended.[3]

In its recommended rules to affiliates for collective bargaining, the American Nurses' Association appears to have avoided the pitfalls of self-restrictive regulation which have so hindered bargaining groups established by the American Society of Civil Engineers. Their agreements set forth wages

[1] Based in part on an interview with Mrs. Mary E. Schmidt, member of California State Nurses' Association and consultant on collective bargaining to ANA. See also *American Journal of Nursing*, XLVI (July, 1946), 437-38; (September, 1946), 630; (November, 1946), 728-29.

[2] A report on the ASCE program was made to the ANA by the latter's attorney. See W. C. Scott, "Shall Professional Nurses' Associations Become Collective Bargaining Agents for Their Members?," *American Journal of Nursing*, XLIV (March, 1944), 231-32.

[3] There are a number of smaller, more specialized nursing associations besides ANA, and a move is now under way to consolidate them. In a proposal for a new structure of organized nurses, the Raymond Rich Associates recommended that the proposed merged association incorporate the program of the California State Nurses' Association. (*American Journal of Nursing*, XLVI [October, 1946], 659-61.) Meanwhile, the National Organization for Public Health Nursing, the largest of the above associations, resolved that "all discussions and negotiations for improvement of personnel policies shall be carried on through professional nursing organizations rather than through organized unions. . . ." (*Public Health Nursing*, XXXVIII [November, 1946], 577.)

and working conditions in detail and provide for a grievance machinery terminating in arbitration, which in no manner precludes adjudication of complaints concerning layoffs, discharges, or other typical sources of grievances.[1]

Far from proscribing union security clauses as do the civil engineers, the ANA regulations encourage their full utilization. Many of the contracts signed by the California group already contain union shop provisions. A principal reason appears to be the desire to eliminate any foothold of organized labor. A further restriction on union rivals is the rule adopted by the 1946 ANA convention which would prohibit "dual" membership once a state affiliate has put its collective bargaining program into effect.[2] Thus any nurse in California who is a union member automatically becomes ineligible for membership in the California State Nurses' Association, and hence, in the American Nurses' Association. As loss of ANA membership means loss of professional status, contacts, and aids, as well as in some cases, position or rank, unions will find it increasingly difficult to compete with ANA bargaining groups.

Since bargaining groups include not only staff nurses but head nurses and supervisors as well, the rules of the ANA provide that each category shall meet separately and draw up its program. The possibility remains, however, that grievances of staff nurses, which may involve relations with member-supervisors, will not be adjudicated to the satisfaction of the complainants or will otherwise result in intra-organization difficulties.

A different and delicate problem with which the ANA must come to grips involves Negro nurses. Many state nurses'

[1] For a typical agreement signed by the California State Nurses' Association, see the one with the East Bay Hospitals (San Francisco area), reproduced in *The Modern Hospital*, LXVII (October, 1946), 83-84.

[2] This rule reads: "Since it is the established policy of other groups, including unions, to permit membership in only one bargaining group, the Association [ANA] believes such policy to be sound for the state and district nurses' associations." Proponents of this rule have pointed out that "Nothing could be more unfair than for a state nurses' association to adopt this policy unless it has a well-organized and effective economic security program." (*American Journal of Nursing*, XLVI [November, 1946], 729.)

associations, especially in the South, exclude Negroes, and there does exist a separate Negro nursing association. The ANA has urged its state affiliates to admit nurses regardless of race, and some reform has been achieved. At its 1946 convention, the ANA urged abolition of any salary differentials and barriers to employment based on race, and voted to permit Negro nurses to affiliate directly with the national association in areas where state bodies exclude them.[1]

Despite these forward steps, the central issue remains in so far as collective bargaining is concerned. In states in which Negroes are excluded from nursing associations, the ANA proposes that they assign bargaining rights to the state association nonetheless. It is questionable whether proper representation for Negroes is feasible under such an arrangement. If the ANA wants its affiliates to act as bargaining agents with union shop contracts and to forbid "dual" membership, it must require that the bargaining groups admit all qualified personnel to membership. It is worth noting here that the record of professional societies in the United States in regard to race discrimination is in many instances no better, and in some instances considerably inferior, to that of trade unions.[2]

The California nurses have demonstrated considerable initiative and foresight in the mechanics of collective bargaining. Realizing that strikes are unthinkable, they have utilized public relations instead. They employ public relations counsel to keep the public abreast of their needs and to bring pressure on hospitals or other institutional bodies reluctant to meet their demands. In so doing, they have been careful to associate their demands with a public viewpoint.[3]

[1] *American Journal of Nursing*, XLVI (August, 1946), 512; (October, 1946), 729. For similar action by the National Organization for Public Health Nursing, see *Public Health Nursing*, XXXVIII (November, 1946), 577.

[2] Thus until recently the American Bar Association excluded Negroes entirely and some of its constituent bodies still do, as do some of the affiliates of the American Medical Association.

[3] For a case study of this technique, see B. J. Ballard, "The Nurses' Staunchest Friend Could Be the Public," *American Journal of Nursing,* XLVI (September, 1946), 586-88.

Thus, when successfully pressing for the forty hour week, they stressed that, far from aggravating the nursing shortage, the shorter work week would improve it because good working conditions encourage entrance to the profession, and married women could remain in nursing positions. The success of public relations tactics in California has induced ANA to include them as an integral part of its recommended collective bargaining program.

The ANA program will in the main affect nurses employed in hospitals and other public and charitable institutions not subject to the National Labor Relations Act. Unlike unions which include nurses as members, the association does not advocate NLRA coverage of such institutions. Because its program does envisage representing nurses in industry—as its California branch already does in a few instances—the ANA has gone on record in favor of separate bargaining units for industrially employed nurses, and its leaders supported the movement initiated by the professional engineering associations, which resulted in the already mentioned amendment to the National Labor Relations Act. Actually, on the basis of the performance of the National Labor Relations Board, the ANA had even less reason for interest in amending the National Labor Relations Act than had the engineering societies. The NLRB uniformly excluded nurses from bargaining units composed of either rank-and-file or white collar employees, and did so despite claims to the contrary on various occasions by unions or employers. Since nurses "constitute [a] well defined professional group," the NLRB placed them in separate bargaining units as a matter of course.[1]

The ANA, however, was quite perturbed because the NLRB placed practical and registered nurses in the same bargaining unit on occasions. Apparently, mainly for that reason, ANA's president charged that the Board did not "evidence

---

[1] *Matter of Electric Auto-Lite Co.*, 9 NLRB 147 (1938); *Matter of Electric Auto-Lite Co.*, 50 NLRB 68 (1943); *Matter of Hudson Motor Car Co.*, 45 NLRB 55 (1942); *Matter of Consolidated Vultee Aircraft Corp.*, 59 NLRB 1276 (1944); *Matter of Bethlehem-Alameda Shipyard, Inc.*, 59 NLRB 1525 (1945). For ANA's position, see the *New York Times*, March 5, 1946.

any great preoccupation with or respect for professional status." [1]

Here again, however, the NLRB appeared blameless. For in the case used by the ANA president as an illustration,[2] the practical and registered nurses were performing very similar, if not identical functions. Thus, the Board's decision was soundly grounded. Its decision here, as its decisions generally, demonstrated considerable preoccupation with, and full respect for, professional status.

SOME CONCLUSIONS AND IMPLICATIONS

The entrance of the professional societies into the collective bargaining field raises many questions concerning the future course of the professions and organized labor. There appears to be a central thesis governing the actions of both groups: that unions and professional societies cannot exist side by side and that inevitably one will triumph to the exclusion of the other. Acting on this belief, whatever its merits, professional societies and unions are each endeavoring to perform the obligations of both and to exclude the other from participation in the life of professional men and women. The policies of the American Nurses' Association are forthright in this regard. Less obvious steps in the same direction are the policies of the American Society of Civil Engineers particularly, and of the other engineering and chemical societies generally, in urging bargaining units selected on individual qualification as determined by the societies and in promoting bargaining agents under the leadership of persons who are professional-society minded. And the National Education Association, which has for years opposed the unionization of teachers, now proposes collective bargaining under its own banner and leadership.

This essay has been confined to a discussion of professional societies as bargaining agents and has, therefore, dealt with union policy only as a motivating force which has led the

---

[1] U.S. Senate, *op. cit.*, p. 1666.
[2] *Bethlehem-Alameda Shipyard*, 59 NLRB 1525 (1945).

professional groups into collective bargaining. It must be noted here, however, that unions are as loath to share the scene with professional societies as are the societies with unions. The American Federation of Teachers (AFL) blames the teachers' financial woes on the National Education Association; the United Office and Professional Workers (CIO) regards professional societies as "employer minded" and generally antagonstic; and the list of unions could be expanded without discovering a dissenter. All urge that societies either be abandoned, or be compelled to restrict their activities to purely technical or noneconomic matters.

The roots of union-professional society antagonisms and fears are not difficult to discover. They stem on the one hand from the conservative, middle-class outlook of most professional persons; and on the other, from the failure of unions to adapt techniques, policies, and programs to the professional level. The "after all, we are all workers" approach has served to alienate many professional persons from the labor movement, who might otherwise be sympathetic. "The terminology of professionalism is fundamentally eulogistic." [1] Unionism's endeavor to organize professional personnel by appeals to worker solidarity, when professionals regard themselves as a group set above the common herd, has been a tactic as self-defeating as it has been persistent.[2] Combined with the professionals' middle-class distaste for trade unionism in general, it has created the demand for a "different" type of collective bargaining agent and thus opened up the field to the professional societies.

It may well be that the American labor movement lacks the initiative and resourcefulness to handle the requirements of professional personnel. Given the need for collective action by employees in many professions—a need that is becoming

---

[1] Oliver Garceau, *The Political Life of the American Medical Association* (Cambridge, Harvard Univ. Press, 1941), p. 5.

[2] In the case of unions adhering to the Communist Party "line," such as the United Office and Professional Workers (CIO), it is philosophically and psychologically impossible to take any other position. The Communist ideals and goals reject any such differentiation or if it exists, seek to eliminate it.

increasingly more obvious—perhaps it can best be met outside organized labor's sphere. If that is the case, perhaps a new type of leadership will develop which will recognize that professional persons have different problems, outlooks, and ideas from the general laboring groups. In such an event, organized labor will be deprived of the aid and strength which professional persons could bring to unionism, and the professionals will probably continue to align themselves with the middle class and others traditionally hostile to trade unionism.

That is not to say, however, that collective bargaining functions should be assumed by professional associations, or that such a development is an unmitigated boon to the public. Indeed, it may be as much a cause for concern as the tendency of unions to take over the functions of professional societies. For in either case, one organization becomes too important in the professional person's life; it represents too many facets of his endeavors; it is at odds with pluralism, a fundamental tenet of democracy, which requires the widest possible distribution of power and responsibility.[1]

It may be argued that this view is exaggerated; that the interests of organizations whether professional societies or unions, have always been expanding; and that they must expand if they are not to stagnate.[2] Certainly, it is not inevitable that these developments prove unhealthy for our democracy, and one can perhaps rely on the good sense of American professional personnel to see that they do not. Yet

[1] Cf. the following: "There is a viewpoint growing increasingly common in progressive labor circles which . . . asserts that . . . a labor union is not properly an industrial organization at all but a *total* organization, one endeavoring to meet the worker's needs on *all* fronts and to represent him in *all* his social interests. . . . This viewpoint is intelligible and consistent. The only trouble with it is that it is utterly incompatible with the notion of a free democratic society. . . . The idea of one great overall organization representing the total interests of its members is essentially totalitarian." Will Herberg, "For ' 'Limited' As Against 'Total' Unionism," *Labor and Nation*, I (April-May, 1946), 53. Of course it is not here implied that professional societies or unions of professional personnel have become "total" organizations, or that they inevitably will be, but the fear is expressed that the exclusion of one by the other is a step in that direction.

[2] See, e. g., Herbert J. Lahne's comment on the above-cited Herberg article, *Labor and Nation*, I (November-December, 1946), 61-62.

the danger cannot be overlooked, especially when it is noted that both unions and professional societies are becoming ever more interested in politics and legislative answers to their problems, and are thus assuming direction in this field as well as in the intellectual, social, and economic aspects of professional life.

Perhaps the combination of the intellectual, political, and collective bargaining functions of professional persons into one organization should not be of concern so long as that organization is a professional society rather than a union. Professional societies, while active in politics, have not entered the arena to the extent of unions. At least at present, they are for the most part managed by personnel drawn from the profession, and are conversant with professional ideals and practices. The same cannot be generally said for the present union leadership in the professional field.

On the other hand, those pillars of the professional society world, the American Medical Association and the American Bar Association, which most other societies seek to emulate, have engaged in practices not unlike those of some of the least responsible unions, e. g., race discrimination, restriction of entry into the calling, unfair competitive practice, and questionable political lobbying.[1] Should it be considered undesirable for one organization to control so many facets of a professional person's life, a distinction based on whether that organization is a professional society or a union may be only one of degree and not one of kind, although admittedly the degree may be significant.

There are other important, though less dramatic, implications of the organization of the professional groups under discussion here. For the most part, they obtain whether organi-

---

[1] See, e. g., the literature on restriction of entry into the medical and legal fields discussed and cited in M. Friedman and S. Kuznets, *Income from Independent Professional Practice*, Publication No. 45 (New York, National Bureau of Economic Research, Inc., 1945), pp. 11-21, 34-39. Note also that on January 18, 1943, the U.S. Supreme Court upheld the conviction of the American Medical Association and the District of Columbia Medical Society for violating the Sherman Act by conspiring to block the activities of Group Health, Inc., a cooperative clinic. See also Garceau, *op. cit., passim.*

zation is by unions or by professional societies. Collective bargaining organizations in the professional fields must solve the dilemma of supervisory members. Potential leadership of the bargaining groups, whether under trade union or professional association auspices, is constantly restricted by the presence and interests of supervisors as well as regular members. This is a problem which confronts teachers and nurses more than chemists and engineers, but it is not wholly absent from the latter groups. Indeed, it is found in almost all collective bargaining organizations composed of white collar groups. The difficulty arises because the potential leader is often fearful to take a stand lest his professional career be judged on the basis of his collective bargaining activity. Perhaps some stratification of professional positions similar to a craft union setup is feasible. At any rate, until some workable arrangement is discovered, nonsupervisory members of these organizations are likely to be reluctant to take positions or to assume leadership for fear of incurring the displeasure of their supervisors and of hindering their opportunities for professional advancement.

Then there is the question of whether the organization of professional engineers and chemists will adversely affect industrial research. It has been argued that if organization occurs on a large enough scale to result in raising the salaries of professional engineers and chemists substantially, the effect will be to reduce the employment of professional personnel and thus to discourage research. If industrial research is discouraged, technological advancement, and hence general employment, will decline.[1]

The basic assumption of this analysis is that the demand for the services of professional engineers and chemists is very elastic, and therefore, that it will decline sharply if their salaries are considerably increased. It is possible that in times of economic stress companies may reduce or liquidate technical

---

[1] See, e.g., S. H. Slichter, "The Responsibility of Organized Labor for Employment," *American Economic Review*, Papers and Proceedings, XXXV (May, 1945), 198-99.

staffs, and they may be more inclined to do so if the salaries of these staffs are quite high.

On the other hand, the research payroll of industry, although large, is relatively insignificant in comparison with its total wage and salary bill. Moreover, the salaries of professional personnel do not move in a vacuum, but are affected by and move in the same direction as those of other employees. Therefore, even a very considerable increase in the salary level of professional engineers and chemists would result in only a small percentage increase in labor costs. In addition, the possible returns from industrial research in terms of lower production costs, new and superior products, and improved methods are so great that it seems probable that the employment of professional engineers and chemists depends more on the anticipated results of their work than on the costs of their salaries. If this analysis is correct, more complete organization of professional engineers and chemists is unlikely to have adverse effects on industrial research, technological advancement, or employment.

The economic and social effects of the organization of teachers and nurses are likely to be different from those of engineers and chemists because of the different nature of the service and because they are mostly public rather than private employees. In the case of teachers, any improvement in salaries resulting from organization may aid in improving the character of the teaching force, which is being rapidly depleted both in quantity and quality by the present low levels of earnings. This is, of course, all to the good. It will also cost money and, therefore, will be reflected in higher taxes. The ramifications of tax incidence cannot be discussed here, but one broad aspect may be noted. States and municipalities, especially in the poorer areas of the country, do not have the tax capacity to support the significant increases in teacher salaries that our educational system requires. Hence, the organization of teachers into more effective bargaining and pressure groups will probably hasten the day of substantial federal aid to education.

The effect of organization in the nursing profession is likely to be somewhat similar to that in teaching. Increased salaries may improve the character of the professional force, but will make it increasingly difficult for private and public hospitals to operate without federal aid. It may also have another effect. By increasing the cost of hospital care, the organization of nurses is likely to hasten the advent of a federal health insurance program, which, in turn, should result in increased demand, and probably pay, for nurses.

CHAPTER SEVEN

The Development of Labor Organization: A Theoretical Framework [1]

by *John T. Dunlop*

"THE FACTS do not tell their own story; they must be cross-examined. They must be carefully analyzed, systematized, compared and interpreted." [2] This conclusion is an indictment of the all too frequent approach to the development of the labor movement,[3] in which "history" and "theory" are separate and non-permeable compartments.

Under the caption of "history of labor" are chronicled what purport to be collections of fact and sequences of fact. Under the heading of "theory of labor organization" are found "explanations" conjured out of inner consciousness with only occasional and convenient reference to the past. The "history" and "theory" of the labor movement can have little meaning in isolation.[4] But it is particularly the failure of theoretical apparatus that accounts for the lack of greater understanding of the development of the labor movement and the paucity of significant research. Indeed, despite all the epoch-making developments in the field of labor organization in the past fifteen years, there has been virtually no contribu-

[1] This essay has benefited from helpful comments by J. A. Schumpeter, A. P. Usher, and Selig Perlman.

[2] Talcott Parsons, *The Structure of Social Action* (New York, McGraw-Hill Book Co., 1937), p. 698.

[3] See E. Wight Bakke, *Mutual Survival, The Goal of Unions and Management* (New Haven, Labor and Management Center, Yale Univ., 1946), p. 12, for a contrast between a "movement" and a "business."

[4] J. B. Bury, *The Idea of Progress* (New York, Macmillan Co., 1932). See the Introduction by Charles A. Beard, pp. ix-xl.

tion to the "theory" and scarcely a reputable narrative of this period exists.[1]

This essay constitutes a re-examination of fashions of thinking in theories of the labor movement. It proceeds from the initial conviction that any theory of the labor movement must first establish its criteria. Just what questions is a theory of labor organization supposed to answer? Only after this task has been explicitly recognized can there be critical discussion of the development of the labor movement.

The body of economic theory attempts to explain the allocation of resources.[2] Business cycle theories present systems of propositions to make intelligible the fluctuations of the economic system. In similar terms, what is the *pièce de résistance* of a theory of the labor movement? By what standards or tests is it possible to prefer one theory to another? What behavior must such a theory explain to be judged a "closer fit" than another model?

EXPLANATIONS OF THE LABOR MOVEMENT

The literature on theories of the labor movement, if carefully analzed, reveals at least four questions which have been the concern of investigators. As far as can be determined, however, nowhere are these questions posed explicitly.

1. How is one to account for the origin or emergence of labor organizations? What conditions are necessary and what circumstances stimulate the precipitation of labor organization? Why have some workers organized and others not?

2. What explains the pattern of growth and development of labor organizations? What factors are responsible for the sequence and form in which organizations have emerged in various countries, industries, crafts, and companies? Since there is great diversity in the patterns of development, any

[1] Selig Perlman's *Theory of the Labor Movement* (New York, Macmillan Co.) was published in 1928. See Horace B. Davis, "The Theory of Union Growth," *Quarterly Journal of Economics,* LV (August, 1941), 611-37, and Russel Bauder, "Three Interpretations of the American Labor Movement," *Social Forces* XXII (December, 1943), 215-24.

[2] Frank H. Knight, *Risk, Uncertainty, and Profit* (London, London School of Economics and Political Science, 1933), Preface to reissue.

theory of the labor movement must account for these differences.

3. What are the ultimate goals of the labor movement? What is its relationship to the future of capitalism? What is its role in the socialist or communist state?

4. Why do individual workers join labor organizations? What system of social psychology accounts for this behavior of the employee?

Most writings on theories of the labor movement have in effect been concerned with one or several of these questions. They show a tendency to seek a single and usually oversimplified statement of the development of labor organization. But the labor movement is highly complex and many-sided. The "history" does not readily lend itself to any single formula.

The pages immediately following constitute a brief summary of the principal contributions to theories of the labor movement. No attempt will be made to present a detailed appraisal of these views; the summary cannot be an exegesis. The discussion is necessarily sketchy. It may be helpful, however, to have in brief compass a summary of views since none exists. Brevity at times has the virtue of concentrating on and compelling attention to essentials.

(1) *Frank Tannenbaum* [1]

To Tannebaum "the labor movement is the result and the machine is the major cause." [2] The machine threatens the security of the individual worker and the wage earner reacts in self-defense through a union to attempt to control the machine. The individual worker seeks to harness the machine and to stem the tide of insecurity by which his life is menaced.

---

[1] Frank Tannenbaum, *The Labor Movement, Its Conservative Functions and Social Consequences* (New York, G. P. Putnam's Sons, 1921).

[2] *Ibid.*, p. 29. As a statement of the origin of labor organizations, this view is to be contrasted with that of John R. Commons, "Whatever may have been its origin in other countries, the labor movement in America did not spring from factory conditions. It arose as a protest against the merchant-capitalist system." (*A Documentary History of American Industrial Society* [Glendale, Calif., Arthur H. Clark Company, 1910], Vol. V, p. 23 [with Helen L. Sumner].)

He intends little more than this security when joining a union, but ". . . in the process of carrying out the implications of defense against the competitive character of the capitalist system he contributes to the well-being of present-day society—a contribution which represents a by-product of the more immediate and conscious attempt to find security in an insecure world." [1]   Tannenbaum sees the labor movement ultimately displacing the capitalistic system by "industrial democracy," "an achievement which is implicit in the growth and development of the organized labor movement." [2]

Tannebaum provides an answer of sorts to at least three of the four questions posed above; he does not examine the pattern of growth of the labor movement. While not concerned with historical detail, Tannebaum finds the origin of labor organizations in a reaction to the machine (question 1). The labor movement creates a new society (question 3). The individual worker joins the union in self-defense in quest of security (question 4).

(2) *Sidney and Beatrice Webb* [3]

A trade union is a "continuous association of wage-earners for the purpose of maintaining or improving the conditions of their working lives." [4]   Its fundamental objective, according to the Webbs, is "the deliberate regulation of the conditions of employment in such a way as to ward off from the manual-working producers the evil effects of industrial competition." [5] The labor organization utilizes, in the well-known schema of the Webbs, the "methods" of mutual insurance, collective bargaining, and legal enactment. The labor organization chooses among these "methods" depending on the stage of development of the society. An era of the master system

[1] These lines are in italics in the original. *Op. cit.*, p. 32.
[2] *Ibid.*, p. 44.
[3] Sidney and Beatrice Webb, *Industrial Democracy* (New York, Longmans, Green & Co., 1897); and *History of Trade Unionism* (New York, Longmans, Green & Co., 1894). Also see Margaret Cole, *Beatrice Webb* (New York, Harcourt, Brace & Co., 1946), pp. 73-83.
[4] *History of Trade Unionism* (1920 ed.), p. 1.
[5] *Industrial Democracy* (1914 printing), p. 807.

requires the enforcement of common rules against "industrial parasitism"; the existence of trusts makes legal enactment the only effective method in many cases. The assumption by government of responsibility for social risks, such as old age and unemployment, greatly curtails the use of the method of mutual insurance on the part of labor organizations.

In the view of the Webbs, trade unionism is ". . . not merely an incident of the present phase of capitalist industry, but has a permanent function to fulfill in the democratic state." [1] The special function of the trade union is in the democratic administration of industry. While consumers acting through cooperatives or entrepreneurs may determine *what* is produced, the democratic society requires a labor organization to provide for the participation of workers in the conditions of sale of their services. In the type of democratic society the Webbs eventually expected (the little profit-taker and the trust superseded by the salaried officer of the cooperative and by government agencies), the unions would more and more assume the character of professional associations.

The Webbs use the term "theory of trade unionism" [2] not to refer to answers to any of the four questions posed in the preceding section but as a statement of the economic consequences of a labor organization, virtually a theory of wages or collective bargaining. The trade union is pictured as having only two "expedients" for the improvement of conditions of employment: [3] the restriction of numbers in the trade and the establishment of uniform minimum standards required of each firm. The Webbs condemned the former monopolist policy. They endorsed the latter application of the Common Rule, for it transfers competition from wages to quality. The device of the Common Rule envisages the gradual improvement in these minimum standards of wages and conditions. It is the duty of the labor organization to strive perpetually to raise

[1] *Ibid.*, p. 823.
[2] *Ibid.*, pp. viii and 795. See note 1 on next page.
[3] *Ibid.*, p. 560.

the level of its common rules. This process may be carried on by collective bargaining or by the use of legislation.[1] Such is the Webbs' "theory of trade unionism," an economic rationalization for the establishment of minimum standards.

What the Webbs called their "theory of trade unionism" would not ordinarily be called a theory of the development of the labor movement. While the Webbs made fundamental and pioneer contributions to the study of trade union government and the narrative of labor organization history, they formulated no systematic, conceptual answers to the first two questions posed in the previous section (the emergence of labor organization and the patterns of development). As for ultimate goals (question 3), the Webbs see the labor union as an instrument of the democratization of both the work community and the wider society as a whole.

(3) *Robert F. Hoxie* [2]

Hoxie starts from the proposition that wage earners in similar social and economic environments tend to develop a "common interpretation of the social situation." [3] The union emerges when group sentiments have been crystallized. It appears as a "group interpretation of the social situation in which the workers find themselves, and a remedial program in the form of aims, policies, and methods. . . ." [4] To Hoxie, the union constitutes a common interpretation and set of beliefs concerned with the problems confronting the worker and a generalized program of amelioration. Such a persistent group "viewpoint or interpretation" [5] Hoxie calls a *functional* type of unionism. His name has come to be associated almost

---

[1] ". . . the whole community of wage-earners . . . may by a persistent and systematic use of the Device of the Common Rule secure an indefinite, though of course not an unlimited, rise in its Standard of Life. And in this universal and elaborate application of the Common Rule, the economist finds a *sound and consistent theory of Trade Unionism,* adapted to the conditions of modern industry; . . ." *Ibid.,* p. 795. (Italics added.)

[2] Robert F. Hoxie, *Trade Unionism in the United States* (New York, D. Appleton & Co., 1921). See the Introduction by E. H. Downey.

[3] *Ibid.,* p. 58.

[4] *Ibid.,* p. 60.

[5] *Ibid.,* p. 69.

exclusively with classification of the functional types he suggests (business unionism, uplift unionism, revolutionary unionism, predatory unionism, and dependent unionism) to the detraction of an understanding of his significant contribution.

The account of the origin of labor organizations which Hoxie gives—a crystallization of group viewpoint and programme of action—leads him to question whether the labor movement has any unity: "Seen from the standpoint of aims, ideals, methods, and theories, there is no normal type to which all union variants approximate, no single labor movement which has progressively adapted itself to progressive change of circumstances, no one set of postulates which can be spoken of as *the* philosophy of unionism. Rather there are competing, relatively stable union types . . ." [1]

Since the labor movement is nonunitary, Hoxie rejects interpretations that look upon trade unionism as fundamentally an economic manifestation of changing methods of production or market developments.[2] The fact of different functional types compels Hoxie to renounce any explanation in environmental terms alone. The subjective factor emphasized in the concept of functional types is equally important.

Hoxie provides an answer to the problem of the emergence of labor organization (question 1) in terms of "group psychology." He accounts for the divergent forms of unionism but is comparatively unconcerned with an explanation of historical development. One of the factors affecting the classification of functional types is the program for social action developed by the group. In this sense, Hoxie indicates the different answers that have been posed to the problem of the relation of the labor movement to the future of capitalism (question 3). But there is no sense of historical development. Here again for Hoxie is reticent to generalize to a "labor movement as a whole" from his "functional types." [3]

[1] E. H. Downey, Introduction to *Trade Unionism in the United States*, pp. xxiii-xxiv.

[2] See the discussion under the heading of John R. Commons which follows in the text.

[3] See, however, *op. cit.*, note 3, p. 59.

(4) *Selig Perlman* [1]

Perlman finds that in any "modern labor situation" there may be said to be three factors operative: "first, the resistance of capitalism, determined by its own historical development; second, the degree of dominance over the labor movement by the intellectual's 'mentality,' which regularly underestimates capitalism's resistance power and overestimates labor's will to radical change; and, third, the degree of maturity of a trade union 'mentality'." [2]   By this last factor Perlman means the extent to which the trade union is conscious of job scarcity. "It is the author's contention that manual groups . . . have had their economic attitudes basically determined by a consciousness of scarcity of opportunity . . . . Starting with this consciousness of scarcity, the 'manualist' groups have been led to practicing solidarity, to an insistence upon an 'ownership' by the group as a whole of the totality of economic opportunity extant, to a 'rationing' by the group of such opportunity among the individuals constituting it, to a control by the group over its members in relation to the conditions upon which they as individuals are permitted to occupy a portion of that opportunity . . . ." [3]

Perlman suggests that there are three basic economic philosophies, those of the manual laborer just indicated, the businessman, and the intellectual. In the United States a "stabilized" unionism was delayed until the labor movement developed job consciousness, until it came to assert a "collective mastery over job opportunities and employment bargains," until wage earners dissociated themselves from "producers" generally who were imbued with the doctrine of abundance and who organized under the slogan of antimonopoly. The American Federation of Labor constitutes a shift in the psy-

[1] Perlman, *op. cit.*

[2] *Ibid.*, p. x.

[3] *Ibid.*, p. 4; also see pp. 237-53. The importance attached to job consciousness is the outcome of one of the few explicit statements on the requirements of a theory of the labor movement. "A theory of the labor movement should include a theory of the psychology of the laboring man" (p. 237).

chology of the labor movement, a recognition of the scarcity of opportunity. [1]

Perlman apparently gives a certain primacy to the role of job consciousness in the labor movement. In fact a labor organization can be regarded as fundamentally a manifestation of "economic attitudes" (see quotation cited above in note 3, page 170). Nonetheless, labor history cannot deny a "truly pivotal part" to the intellectual. The character of the labor movement in any particular country must depend on the particular combination of the role of the intellectual, the resistance of capitalism, and the development of job consciousness.

Perlman is seen to treat in one way or another all four criteria posed in the previous section. Labor organizations develop from a concern with the scarcity of job opportunities (questions 1 and 4). The pattern of development of organization in a particular country depends upon the particular combination of the three factors operative in any "modern labor situation" (question 2). The relation of the labor movement to the future of capitalism is peculiarly influenced by the role of the intellectual (question 3).

(5) *John R. Commons* [2]

Commons believed that labor history should be understood in terms of the interaction of "economic, industrial, and political conditions with many varieties of individualistic, socialistic and protectionist philosophies." [3] He treats labor history as a part of its industrial and political history.

[1] Perlman disagrees with the Webbs' view that there is a tendency for unionism to give up the principle of restriction of numbers in favor of the device of the Common Rule. *Ibid.*, pp. 295-98. Also see *Labor in the New Deal Decade,* Three Lectures by Selig Perlman, . . . at the ILGWU Officers Institute, New York City, 1943-1945 (Educational Department, International Ladies' Garment Workers' Union, 1945).

[2] John R. Commons, Ed., *A Documentary History of American Industrial Society,* 11 Vols. (Glendale, Calif., Arthur H. Clark Co., 1910-11). In particular see the Introduction, Vol. V, pp. 19-37, written with Helen L. Sumner. Also John R. Commons and Associates, *History of Labor in the United States,* 2 Vols. (New York, Macmillan Co., 1918), in particular Vol. I, pp. 3-21.

[3] Commons and Associates, *op. cit.,* Vol. I, Introduction; p. 3.

Commons' thinking on the origin and emergence of labor organization involved an appraisal of the writings of Marx, Schmoller, and Bucher. He posed the problem of explaining the emergence of the labor movement in terms of the growth of new bargaining classes—the wage earner and the employer. He traced the gradual evolution of the employee-employer relationship from the merchant-capitalist dealings with a journeyman. The growth of the market separates from the merchant-capitalist the functions of the custom merchant, the retail merchant, and the wholesale merchant. The employer remains.[1]

While Commons recognized that the changing modes of production influenced to some extent the emergence of labor organization, he attached primary importance to the market expansion. "The extension of the market took precedence over the mode of production as an explanation of the origin of new class alignments." [2]

The pattern of uneven growth in the American labor movement Commons attributed to the fluctuations in economic conditions. Periods of prosperity produced organization while depressions saw the labor movement subside or change its form to political or social agitation.[3]

The theoretical system of Commons seems to have been concerned only with the emergence and the pattern of development of the labor movement (questions 1 and 2 above).

(6) The Marxist View

To Karl Marx, the trade union was first and foremost an "organizing center." [4] It provided the locus for collecting the forces of the working class. Without organization, workers competed with each other for available employment. "The trade union developed originally out of the spontaneous attempts of the workers to do away with this competition, or at

[1] *Ibid.*, p. 106.
[2] *Ibid.*, p. 28.
[3] Commons, Ed., *Documentary History* . . . . Vol. V, p. 19.
[4] A. Lozovsky, *Marx and the Trade Unions* (New York, International Publishers Co., 1935), p. 15.

least to restrict it for the purpose of obtaining at least such contractual conditions as would raise them above the status of bare slaves." [1]

The labor organization provided for Marx the focal point for the functional organization of the working class toward a change in the structure of society. Just as the medieval municipalities and communities were the center of organization of the bourgeoisie, so the trade union for the proletariat. Thus, in addition to its original tasks, the trade union was to learn to take on additional duties, to become the center for organizing the working class for its political emancipation.[2]

It is imperative to distinguish the role of the trade union under capitalism from that after the successful revolution of the proletariat. Left to themselves, labor organizations would remain within the capitalistic framework. Lenin has put this point succinctly. "The spontaneous labour movement, able by itself to create (and inevitably will create) only trade unionism, and working-class trade-union politics are precisely working-class bourgeois politics." [3]

In terms of the fundamental questions posed above, it is apparent that Marx and Lenin, insofar as they formulated a theory of the labor movement, were concerned with the origin or emergence of labor organizations (question 1) and their ultimate relationship to capitalistic society (question 3).

A critical comparison of these views is beyond the scope of this essay. There are important similarities of analysis and emphasis that appear at once and more that would be evident save for differences in language. A rather sharp cleavage emerges, however, between writers such as the Webbs and Commons, who look upon the labor movement primarily as the manifestation of economic developments, and those, such as Perlman and Hoxie, who choose to emphasize the habits of

[1] *Ibid.*, p. 16. (Italics deleted.)
[2] Paul M. Sweezy, *The Theory of Capitalist Development* (New York, Oxford Univ. Press, 1942), pp. 312-13.
[3] V. L. Lenin, *What Is to Be Done?*, Reprinted from *The Iskra Period* (New York, International Publishers, 1929), p. 90.

mind of wage earners. Compare the *key concepts* of "common rule" (Webbs) and "expansion of the market" (Commons) on the one hand with "job consciousness" (Perlman) and "functional type" (Hoxie, a persistent exponent of the group viewpoint or interpretation). The Webbs and Commons built their models of the trade union out of changes in observable economic institutions. Hoxie and Perlman were imbued with the necessity of a "psychology" of the labor movement and hold the notion that the outlook of the worker upon his world and his destiny is the cornerstone of a model of trade union development.

This cleavage represents a fundamental failure in the formulation of "theories of the labor movement." For certainly, there are significant interrelations between the outlook of members of a community and the economic institutions. Consider, for instance, the shedding of the "producer class" complex of the American labor movement. Commons explains the development in terms of the final development of the national market while Perlman emphasizes that job consciousness and the belief in scarcity of work opportunities had asserted itself. These developments are clearly not independent.

The sections which follow are intended to present a more generalized and more integrated understanding of the development of the labor movement. The next section provides a scaffolding or generalized theoretical framework for an approach to the labor movement.

THE DETERMINANTS OF LABOR ORGANIZATION

The labor movement, or any similarly complex social organization, may be fruitfully explored by an examination of four interrelated factors: technology, market structures and the character of competition, community institutions of control, and ideas and beliefs.

1. Technology. This term includes not only changes in

machinery and in methods of production but concomitant developments in the size and organization of production and distribution units.

2. Market structures and character of competition. The term comprehends the growth of markets, the changes in the locus of financial control as distinguished from the size of production units, the development of buying and selling institutions in both product and factor markets, and the emergence of specialized functions and personnel within these organizations.

3. Wider community institutions. This phrase is intended to include among others the role of the press, radio, and other means of communication in the society, the formal educational system for both general and vocational training, the courts, governmental administrative agencies, and political parties and organizations.

4. Ideas and beliefs. This caption is a short cut for the value judgments and mores that permeate and identify a social system.

Such a comprehensive scaffolding or method of approach does not in itself constitute a theory of the labor movement. It claims only to facilitate the development of such a theoretical system. It compels reflection on the range of mutual influences operative in any society. Such a comprehensive framework of reference assists in asking significant questions; the complex interrelations between the labor movement and any society are sharpened. The labor movement is seen in the context of its "total" environment. This fourfold scheme is a set of preliminary tools through which the labor movement may be reconnoitered and analyzed. The facts of labor history may more readily be cross-examined.

It must be emphasized that these four factors are intended not merely to facilitate the cross-sectional study of the labor movement at any one given time but even more to assist in the analysis of the growth and change of the labor movement over time. The interaction among technological and market factors, community institutions, and ideas and beliefs must be used to account for the development of the labor movement.

Social systems or institutions go through periods of relative stability and through other periods of spectacular and tortuous change. Periods of stability may be regarded as involving a certain equilibrium among these four factors. That is, a given system of technology and markets requires or is compatible with only a limited number of community institutions and value judgments and ideas. The converse is equally true; a given system of ideas and community organization is compatible only with particular types of market and technological arrangements. In these terms, equilibrium in the social system may be said to exist when these four groups of factors are compatible one with another. Equilibrium may involve an unchanging condition or rates of change among the factors which are congruous. Change the technology of a system and there are required alterations in the other three factors, or change the value judgments and ideas of a community and there must be changes in market systems and technology.

The actual course of history does not disclose the isolated reaction to the change in a single factor any more than a series of prices reveals directly the unique effects of shifts in demand or movements along demand schedules. A comprehensive theory of a society should indicate the result of varying one of these factors—the others unchanged—when the system as a whole is in initial equilibrium. The actual course of events consists in continuous and inseparable interaction between the secondary effects of the initial change and new impacts on the social system.

The procedure suggested in this section would analyze the labor movement by indicating the change in each of these four factors over the past and the consequent impact on the emergence and the manner of growth of the labor movement. The labor movement is seen as the product of its total environment. As labor organizations grow they become an independent factor affecting the course of their own destiny.

LONG-RUN TRENDS IN UNION GROWTH

In thinking of the development of the labor movement, it will be helpful to distinguish between long-term trends and variations around these tendencies. The evolution of social institutions does not take place at uniform rates. The process is more like waves eating away at the base of a cliff, which eventually crashes into the sea.[1] The present section will be concerned with the trend aspects of the development of the labor movement, while that which follows will adapt this analysis to the pulsation of growth of labor organization.

No working community is ever completely unorganized. Any group of human beings associated together for any length of time develops a community in which there are recognized standards of conduct and admitted leaders. ". . . in industry and in other human situations the administrator is dealing with well-knit human groups and not with a horde of individuals."[2] A group of workers which continues together will establish standards of a "fair" day's work and acceptable norms of behavior in the views of the working group as a whole. Not everyone, of course, will conform to these standards, but there will be recognized norms. In the same way one worker will soon be recognized as a person whose judgment is sought on personal problems; another will be regarded as having superior skill, whose advice on the technical aspects of the job is highly regarded; still another will be accepted as spokesman in expressing the feelings of the group to the management. At times these functions may be combined in the same person. Whenever human beings live or work together the informal group develops. This fact is true today; it no doubt preceded the first formal labor organization.

---

[1] For a discussion of historical change refer to Melvin M. Knight, Introduction to Henri Sée, *The Economic Interpretation of History* (New York, Adelphi Co., 1929), pp. 9-37.

[2] Elton Mayo, *The Social Problems of an Industrial Civilization* (Cambridge, Harvard Univ. Press, 1945), p. 111. Also see F. J. Roethlisberger and William J. Dickson, *Management and the Worker* (Cambridge, Harvard Univ. Press, 1940); F. J. Roethlisberger, *Management and Morale* (Cambridge, Harvard Univ. Press, 1942).

Formal trade union organization has on many occasions been precipitated out of this type of informal organization. Some danger to the stability and security of the informal group frequently serves as the immediate occason for formalizing an organization. The threat may come from the management in the form of a wage reduction or a substitution of women on men's jobs, or the arbitrary discipline of a member of the work community. The threat may have its origin outside the firm, as in the introduction of machinery made necessary by competitive conditions. Very frequently the formal organization may last for a short time, only during the period of greatest immediacy of the danger.

The formal group may be assisted and encouraged by outside organizers. The initiative may be taken by the professional organizer, or he may be called in after an initial step. The congealing of these informal organizations into formal structures follows no uniform pattern. The "intellectual" does not here receive the prominence in the development of the labor movement subscribed to by some writers. There can be little doubt that, in any going institution, "rationalizations" are developed—a task necessarily intellectual in content. Such formal statements often help in extending organization. The processes of rationalization are here treated as an essential step in the growth of the union movement, but the "intellectual" does not have a dominant role.

Wage earners join unions for a great many different reasons. They generally involve various aspects of the relation of the individual workman to his immediate work community and, at times, his relation to the larger locality and national life.[1] The fundamenal point, however, is that any analysis of the development of labor organizations must proceed from the recognition that work communities, prior to formal organization, are not simply random aggregates of individual workmen. Typically, informal coagulations exist. While every labor organization probably has not grown out of nor

[1] E. Wight Bakke, "Why Workers Join Unions," *Personnel*, XXII, No. 1 (1945).

adopted the leadership of the informal group, it is difficult to conceive of a labor organization which has not been substantially influenced by these basic facts of any work community.

There have been, no doubt, many cases in which the informal organization has been precipitated into dramatic formal action only to lapse quickly and pass away. There have been many such outbursts against arbitrary behavior and substantial grievances. But in some circumstances continuing organization has developed and in others it has lapsed. The discussion which follows suggests, with reference to the American scene, two factors that were necessary to the emergence of organization historically and two that have been decisive in determining the trend of development.

(1) How is the student of labor organization to account for the location in the productive process of the emergence of continuing unions? Successful organization has required that workmen occupy a *strategic* position in the technological or market structures. In any *technological* process for producing and distributing goods and services, there are some workers who have greater strategic position than others; that is, these workers are able to shut down, to interrupt, or to divert operations more easily than others. They furnish labor services at decisive points in the productive stream where the withdrawal of services quickly breaks the whole stream. The productive process has its bottlenecks. Frequently these workers are skilled. The term strategic, however, is not identical with skill. It means sheer bargaining power by virtue of location and position in the productive process. Locomotive engineers, loom fixers in the textile industry, molders in the casting industry, and cutters in the garment industry well illustrate the concept. The withdrawal of the services of these relatively few men almost immediately compels, for technological reasons, the complete shutting down or diversion of operations of the plant.

Analogously, in the *structure of markets* there are firms, and consequently there are employees, who are in strategic

positions to affect the whole stream of production and distribution. Employees are technologically strategic by virtue
of their position *within* an individual firm. Workers are in a
strategic position, marketwise, by virtue of their position in the
structure of markets. In the market framework they can most
readily exact a price. Not only are the teamsters in a position
to tie up operations (technological position), but also their
employers are in a position to pass on cost increases to their
customers (market position). Another illustration would be
a craft, such as the bricklayers, where cost increases may be
passed on to the small house-builder whose bargaining position is such as to force absorption. The musicians constitute
probably an even better example. The technological and market strategic positions are never completely disassociated,
although it is helpful to make the conceptual distinction.

Labor organization emerges among employees who have
strategic market or technological positions. They have bargaining power. They can make it hurt. These strategic employees may be regarded as "points of infection" or "growth
cones," to borrow the latter term from embryology, for the
spread of labor organization.

How far will organization spread around the original
"point of infection"? In some instances organization is confined to these most strategic workers and a pure craft union
may result. In other instances, these workers become the
nucleus of the organization that encompasses other workers
in the same plant. The cell wall of the organization may be
pushed coextensively with the plant, and an industrial union
result. The boundary line may be drawn any place in between and may in fact fluctuate a good deal over time. The
analogous point applies to the growth of unions in different
types of firms. The boundary line of the union may be
stopped from crossing into firms with different product market
conditions. The phenomenon of a union organized in commercial building but unable or uninterested in pushing into
housing is familiar in construction.

There are barriers to extending the cell wall of organization that arise within the strategic group of workers themselves as well as from the opposition of those outside this nucleus. On occasions, the most strategic group will prefer to remain so purist that developments resulting in differentiation of work among these strategic workers will produce a split in the cell and two organizations result. Expanding the group would dilute the gains of organization for the existing nucleus. Labor organizations in the printing industry in this country have taken this pattern of development. From the original group of strategically positioned printers have split off the pressmen, the photo-engravers, the stereotypers, the bookbinders, and others, as specialized operations have developed.

Resistance to the expansion of the strategic group may arise from the fact that those outside the nucleus may have such high rates of turnover as to make organization impossible. Thus the butchers in retail outlets did not originally include part-time employees around these stores. The boundary line of the union may be confined because those outside may feel that they can enjoy any benefits won by the strategic group without the costs of organization. It is a mistake to interpret historically the structure (in the sense of boundary lines) of American trade unionism, primarily in terms of a slavish following of the "principle of craft unionism." This analysis suggests a more general view.

Necessary to the emergence and growth of permanent labor organizations have been workers who are located in strategic positions in the market or technological framework. Organization may be treated as expanding from these centers in different patterns and to varying extents. It may be helpful to illustrate this formal analysis with examples from the early growth of labor organizations. In both the men's and women's clothing industry the first group organized was the cutters.[1] Their key position in the technological operation of the making of garments gave them a dominant position in early organ-

---

[1] See Joel Seidman, *The Needle Trades* (New York, Farrar and Rinehart, 1942), pp. 81-92; also Elden La Mar, *The Clothing Workers in Philadelphia* (Philadelphia Joint Board, Amalgamated Clothing Workers, 1940), pp. 46-47.

izations in these industries. For a while, organization was concentrated in this group. Later the cutters became the nucleus in the women's garment industry for the International Ladies' Garment Workers' Union.

Consider the development of the coal mining industry. Organization was first significant among the contract miners. As a "petty contractor," the miner owned his own tools, purchased his own powder, and worked without supervision. Starting from these strategic employees in the early coal mining industry as a nucleus, organization among the miners gradually expanded to include in a single organization all employees, including those who worked above ground as well as underground.[1]

In the cotton textile industry, the loom fixer has had a position of technological prominence. The failure to keep the looms in running order would soon force the shutdown of the weaving shed. There are other strategic groups of employees, such as the spinners and the slasher tenders. In a sense, one finds multiple points of organization in this industry. In some cases the craft-like union resulted and in others the nucleus expanded to include sufficient other groups to be designated as a semi-industrial arrangement.

In the steel industry, the Amalgamated Iron, Tin, and Steel Workers Union was formed out of strategically located groups in various branches of the industry. The boilers and puddlers in the making of iron, and the heaters, rollers, and roughers from the finishing operations, formed the bulk of organization.[2] This nucleus failed to expand and in fact could not maintain its own position until the emergence of the CIO. These illustrations could be multiplied many times: the linemen in the growth of the Brotherhood of Electrical Workers,[3]

[1] Edward A. Wieck, *The American Miners' Association* (New York, Russell Sage Foundation, 1940), pp. 75-77 and 85-86.

[2] J. S. Robinson, *The Amalgamated Association of Iron, Steel and Tin Workers* (Baltimore, Johns Hopkins Press, 1920), pp. 9-21.

[3] Michael A. Mulcaire, *The International Brotherhood of Electrical Workers* (Washington, The Catholic University of America, Studies in the Social Sciences, Vol. V, 1923).

the jiggermen and kilnmen in the pottery industry,[1] and the blowers, gatherers, flatteners, and cutters in the flat glass industry.[2] A union leader described an organizing drive as follows: ". . . we had all of the polishing department, and those men were the core of our whole organization."[3] Such instances provide flesh and blood to the formal scheme outlined above. The simple notion again is a strategic nucleus, which may expand in different patterns, depending on conditions and ideas within the union and the environment without.

The analysis that has just been outlined must be thought of as applicable to the task of understanding the development of the American labor movement in the context of community institutions which prevailed prior to the Wagner Act. Organization by ballot rather than by the picket line places much less emphasis upon strategic employees in the technological and market scene. Organization may proceed instead from those most susceptible to union appeals for votes. Furthermore, the unit or boundary which a union would select for an election is apt to be quite different from that which it would select to defend on the picket line. It has not been generally recognized that the Wagner Act has had as much effect on the organizing strategy and structure of labor organizations as upon relations with the employer.[4]

The concept of strategic workers cannot be as useful to an understanding of the development of the labor movement today as it is for the explanation of the past. Still it may help to explain stresses and strains within unions and particular wage policies.

[1] David A. McCabe, *National Collective Bargaining in the Pottery Industry* (Baltimore, Johns Hopkins Press, 1932), pp. 4-7.

[2] Window Glass Cutters League of America, *A History of Trade Unions in the Window Glass Industry* . . . , reprinted from the *Glass Cutter*, March-September, 1943.

[3] "From Conflict to Cooperation," *Applied Anthropology*, V (Fall, 1946), p. 9.

[4] The interpretation of the rise of the CIO as a repudiation of the principle of craft unionism neglects the adaptation in structure to these new conditions. A fruitful research enterprise would study these effects of the Wagner Act on union structure.

(2) A second necessary condition in the emergence of organization is the view of the employees that they shall look forward to spending a substantial proportion of their lifetime as workmen. This factor has been gradually developing over the past hundred years and has been influenced by the rate of increase in gainful employment. It is also necessary that a substantial proportion in any given work community look forward to remaining in the same or similar work community. Negatively, organization is difficult, if not impossible, where individuals expect to work themselves out of the status of wage earners, or where they expect to remain wage earners but a short time because of anticipated withdrawals from the labor market, or where the rate of turnover and migration is so rapid and so erratic and random as to preclude stability in organization. In a period or in situations in which individual employees expect to become foremen and then owners of their own business, permanent and stable organization is virtually impossible. One of the problems of organizing women arises from the fact that they expect only a short working life and then plan to retire to the more arduous duties of the household. Migratory labor has been notoriously difficult to form into permanent organizations.[1]

(3) Certain types of community institutions stimulate, and others retard, the emergence and growth of labor organizations. ". . . there had developed, in effect a double standard of social morality for labor and capital. . . . The story of the gradual modification of this double standard can be read in the history of labor organization and in the record of social legislation on state and federal governments over the past fifty years."[2] The legal system may actually preclude organization, as would have been the case had the doctrine of the early conspiracy cases been generally applied. This is not to

[1] Carleton H. Parker, *The Casual Laborer and Other Essays* (New York, Harcourt, Brace, and Howe, 1920). Also see Stuart Jamieson, *Labor Unionism in American Agriculture*, Bulletin 836 (Bureau of Statistics, Washington, 1945).

[2] Samuel Eliot Morrison and Henry Steele Commager, *The Growth of the American Republic* (Revised and enlarged edition, New York, Oxford Univ. Press, 1937), Vol. II, p. 153.

suggest that the passage of a law could have wiped out all organization. Such a legal doctrine, however, acted as an obstruction to the growth of organization. Analogously, a policy of government to encourage organization, such as adopted in the Wagner Act, tends to accelerate the growth of labor unions.

The role of the wider community influence on the emergence and pattern of growth of the labor movement must be more broadly conceived than the legal system.[1] Both the struggle for free public schools and the impact of widespread general and technical education have left their mark on the American labor movement. The labor press has drawn heavily on the conventions of the daily newspaper. The hostility of the ordinary press to labor organizations over much of the past in this country in turn helped to set the tone of the labor press.

The *emergence* of labor organizations has been related in preceding pages to the strategic position of wage earners in a market and technological setting. But the subsequent form of the labor organization will be decisively molded by the environment of these wider community and national institutions. In some contexts the labor organization has developed into an almost exclusively political body; in others political activity is minor. Special local or industry conditions, such as prevail in the field of municipal employment, may lead to substantial political activity even though the dominant pattern in the country may involve little such action.

The relation of the labor movement to the future of capitalism (question 3, page 165) must not be viewed narrowly as an issue of the extent or character of political activity. The growth in modern technology in the setting of the business corporation has gradually yielded a society predominately made up of wage and salary earners. Wage earners have constituted a minor element in previous communities made up

---

[1] See W. Lloyd Warner and J. O. Low, "The Factory in the Community," in *Industry and Society*, William F. Whyte, Ed. (New York, McGraw-Hill Book Co., 1946), pp. 21-45.

largely of self-employed farmers, serfs, slaves, or peasants.
Unique in human history has been the creation of a society
where the vast majority of persons earn a livelihood as wage
and salary earners. (Two-thirds of the national income is
wage and salary payment). Under these circumstances when
wage earners organize into labor organizations, as traced in
previous sections, these bodies may be expected to exercise
considerable political power in the community. The center
of political power ultimately shifts as the character of the
groups within the community changes.

If the locus of political power shifts to the degree that the
labor organization becomes the dominant political power,
there is growing evidence that the function and role of the
union changes. The attitude toward the right to strike, compulsory arbitration, and production drives shifts away from
the customary patterns under capitalism. This transition cannot but involve serious controversy within the labor movement.

(4) Over and above these technological, market, and community influences on the labor movement has been the system
of values, the ethos, and the beliefs of the community. Professor Schlesinger has summarized the traditional attributes of
the American most noted by foreign observers: "a belief in the
universal obligation to work; the urge to move about; a high
standard of comfort for the average man; an absence of permanent class barriers; the neglect of abstract thinking and of the
aesthetic side of life . . ." [1] Many of these characteristics
are to be traced to the "long apprenticeship to the soil."

It should not be hard to understand why labor organization
would be difficult in a day in which men believed that individual advancement was to be achieved solely by work,[2] where
leisure was a vice, where economic destiny depended solely

[1] Arthur Meier Schlesinger, "What Then Is the American, This New
Man," reprinted from the *American Historical Review*, XLVIII (January,
1943), pp. 3-4.
[2] "What qualities of the national character are attributable to this long-
persistent agrarian setting? First and foremost is the habit of work." (*Ibid.*,
p. 10.)

upon one's ability to work and save, where poverty could only
be the reward for sloth, where the poor deserved their fate,
and where the public care of the impoverished was regarded
as encouragement of idleness. As Poor Richard says:

Employ thy Time well, if thou meanst to gain Leisure;
And, since thou art not sure of a Minute, throw not away an Hour.

Trouble springs from Idleness, and grievous Toil from needless
Ease.

For Age and Want, save while you may,
No Morning Sun lasts a whole day.

I think the best way of doing good to the poor, is, not making them
easy *in* poverty but leading or driving them *out* of it.

These admonitions of Benjamin Franklin [1] are hardly the
ideal text for the organization of a labor union. This set of
ethical standards which has pervaded the ethos of the American community until recently places the economic destiny of a
workman in his own hands rather than in a labor union.

The political and economic philosophy of the founding
fathers, beyond standards of individual behavior, came to be
adapted to the advancing order of corporate business. "This
ideology was derived in part from deep-rooted folk ideas, in
part from the sanctions of religion, in part from concepts of
natural science. But whatever the source, its arguments rested
upon the concepts of individualism, equality of opportunity,
and the promise of well-being under a profit economy. The
conservative defense, crystallized by business leaders and by
allied members of the legal, educational, and literary professions, was popularized in sermons, speeches, novels, slogans,
and essays. It became part and parcel of American popular
thought." [2]

[1] "The Way to Wealth," Preface to *Poor Richard Improved* (1758).
[2] Merle Curti, *The Growth of American Thought* (New York, Harper
& Bros., 1943), p. 656. See pp. 605-56. Also, Vernon Louis Parrington,
Main Currents in American Thought, Vol. 3, *The Beginning of Critical
Realism in America* (New York, Harcourt, Brace & Co., 1927).

Moreover, the dominant economic thinking on the determination of wage rates (the wage-fund doctrine), by the community, could hardly have been favorable a hundred years ago to the growth of labor organizations. ". . . there is no use in arguing against any one of the four fundamental rules of arithmetic. The question of wages is a question of division. It is complained that the quotient is too small. Well, then, how many ways are there to make a quotient larger? Two ways. Enlarge your dividend, the divisor remaining the same, and the quotient will be larger; lessen your divisor, the dividend remaining the same, and the quotient will be larger."[1] There was no place for a union; it could serve no legitimate function. The intellectual climate of political economy changed and became more conducive to labor organization over the years.

The *trend* of standards of personal morality and social and economic philosophy has moved in directions more congenial to the flowering of unionism. Contrast the entreaties of Poor Richard and Horatio Alger with the admonitions of Sir William Beveridge! Leisure is now a virtue rather than a vice; saving may be a community vice rather than the epitome of individual morality; the economically less fortunate are to be sustained by comprehensive social security rather than to be left to sink or swim. The trade union has a more nourishing ethos.

The dominant ethical judgments pervading the community have been a vital factor influencing the growth of labor oranization not only as they affect the individual workman but also as they shape and mold the character of the labor organization itself. The primacy of property rights in the American tradition is partly responsible for the dominance of the concept of exclusive jurisdiction in the American Federation of Labor constitution. Each union "owns" its jurisdiction in the same

---

[1] A. L. Perry, *Political Economy*, p. 123, quoted in Francis A. Walker, *The Wage Question* (New York, Henry Holt & Co., 1886), p. 143. Compare this with the statement by the Webbs, "Down to within the last thirty years it would have been taken for granted, by every educated man, that Trade Unionism . . . was against Political Economy. . . ." *Industrial Democracy*, p. 603.

way that a businessman owns a piece of property. These community values have also decisively determined the attitude of the community toward social insurance. It is no accident that the American Federation of Labor was opposed to a program of compulsory insurance until 1932.[1]

The environment of ideas and beliefs in which the labor organization developed has included the special role of the labor intelligentsia or the intellectual. "Capitalist evolution produces a labor movement which obviously is not the creation of the intellectual group. But it is not surprising that such an opportunity and the intellectual demiurge should find each other. Labor never craved intellectual leadership but intellectuals invaded labor politics. They had an important contribution to make: they verbalized, supplied theories and slogans for it, . . . made it conscious of itself and in so doing changed its meaning." [2] The formulation of a creed or folklore or rationalization is an important function in the development of the labor movement, just as in any organization. The function needs to be kept in proportion. In the American scene this process seems not to have been the province of a special class nor fashioned through different means in labor organizations than in other groups in the community. The English and Continental experience is different in this respect.

This section has sketched some suggestions toward an analytical view of the emergence and development of the labor movement out of its total environment, regarding that environment as the technological processes, the market structure, the community institutions, and the value judgments of the society. The emphasis has been upon the long-term *trend* of development.

SHORT-RUN VARIATIONS IN TRADE UNION MEMBERSHIP

The growth of the labor movement has not been uniform and the four factors which have been used to approach the

[1] See George G. Higgins, *Voluntarism in Organized Labor in the United States, 1930-1940* (Washington, Catholic University of America Press, 1944).

[2] Joseph A. Schumpeter, *Capitalism, Socialism and Democracy* (New York, Harper & Bros., 1942), pp. 153-54.

long-term trends in the labor movement were not all operative at the same rate. This section is concerned with the deviations from trend, in particular the periods of advance in labor organization.

Even a cursory view of the American labor movement identifies seven major periods of rapid expansion in organization. The following tabulation identifies these periods; it also notes the estimated membership [1] of the organizations at the end of a given period.

Periods [2]	Dates	Membership
Awakening	1827-1836	300,000
Nationalism	1863-1872	300,000
Great Upheaval	1881-1886	1,000,000
Mass Advancement	1896-1904	2,000,000
First World War	1917-1920	5,000,000
New Deal	1933-1937	8,000,000
Second World War	1941-1945	14,000,000

These seven periods can be divided into two distinct types. The dominant characteristics of a period do not preclude some elements of the opposite type. The first group of periods were years of wartime, with rapid increases in the cost of living and stringency in the labor market. This group includes the periods of Nationalism (1863-1872), Mass Advancement (1896-1904), the First World War (1917-1920), and the Second World War (1941-1945). The rapid expansion in membership is to be explained almost entirely by developments in the labor market: the rapid rise in the cost of living and the shortage of labor supply relative to demand. Under these circumstances a trade union helped to enable wage earners to increase their wages to an extent more closely approximating the rise in prices. The individual worker joined unions to

[1] In any organization it is not always clear who should be counted as a "member." In the case of a union, depending upon the purpose, the significant figure may be those who have signed membership cards, pay dues regularly, attend meetings, vote for the union in a NLRB election, or support the union by joining a strike.

[2] The titles used in Commons and Associations, *op. cit.*, have been adopted for the first four periods. The membership figures for these periods are from the same source.

push up his wages; the tightness in the labor market and the general level of profits enabled the union to achieve results. Organization in these instances may be regarded as predominately a market reflex.

Contrasting with these years is the second type of period, to be regarded as one of fundamental unrest. Organization of unions represented a basic dissatisfaction with the performance of the economic system and the society in general. Such were the years of Awakening (1827-1836), the Great Upheaval (1881-1886), and the New Deal (1933-1937). It is these three periods which call for special explanation.

It is well established in the analysis of economic fluctuations that modern capitalism has moved in certain long waves.[1] These long waves or Kondratieff cycles are generally regarded as approximately fifty years in length with twenty-five years of good times and twenty-five years of bad times, and are distinguished from the shorter business cycles. Professor Alvin H. Hansen's dating scheme is typical.[2]

Good Times	Bad Times
1787-1815	1815-1843
1843-1873	1873-1897
1897-1920	1920-1940
1940-	

The long wave represents a fundamental structural period in modern capitalism. The first of these waves has been designated as that of the Industrial Revolution, the second the Age of Railroads, and the third the Electrical Period.[3] The fourth may be known as that of the airplane and atomic power.

For the present purposes it is significant to note that each one of the three periods of major upheaval and fundamental unrest came at the bottom of the period of bad times in the long wave. The period of good times in the long wave is

[1] Joseph A. Schumpeter, *Business Cycles, A Theoretical, Historical, and Statistical Analysis of the Capitalist Process* (New York, McGraw-Hill Book Co., 1939).

[2] Alvin H. Hansen, *Fiscal Policy and Business Cycles* (New York, W. W. Norton & Co., 1940), p. 30.

[3] Schumpeter, *Business Cycles . . .* , I, pp. 220-448.

associated with a cluster of major innovations. There follows a period of generally declining prices (1815-43, 1873-97, 1920-40), during which the shorter business cycles are severe and intense. The three major periods of upheaval follow severe depressions. It is suggested that after prolonged periods of high unemployment for a substantial number in the work force and after years of downward pressure on wages exerted by price declines, labor organizations emerge which are apt to be particularly critical of the fundamental tenets of the society and the economy.

These three fundamental periods of upsurge in the labor movement must also be related to important developments in community institutions and ideas or value judgments. Thus, the first period was the Age of Jacksonian Democracy, the second the Populist, and the third the New Deal. The labor movement of 1827-1836 has been treated as an alignment of "producer classes."[1] The Knights of Labor in the period 1881-1886 has been referred to as the last great middle-class uprising. The expansion of the labor movement in the New Deal period was primarily a working class movement. The first period rallied around the slogan of free education, the second used the watchword of shorter hours, the third was characterized by the accent on security.

CONCLUDING REMARKS

The scaffolding may now be removed. In the distinctive pattern of growth of the labor movement in this country, one sees in outline form the way in which technology, market structure, community institutions, and the ethos factors have interacted together to yield the labor movement considered as a whole. Special types of these factors in operation in specific industries and localities account for the divergent types and forms of unionism which have developed within the generalized framework. For example, the migratory character of

[1] At the third meeting of the Working Men's Party in New York it was not the employers who were given 5 minutes to withdraw but "persons not living by some useful occupation, such as bankers, brokers, rich men, etc." Commons, Ed., *Documentary History* . . . , V, p. 24.

agricultural work and the lumber industry, together with the absence of stability of community, help to account for the type of unionism that originally emerged in this sector, illustrated by the IWW. The unions in the field of local or national government employment have become lobbying agencies by virtue of the practical prohibitions to effective collective bargaining. These specialized forms or species are variations from the main pattern of growth and development arising from special types of environments. In the same way, peculiar national characteristics shape the operation of these factors in comparing labor movements in various countries.

The framework of approach to the labor movement presented here is intended to be suggestive for a renewed interest in the writing of the history of the labor movement in general and in particular sectors. The emphasis upon the interrelations and mutual dependence of four groups of factors has served as the basis for this analysis. Not only is the analysis schematic, but it must be recognized that any simplified schemata must abstract from many complexities of behavior. The formal analysis must not leave the impression of the labor organization as primarily rationalistic. Professor Knight has well said that there is need for "some grasp of the infinitely complex, intangible, and downright contradictory character of men's interests, conscious and unconscious, and their interaction with equally intricate mechanical, biological, neural, and mental processes in forming the pattern of behavior. The great vice is over-simplification . . . ." [1]

[1] Knight, *op. cit.*, p. xxix.

PART TWO

Wages and the Labor Market

CHAPTER EIGHT

Results and Implications of Some Recent Wage Studies

by *Richard A. Lester*

DESPITE voluminous statistics and numerous studies, our knowledge of wages has remained largely superficial. Understanding of the underlying factors in wage determination and wage differentials has been impeded by the tendency of economists to confine their wage theorizing within conventional limits.

Explanations of wages and wage changes have been highly mechanistic. Commodity market concepts are rigidly applied to labor markets; wage theory is regarded merely as a part of price theory. Allowance has not been made for the marked differences between employers' wage and employment policies and their policies regarding commodity prices and purchases. Lack of an adequate theory of human behavior in the workshop and in the labor market has resulted in neglect or insufficient recognition of the importance of workers' reactions to wage payments, of management's response to wage changes, and of company and union wage policies.

Students of labor have long been dissatisfied with the narrow, one-sided character of conventional wage theory. The development of a more adequate and inclusive explanation of wage change and wage patterns has, however, been retarded by inadequate factual information, by lack of searching wage studies.

Industrialists and trade unionists have found conventional wage theory too abstract and unrealistic for practical application and have, therefore, largely disregarded it. Instead employers and union officials have developed their own wage

197

principles, policies, and practices, independent of the marginalist theory of the textbooks. An adequate explanation of wage determination and wage patterns in our economy must take into account such policies and practices.

Some of the data needed for the development of a more satisfactory explanation of actual wage scales are being provided by recent studies of company wage policies, of geographic and interplant wage differentials, and of wages under industrywide collective bargaining. This essay discusses the results of such studies and indicates their implications for wage theory and national policy.

COMPANY WAGE POLICIES

Company wage and price policies generally differ markedly. In pricing their products, manufacturing concerns may quote a price at the mill or the basing point, or a uniform delivered price for each zone or section of the country, or a uniform price for any location in the country. Companies may also quote wages on a local plant basis with scales varying from plant to plant in a multi-plant company, or may offer a uniform scale for all plants in a district or section of the country, or may pay a uniform scale in all the company's plants throughout the country regardless of community wage levels. The most prevalent practice for manufacturers of trademarked products is to quote uniform delivered prices for a district or the whole country. On the other hand, the policy followed by at least four out of every five firms is to base their wages on levels prevailing within each locality, which means non-uniformity in company wage scales within districts or regions.

Seldom are company wage and price policies on the same basis—local, district, or national. Companies that follow the policy of a uniform wage scale nationally, like the Ford Motor Company and the large glass companies, are more likely to quote prices that vary from locality to locality depending upon the distance from producing centers (f.o.b. Detroit or location of nearest competing mill). Companies that follow a policy of varying plant wage scales with wage levels in the

locality are likely to quote the same delivered or retail price
(the seller absorbing differences in freight costs) for their
products throughout a zone or the country. That is true, for
example, in the case of rubber tires, electrical equipment,
business machines, plumbing fixtures, insulation board, hard-
ware, pharmaceutical products, and nationally advertised food
products like canned goods, cereals, and candies.[1] Thus,
Southern plants producing rubber tires have had wage scales
20 to 25 per cent under average Northern scales for comparable jobs, while tires are sold at one list price for the entire
country; yet, the United Rubber Workers (CIO) claim, and
some company data confirm the claim, that output per man-
hour and labor effectiveness in rubber tire production in
Southern plants has been equal to or greater than that in
Northern plants.

In a few branches of industry, like women's full-fashioned
hosiery and men's suits, company prices and wage policy may
be on practically the same basis—the net price to the buyer
of the product identical in every locality and wage scales
approximately uniform for all plants of the large concerns that
operate in the North and are organized by the American Federation of Hosiery Workers or the Amalgamated Clothing
Workers.

The common practice of geographic price uniformity and
independent local wage scales may enable a company to reduce competition among sellers in its product markets, to
reduce competition among buyers in the labor market, and to
stimulate competition on the sellers' side of the labor market,
especially intermarket rivalry. Freight absorption by the
manufacturer eliminates geographical location of mills as a
competitive factor in sales, facilitating complete, nationwide
uniformity in price between competing companies. The local

---

[1] For a discussion and classification of the geographic price structure and
practices in many branches of American industry, see *Price Behavior and
Business Policy*, Monograph No. 1 (Washington, Temporary National Economic Committee, 1940), Part II, pp. 269-345, and Vernon A. Mund, "The
'Freight Allowed' Method of Price Quotation," *Quarterly Journal of Economics*, LIV (February, 1940), 243-45.

prevailing rate policy in the labor market may stimulate inter-community rivalry in the selling of labor, while permitting buyer cooperation in local wage uniformity so as to avoid competitive upbidding of local wage scales. That manufacturing companies customarily quote the prices for their branded products in commodity markets and for their employees in labor markets may aid them in exploiting the monopolistic elements of their position in each market.

Contrasting company wage and price policies also arise out of the differences between labor and commodities and between labor markets and commodity markets. A number of firms believe that to obtain and maintain employee morale, good labor relations, and a high-quality labor force, the company should aim to lead competitors in wage increases and to pay wages somewhat above competitors in each locality. Similar policies are not generally followed by the same companies in purchasing nonhuman factors of production (raw materials, fuel and power, plant and equipment),[1] nor are company policies designed to maintain good customer relations in the company's product markets exactly comparable in respect to leadership in price change or to relative price position. Likewise, company price policies lack an exact counterpart to job evaluation as a method of price determination. Actually many companies have not been able consistently to adjust their scales to wage changes in local markets either because of insufficient flexibility in their job evaluation program or because of a desire, for purposes of employee good-will, to make wage level changes at the same time for all occupations and all plants of the company.

With the spread of unionism, a number of companies that in the 1920's paid scales well above the wage levels of competitors and led in wage increases, have been seeking to eliminate their differential above competitors and to cooperate

---

[1] True, companies may purchase high-quality materials, fuel, or equipment at higher prices but normally they do not seek to lead in establishing new prices for such material items nor are they likely to pay above-market prices for them in order thereby to influence quality, morale, and seller loyalty to the buying firm.

with the industry so that wage changes are made simultaneously with competing firms. One of four companies reporting such a shift toward industry uniformity has practically eliminated a company wage differential averaging 20 to 25 per cent above the industry in the early 1920's. Such companies have become convinced that, with labor unions in their plants, it is no longer possible to obtain differential advantages in terms of employee loyalty and output by means of a policy of wage leadership, and that such a policy carries with it the grave risk that the union will contest each new demand with the leading company first in order to use it as a pattern-setter for the industry.

The growth of unionism is revealing the unsubstantial character of wage scales based on "prevailing local rates." The weakness of such a "prevailing rates" policy is indicated by practices in industries like oil. As one oil company explains, "Our rates are generally the same as those paid by the industry, which are either set by us and met by others in the industry or set by the latter and met by us." Thus, when Sinclair Oil, which recently has tended to assume the role of wage leader, raises rates in a locality, other oil companies operating in the area follow suit.

Market rates are really whatever the companies desire them to be or what the unions, by the means at their disposal, can establish as the going rates in the locality. Consequently, the widespread company policy of standing ready to pay equal to or above prevailing community rates is a standing invitation to the unions to press for increased local rates. This a union may do either by using the organized company that is currently in the weakest position to set the pattern for a wage increase in the community; or by playing companies off against one another, threatening to strike one at a time; or by announcing wage demands concurrently with organizing activities, thus causing unorganized firms to raise wages in order to forestall unionization of their plants.

With companies following policies that result in uniform zone or national prices, the unions can obtain wage increases in a community without local increases in the prices of manufactured goods. The head of the Teamsters' union (AFL) in Seattle, Washington, has frequently pointed out that wage scales for Seattle truck drivers have been raised by the union to a level almost double the pay for similar work in some Southern cities of comparable size, yet manufactured products have generally cost no more delivered in Seattle than in the low wage Southern cities. That is a strong union argument for local wage increases as a means of improving real income in a locality, a fact that should cause marginal productivity economists to ponder.

Company decisions on changes in plant wage levels have often been made on grounds that run counter to the precepts of conventional wage theory. Of the factors influencing companies in wage level changes, three stand out in the answers obtained in the latter half of 1946 from more than a hundred companies (in fifty interviews and seventy-nine questionnaire returns). They are: (1) rates paid by other firms in the area or industry, (2) union pressure, and (3) changes in the cost of living. Although nine-tenths of the firms reported their general wage policy to be one of gearing their scales to prevailing local and industry rates, union pressure and cost of living (which are stressed about equally) are stated each to play a role in determining wage scale changes that is almost as important as prevailing rates. Such stress on cost of living, along with frequent mention of a desire to pay "fair" or "decent" wages per se, indicates the significance of ethical and nonmarket considerations in the wage policies of a considerable number of firms.[1] From his study of wages and profits in the paper industry from 1929 through 1939, Professor Maclaurin also found that the wage policies of a great many companies evidenced other motives than merely pursuit of profit maximization and that "in many cases the maintenance of a

---

[1] More detailed data from the study referred to in the text are contained in a forthcoming report of the Industrial Relations Section of Princeton University entitled *Company Wage Policies*.

contented working force appeared to be an objective in itself." [1]

REGIONAL DIFFERENTIALS

Knowledge of the factors underlying geographic wage differentials has been most meager. Lacking systematic studies of the effects of community wage levels upon industrial location and expansion, little is known about the economic consequences of relatively high wages in some cities, areas, or regions.

Explanations of geographic wage differentials include a host of factors: cost of living, labor productivity, labor-capital ratios, abundance of natural resources, distance from main markets, comparative extent of union organization, type of industry, size of firms and communities, and many other things. In explaining size-of-city differentials and North-South differentials, economists have usually emphasized assumed differences in cost of living, in labor productivity, and in relative scarcity of labor and capital equipment.

Recent studies [2] indicate that such assumptions are, in many cases, of questionable validity and that the actual situation is much more varied and complex than economists have presumed. With regard to North-South wage differentials, for example, my investigations have revealed that some industries have no South-North wage differential, that in industries with a substantial North-South differential a significant number of industrial plants in the South have no such differential, and that the variation in wage scales between Southern firms in the same industry and in the same community may be as great

[1] W. Rupert Maclaurin, "Wages and Profits in the Paper Industry, 1929-1939," *Quarterly Journal of Economics*, LVIII (February, 1944), 225-26.

[2] The studies referred to are summarized in the author's paper on "Southern Wage Differentials: Developments, Analysis, and Implications," presented at the Annual Meeting of the Southern Economic Association in November, 1946, and published in the April, 1947 issue of the *Southern Economic Journal*. An earlier, more popular summary appeared in the Winter, 1946, issue of the *Virginia Quarterly Review* under the title, "Must Wages Differ North and South?"

as, or greater than, the average North-South wage differential for comparable jobs in the industry.

Not only does the pattern of North-South wage differentials vary from industry to industry but also it varies from occupation to occupation in the same industry, differs for the same occupation between industries, and, for the same industry or occupation, shows significant differences between sections of the South (Southeast and Southwest, Upper Southeast and Lower Southeast). Furthermore, South-North differentials in allied industries or in industries drawing on the same type of labor often move in opposite directions. For example, more than half of the average South-New England wage differential for cotton textiles disappeared between 1924 and 1933 (Southern average rising from 61 to 83 per cent of the New England average), while during the same period the South-New England differential for farm wages covering the same states increased by one third (Southern average falling from 45 per cent to 29 per cent of the New England average). Such varied data and conflicting movements indicate how misleading it is to talk of *a* or *the* South-North wage differential.

To a considerable extent the actual variations in South-North wage differentials between industries, occupations, sections of industries, and sections of the South cannot be fully explained or justified on economic grounds. For example, the rubber companies have been hard pressed to explain why Southern wage scales in tire plants should average 20 to 25 per cent below the average for comparable jobs, and for equivalent labor output, in the North, when in allied industries like automobiles, oil, and aircraft (two of the "big four" rubber companies have also been manufacturing aircraft) South-North differentials have been absent or relatively insignificant. A number of large companies with plants in the South have stated to the author that some of the existing wage differentials between their Southern and Northern plants were not fully justified in spite of the fact that South-North differentials in most industries have narrowed considerably during the past two or three decades.

Stated reasons for South-North wage differentials vary from industry to industry, employer to employer, and economist to economist.

A significant number of Southern employers contend that no basis or need now exists for a South-North differential, while other employers in the same industry and same general circumstances insist that some differential is necessary if the industry is to continue to maintain its relative position in the South. Two explanations are offered for this diverse response from business executives similarly situated. First, a wide variation in the abilities of plant management prevails in the South, as is confirmed by the significant differences that exist in labor effectiveness or productivity under comparable plant conditions and by statements of industrial engineers with extensive consulting experience in the South. Second, the reasons offered by some employers are unreasoned rationalizations that fail to weigh the factors favorable and unfavorable to Southern manufacturers and strike an honest net balance. In questionnaire replies and in interviews, a Southern employer will frequently explain the numerous advantages that Southern plants have over Northern plants in his industry, yet will point to some one factor (greater distance from main markets, lower cost of living, or relative skill of workers) and insist that for that one reason alone a South-North wage differential is necessary.

A number of studies have been made of the relative effectiveness or productivity of Southern and Northern labor on comparable jobs and under comparable conditions. They indicate that, in many Southern plants, labor is fully as efficient or productive as Northern labor.[1] Of 41 replying firms with over one million employees in plants in both regions, 23 reported the efficiency of factory labor in their Southern plants equal to or (in four instances) above that of labor in their Northern plants, yet a majority of those 23 concerns were paying wage scales in the South averaging from 10 to 25 per

[1] See "Effectiveness of Factory Labor, South-North Comparisons," *Journal of Political Economy*, LIV (February, 1946), 60, footnotes 4 and 5.

cent lower than in the North.[1]   In terms of actual output, 5
interregional firms with Southern wage scales 10 to 20 per cent
below their Northern scales reported higher output per man-
hour (up to 26 per cent higher) in their Southern plants than
for comparable operations in the North.[2]

Such data on labor effectiveness and productivity between
regions indicate that it is unsafe to generalize about regional
labor productivity from the experience of a few individual
firms, that any relationship between regional wage differentials and labor-productivity differentials is tenuous and uncertain, and that the facts fail to support the view that substantial regional differentials in wages are due to differences in
physical output of labor.   The marked differences between
interregional concerns in labor output per man-hour, where
those firms are producing the same article, use the same type
of labor and equipment, and are located in the same or similar
cities, seem to point to the important role that management
plays in productivity differences.

Economists insist that employers vary the proportions of
labor and capital used in manufacture according to the cost of
labor compared with the cost of purchasing and operating
capital equipment.   On such grounds, they presume that
Southern manufacturing plants use production techniques requiring more labor (the cheaper factor) and less mechanical
equipment than is the case in the higher wage Northern plants
producing the same articles.   However, available data raise
doubts about the general validity of such contentions.   Census
data indicate that the electrical energy used per man-hour
worked by wage earners in Southern manufacturing has generally averaged well above the average for the North and
North Central states in most of the outstanding Southern manufacturing industries.   Such data seem to indicate in general
a greater degree of mechanization of operations in the Southern plants included in the census, as is to be expected in view

[1] *Ibid.*, p. 64, Table 2.
[2] *Loc. cit.*

of the fact that, generally speaking, the Southern plants are newer and more modern in such industries as furniture, hosiery, cotton textiles, pulp and paper, and rubber.

To test further the economists' assumptions regarding wage influences on the ratio of labor to equipment, executives of interregional firms with plants in the South and the North were asked whether lower wage rates in the South had *themselves* caused the companies to use production techniques or methods in their Southern plants that require more labor and less machinery than the proportions used in their Northern operations. Of 44 firms replying, 42 answered flatly "No," that in the construction and equipping of their Southern plants they had not been influenced by regional differences in wage scales. The Southern wage scales of those 42 concerns averaged about 12 per cent under the scales in their Northern plants and 10 of them had Southern scales averaging 20 to 30 per cent below their Northern rates for all comparable jobs.[1]

The view that geographical wage differentials rest on cost of living differences also fails to meet the test of statistical facts. U.S. Bureau of Labor Statistics studies of estimated cost of living for wage earners in 31 large cities (9 in the South) and 10 small cities (5 in the South) in 1938 and 1939 indicated that living costs in the Southern cities averaged only 3 or 4 per cent under the cost of the same plane of living in comparable Northern cities.[2] Indeed, the cost of a "maintenance" level of living for a manual worker's family of four persons in June, 1939, was higher in 6 of the large Southern cities (Atlanta, Houston, Jacksonville, Memphis, Norfolk, and Richmond) than in 3 of the large Northern cities (Buffalo, Indianapolis, and Kansas City). Of the 10 small cities, one in the North had the lowest living costs based on Northern consumption patterns and the second lowest total costs based

---

[1] *Ibid.*, p. 69.

[2] "Differences in Living Costs in Northern and Southern Cities" and "Estimated Intercity Differences in Cost of Living, June 15, 1939," *Monthly Labor Review*, XLIX (July and November, 1939), 22-38 and 1164-67.

on customary wage-earner purchases in the South. In short, cost of living differentials between the South and the North are as varied as patterns of South-North wage differentials.

Furthermore, cost of living differentials do not correspond closely with wage differentials between cities. For large cities, the U.S. Bureau of Labor Statistics has published both estimated cost of living for a manual worker's family and indexes for the level of average hourly entrance rates for adult male common labor, as well as a composite wage index based on 26 occupational groups in manufacturing for 1943. Comparisons can be made for 22 identical Northern and Southern cities for the middle of 1941 and the middle of 1943.[1] Ranking the 22 cities from the highest to the lowest in each of the two factors (cost of living and wage level), one finds that a city's rank for living costs, on the average, is 5 ranks away from its rank for wage level in 1941 and 6 ranks away in 1943, using either common labor rates or the composite-occupational index. For 5 or 6 of the cities the two rankings differ by 10 to 16 ranks in both years. Consequently, in some cities the cost of living is considerably below the 22-city average and wage levels well above such an average, while for other cities the situation is reversed. Especially is the correlation likely to be low if one compares living cost differences between Northern and Southern cities with South-North wage differentials, industry by industry, for the same cities.

Neither singly nor in combination do cost of living, ratio of labor to capital, or labor productivity adequately explain geographical wage differences. In the case of South-North differentials, such factors as relative population growth (which has been greater in the South), relative growth of the industry in the South, extent of union organization, and quality of management probably have been more important and influential than cost of living or labor-capital ratios during recent dec-

[1] For source of data, see *Monthly Labor Review,* LII (May, 1941), 1231; LIV (January, 1942), 165; LVII (October, 1943), 805; LIX (August, 1944), 243; and *Journal of the American Statistical Association,* XL (June, 1945), 177.

ades. (Quality of management and labor productivity are closely related.) Company wage policies, trade unionism, race differentials, community attitudes, tradition, and historical accidents have also played a part.

With a variety of influential factors affecting regional wage differentials and wide diversity in such differentials, it is evident that no single explanation of them will be adequate. One must think of wage differentials in terms of a range of possibilities or an area of indeterminateness and not seek by means of one simple principle of economic calculation to discover a unique answer, which then can be assumed to constitute the one and only "equilibrium" rate. The notion of limits in terms of a range is developed more fully below.

LOCAL WAGE DIVERSITY

Studies of wages indicate that significant differences prevail in the hourly rates being paid by firms in a single community for equivalent labor on similar jobs. Instead of one "prevailing rate" for the same grade of labor in the same locality, there is a band of hourly rates with firms, even in the same branch of an industry, maintaining important differentials in local wage levels over long periods of time. Such wage diversity for practically identical work is likely to be prevalent especially where labor unionism is unimportant or has only recently been established.

In some communities the wage level of the highest paying plant may average 35 or 40 per cent above the level of the lowest paying plant for the same jobs under the time method of payment, and such an interfirm range or spread in one community may be two or three times the spread in other communities.[1] The interfirm variation or dispersion in wage scales [2] in some communities is almost as great as for a whole region or for the entire country, indicating no more wage uniformity in a

[1] See my article, "Wage Diversity and Its Theoretical Implications," *Review of Economic Statistics*, XXVIII (August, 1946), 156, Table 2.

[2] As measured by coefficients of average deviation, i.e., average deviation from the arithmetic mean expressed in percentage of the mean.

single labor market than for an area that includes a multitude of labor markets with widely differing economic conditions.[1]

Why does such interfirm diversity in wage rates exist and persist in the same locality for workers of equal skill, ability, and effectiveness?

A part of the explanation may lie in interfirm differences in nonwage factors—differences in physical conditions of work, in stability of employment, in advancement possibilities, in company benefit programs, in vacations and paid holidays, etc. However, the higher wage firms, generally speaking, also have the most favorable nonwage conditions. Hence, "true" wage differences of significant size seem to have prevailed in many communities and over long periods of time without correction by market forces.

Company wage policies and practices largely account for real wage differentials in a locality.[2] Some companies consciously pursue a high wage policy so that their plants are always among those paying the highest wages in each location. That is true, for example, of the oil and automobile companies. On the other hand, cotton textile mills and plants processing food tend to be among the low wage establishments in industrial centers. Differences in wage-paying ability between industries and firms help to explain the wage level policies of companies. Employers also differ in their policies concerning wage increases and area levels. Some multi-plant companies provide wage scale uniformity over wide geographic areas; others have a different scale at each plant. Company wage increases may be given in cents per hour or in percentage terms, straight across the board or differentiated by occupation, according to merit ratings or automatically by length of service. Some companies have job evaluation plans to which they adhere rigidly; others have no such plans, evaluate a job differently, or give market changes priority over the results of systematic job evaluation. Also, interplant varia-

[1] See "Wage Diversity and Its Theoretical Implications," *op. cit.*, especially Table 3.

[2] See, for example, John W. Riegel, *Wage Determination* (Bureau of Industrial Relations, University of Michigan, 1937), pp. 8-9.

tions in wage scales arise from historical accidents, tradition, and differing notions as to what are "fair" wages.

In pricing labor, a firm's long-run and short-run interests may conflict. A company desiring to preserve its good reputation in the labor market and to maintain employee "loyalty," would hesitate to discharge a large section of its work force in order to hire other labor offering to work at lower wages. And, because of the various costs involved, including employee discontent, it would hesitate to pursue a policy of raising and reducing its occupational wage rates with every change in current rates in the local market. On the supply side, the amount of labor available to a firm at various wage rates is influenced by all kinds of nonwage factors such as personal friendships of the employees, human quality of the supervision, accumulated seniority of workers, etc.

For such reasons, interplant uniformity of hourly rates for the same grade of labor in an industrial community is not normal and has been relatively rare. It is likely to occur under only four conditions: (1) common or combined action by employers, (2) collective action by employees, (3) joint action by labor and employer groups, or (4) compulsory action by government. In other words, uniformity in wage rates is evidence of concerted action and restraint of competition. Consequently, it is wrong to assume that, in the absence of collusive or compulsory forces, there will be a single "prevailing rate" paid by all firms in a locality for the same class and quality of labor. Competitive forces in the labor market apparently do not tend to enforce a single rate but result in a variety of rates for identical work.

EFFECTS OF INCREASING UNIFORMITY IN WAGE SCALES

During the past decade, wage differentials between local firms, between industries, and between regions of the country have, in general, been considerably reduced. Significant factors in such reduction have been labor union policies, relatively "full" employment, more widespread knowledge of wage scales being paid, and governmental influences, especially under the National War Labor Board. Union policies probably have been, and will continue to be, the most important force in the trend toward uniformity in wage scales both geographically and between companies.

As indicated in the discussion of company wage policies, many high wage firms that were wage leaders in the 1920's believe that a significant company differential above the average wage level for their industry no longer pays with widespread unionism, and they have come to favor a greater degree of company uniformity in wage policy for reasons of strategy in dealing with unions as well as for reasons of labor cost per unit of output under union conditions.

Interesting in this connection are the replies of some 50 business firms giving definite answers to the question: "Would your company be adversely affected by a policy of uniform wage scales for all firms in your industry—either uniform nationally or uniform within a region of the country?" Almost half of the companies replied that they would not be adversely affected, stating such reasons as "we are the highest paying firm in the industry," "the trend is in that direction," it "would prove advantageous" for the industry, "it would emphasize competition," especially in management, and "where standard prices are charged for products throughout the country, uniform wage scales should be paid." The fact that a large number replied their company would not be adversely affected because it was one of the highest wage firms in the industry seems to lend support to other evidence indicating that the payment of top wages may not be accompanied by a compensating differential in labor output.[1]

Companies replying that they would be adversely affected by national or regional uniformity in wage scales for an industry gave such reasons as: "uniform rate schedules would tend to minimize competition," "uniformity of wage scales is mo-

---

[1] See, for example, W. Rupert Maclaurin and Charles A. Myers, "Wages and the Movement of Factory Labor," *Quarterly Journal of Economics*, LVII (February, 1943), 251-53.

nopoly," it "would disregard demand and supply," "because of our relative inefficiency compared to some of our large direct competitors," and "it would lead toward industry-wide collective bargaining, a procedure to which this company is opposed." Companies in industries subject to national or regional bargaining generally have favored uniformity in wage scales as a means of stabilizing labor costs, providing "fair" competition, eliminating "whipsawing" on wages by the union playing one firm against another, and avoiding wage differentials based on differences in the wage-paying ability of individual firms.[1]

Applying commodity market reasoning, economists have contended that "Under a free labor market, different wage rates for the same kind of labor could not long exist," [2] that "We have a real problem of different wage rates for the same work only when there is not a free labor market—when there is labor monopoly," [3] and that "Labor is properly priced and allocated in a competitive system if, say, all unskilled labor in a particular market sells at the same price. . . ." [4]

Although favoring price uniformity for equivalent labor in local labor markets, economists have not generally favored uniformity in wage scales over wide geographical areas that include many local labor markets. Regional or national uniformity in wage scales has been called economically "unsound" because it fails to allow wage adjustments to labor supply and demand in each local market, with a resulting threat of "wage distortion" unemployment. It is contended, for example, that "a differential between North and South wages is needed to improve the geographical distribution of both labor and capi-

---

[1] See R. A. Lester and E. A. Robie, *Wages under National and Regional Collective Bargaining* (Industrial Relations Section, Princeton Univ., 1946), pp. 54, 67, 77, 88, and 91.

[2] Fred R. Fairchild, *Profits and the Ability to Pay Wages,* Popular Essays on Current Problems, Vol. 1 (The Foundation for Economic Education, Inc., August, 1946), p. 16.

[3] *Ibid.,* p. 16.

[4] Charles E. Lindblom, "Collective Bargaining and the Competitive System," *Canadian Journal of Economics and Political Science,* XI (November, 1945), 571, footnote 19.

tal . . . to accelerate the movement of capital into the South and of labor into the North." [1]

Such contentions raise interesting questions. A number of interregional concerns have followed a practice of paying identical scales in their Northern and Southern plants. Have the uniform wage scales paid by the Ford Motor Company, certain rayon companies, or the flat and flint glass companies, represented "distorted" wage structures? Is the uniform piece-rate structure in full-fashioned hosiery from Massachusetts to California, or the complete uniformity in time rates in pulp and paper in the three West Coast states, an example of "wage distortion"? And if so, does the same reasoning apply to product prices? Do nationally or regionally uniform prices for trademarked articles constitute "price distortions" because such prices are not adjusted to local demand and supply conditions or to differences in cost of production at each plant or in each locality?

Comment has already been made on the tendency for geographic uniformity in price to encourage local wage increases and unformity in wage scales. If the purpose is to distribute resources according to demand, supply, and cost in order to facilitate the economic location and expansion of industry, then mill-base prices related to local costs of production are the most effective means. Independent price scales for each mill based on its costs would, for example, be much more efficacious in achieving expansion of tire production in the South than the present arrangement of uniform national prices for tires with production supposed to be distributed between localities and regions according to the profits from each plant. Individual plant profits are obscured in a multiple-plant company offering uniform delivered prices and absorbing the varying costs of freight to the buyers' places of business.

[1] Sumner H. Slichter, "The Responsibility of Organized Labor for Employment," *American Economic Review*, XXXV, Supplement (May, 1945), 196. See also Slichter, "Wage-Price Policy and Employment," *American Economic Review*, XXXVI, Supplement (May, 1946), 315, and John V. Van Sickle, "Regional Aspects of the Problem of Full Employment at Fair Wages," *Southern Economic Journal*, XIII (July, 1946), 36-45.

Price and wage uniformity bring up the question of monopolistic elements in labor and product markets. Monopoly in the labor market has never been prosecuted as such, presumably because the market is local and difficult to define, monopolistic elements are almost bound to be present on the buying side, and, until recently, a legal bias existed in favor of employers. Obviously in company towns one employer may have complete monopoly of the local labor market, and, until a labor union enters the picture, monopolistic determination of wages may be easily achieved among employers who quote the scales they pay and who may refrain from bidding wages up or hiring labor away from one another.

Given monopolistic elements in labor markets and local wage diversity where labor has not been organized, what are likely to be the economic effects of trade union or governmental policies designed to achieve more wage uniformity locally and over wide geographic areas? What company adjustments are to be expected when "true" wage differentials are reduced or eliminated in a locality or between regions?

Experience fails to confirm a priori conclusions based on traditional theory. In the mid-1920's, Southern wage scales averaged only about 65 per cent of Northern scales in cotton textiles and pulp and paper, and 75 per cent of Northern scales in seamless hosiery. Since then, the South-North differential in those three industries has been practically eliminated, yet in each industry employment in the South has continued to expand relative to the North.

With a reduction in the South-North wage differential in the men's cotton garments and wood furniture industries under the Fair Labor Standards Act in the period from mid-1938 to March, 1941, employment expanded most in the firms in which wage scales were increased the most.[1] In wood furniture, where the average South-North differential in wages had apparently experienced no permanent change in the previous

[1] For further discussion of these two cases see my article, "Shortcomings of Marginal Analysis for Wage-Employment Problems," *American Economic Review*, XXXVI (March, 1946), 75-77.

forty-five years,[1] not only did employment in Southern plants increase 26 per cent whereas it decreased slightly in competing Northern firms during the period (October, 1937, to February, 1941), but, within the South, employment expanded more than twice as fast in the lower wage firms whose wages increased 10 per cent as it did in the higher wage firms where the increase in wages was less than 2 per cent.

During the past two decades, many firms have raised their wage scales by 10 or 15 per cent for purely local reasons—such as the location of a new, high wage plant in the same small community, the threat of union organization in the plant, negotiation of the first union contract following organization, etc.—that have no effect on all the other plants in the industry. Most of the firms could be fairly certain that, under the circumstances, such an independent increase in wages would leave their wage level, at least for many years, raised by that amount relative to the scales paid by practically all of their competitors. A number of plants so affected were Southern cotton yarn mills, weaving mills, and full-fashioned hosiery mills, all producing "grey goods" (undyed, unbranded, standard items for the grey goods markets) in highly competitive industries characterized by a large number of small firms. Employment data and interviews covering such firms indicate that, as a group, they met such independent wage increases without curtailing operations and employment relative to the rest of the industry.

Experience with uniformity in company wage scales under national, regional, and citywide collective bargaining also indicates that differentiated increases raising the low wage firms up to the uniform scale have not led to any special tendency for such firms to curtail their operations or to go out of business.[2] Many industries under national collective bargaining and wage uniformity, such as full-fashioned hosiery, men's clothing, pressed and blown glassware, silk and rayon

[1] Data from my article, "Trends in Southern Wage Differentials since 1890," *Southern Economic Journal*, XI (April, 1945), 330-31.

[2] Lester and Robie, *op. cit.*, and Chapter 2 in this volume.

dyeing and finishing, and bituminous coal, contain a hundred or more firms, no one of which accounts for more than a minor fraction of the industry's total output. In those industries, the small companies seem not to have been at a relative disadvantage under such uniformity.

Why has experience been so contrary to the presuppositions of orthodox economic theory?

Conventional theory is based on an erroneous conception of business management and management policies. Faced with a relative wage increase, business executives generally are not inclined to curtail operations. Such action would be contrary to their psychology. Usually it would also be an irrational reaction. The theorists generally have assumed diminishing returns with increased employment even in a plant already constructed and equipped, whereas data from 33 Southern companies show that normally businessmen anticipate increasing returns (and profits) up to 100 per cent of plant capacity.[1] For all 33 firms, variable costs per output unit (and judging from interviews, particularly labor costs per unit) tend to increase, on the average, about 25 per cent whenever the scale of plant operations declines from 100 per cent to 70 per cent of plant capacity. If businessmen think that their unit variable costs (to say nothing of their overhead costs per unit) change in that fashion they will not be prone to curtail operations and employment because of a wage increase.

Wide differences exist in management effectiveness under similar circumstances and compensation. Experience has indicated that wage increases frequently serve as a stimulus to management to make improvements in plant organization and operations that would have been profitable to institute prior to the wage increase. If existing management fails to make such improvements, new management personnel may.

Interesting in this connection are replies from executives of 43 Southern concerns in the summer of 1945 to the question

[1] As they define such capacity. See "Shortcomings of Marginal Analysis for Wage-Employment Problems," *op. cit.*, pp. 68-71.

how their firm would be likely to adjust to a 50 per cent reduction in the average South-North differential in their industry during the first three years after the defeat of Japan.[1]   As wage scales for the replying Southern concerns averaged 18 per cent under the comparable average for their competitors in the North, the question involved an average increase of 11 per cent in the wage scales of the Southern firms, assuming no change in the wage levels of their Northern competitors.   The replying executives gave most frequent mention and greatest emphasis to improvements in efficiency through better production methods, organization, supervision, incentives, workloads, etc.   Second in importance in their answers was the installation of labor-saving machinery, which was stressed particularly by firms with high ratios of labor cost to total cost.   Almost as significant as labor-saving machinery in number of times mentioned and average weight given was increased sales efforts in order to expand sales and production.   Stress on sales efforts is an understandable adjustment in view of the importance of operations at or near 100 per cent of plant capacity if unit variable and unit overhead costs are to be kept at a minimum.   Increased sales efforts would tend to result in a volume of production and employment greater than would otherwise occur—a result directly contrary to the employment effects expected to follow from such a wage increase according to conventional economic theories.

Orthodox economic theory assumes that adjustments in employers' employment, wages, and prices are governed by calculated marginal productivity.   However, available data indicate that manufacturing companies of any size do not consistently pursue a policy of varying (especially reducing) the volume of employment in their plants in an attempt to keep the cost of the last unit of labor actually employed equal to some estimate of the net addition to the company's receipts attributable to that unit of labor.   Such calculation would be difficult in companies in which the scale of plant operations

[1] The data for this paragraph are taken from *ibid.*, pp. 77-81.

varies so that the cost of production per unit of output differs over time, the company produces and sells more than one article so that common and joint costs are involved, and production includes a number of processes in the company as, for example, assembly line operation, so that the value contribution of any one worker is practically indistinguishable.[1] The infrequency of change in companies' price scales, wage scales, and (often) total volume of employment seems to indicate that businessmen are not constantly, or even frequently, calculating and acting on marginal principles. That most businessmen do not consciously engage in such marginal estimates and calculations seems also to be indicated by the fact that five out of six industrial companies (representing three-fourths of all manufacturing production) do not have total cost data on a product-by-product basis [2] and, therefore, cannot even calculate total costs per unit of output.

Other difficulties stand in the way of any attempt by employers to operate on marginal principles in the labor market. For example, plants are designed and equipped for a work force of a certain size; companies generally make across-the-board wage increases or decreases; monopolistic elements are important in both product and labor markets. Reduction in an employer's work force generally involves significant costs to the employer in the form of adverse effects on the morale of the remaining employees, a tendency for workers to restrict output in the face of reductions in the work force, a need to shift workers to different jobs with changes in the scale of plant operations, and possible increases in the employer's tax rate under experience rating in unemployment compensation. How union policies and provisions of union agreements pre-

[1] See, for example, Wilford J. Eiteman, "The Equilibrium of the Firm in Multi-Process Industries," *Quarterly Journal of Economics*, LIX (February, 1945), 280-286.

[2] Data from *A Report on Cost Accounting in Industry* (Accounting Department, Office of Price Administration, June 30, 1946), pp. iii and iv. See also Martin L. Black, Jr. and Harold B. Eversole, "Cost Accounting in Price Determination," *Journal of Accounting*, LXXXII (November, 1946), 370-71.

sent additional obstacles to strict application of payment and employment according to marginal principles is well explained in Chapter 10 of this volume.

The conclusion that can be drawn from the above data and discussion is that employment in a manufacturing plant already constructed and equipped is largely determined by the volume of sales and anticipated orders, and not by variations in labor costs. Within rather wide limits, output and employment are usually a function of the volume of present and prospective demand at the prevailing prices. The prices are either market-determined or, for trademarked articles, are influenced by the price policies of competitors. In such cases, price changes are normally infrequent and made by all competing firms at the same time. Also, prices of branded articles are generally uniform over wide geographic areas, regardless of differences in demand, supply, or cost conditions between localities within a uniform price zone. Geographic uniformity for wage scales seems to present no greater economic problems than similar price uniformity. Indeed, as already indicated, such price uniformity both encourages and justifies attempts at corresponding wage uniformity.

For both wages and prices, companies generally follow a leader or a pattern of leadership in industries where prices are not market-determined. It is possible that a large firm customarily serving as a price leader may, in altering its prices, take into account some rough guesses concerning the elasticity of demand for its various products—the variations in money volume of sales with changes in price. However, inquiry indicates that even price leaders have only the vaguest notions of demand elasticities for the numerous products manufactured by such leaders and that the price conformers or followers—the overwhelming numbers constituting the bulk of American industry—generally take no, or practically no, account of theoretical demand elasticities in determining their prices and employment.

Price-conforming firms or leadership followers adjust their production and employment (perhaps expanding in some lines and contracting in others), not according to hypothetical slopes of demand curves or presumed changes in their elasticities, but according to the actual and anticipated volume of sales for the products that they manufacture. Under price leadership, executives of a nonleading firm tend to base their production, employment, and sales policies on some notion of total present and prospective sales for the products that the firm makes and the share of such totals that the firm is likely, or seeks, to obtain. They think more in terms of the firm's relative position in the industry than in terms of hypothetical, static curves and marginalist calculations. Thus, acceptance of price leadership tends to eliminate much of the possible, practical significance that the notion of demand elasticities might have for the theory of production and employment in the individual firm.[1] It is for such reasons that employers do not react to alterations in their wage scales, or even the elimination of interfirm wage differentials, by making the changes in the firm's production and employment that the marginalists postulate.

IMPLICATIONS FOR THEORY AND POLICY

Wage theory is so unsatisfactory, partly because it has so much to explain—(a) the general level of wages and its movements, (b) occupational differentials and their changes, (c) geographic differentials and alterations in such differentials,

---

[1] Such explanations of employer behavior as that above are difficult for a marginalist to grasp because they do not fit into his conceptual framework. Thus, to an explanation by the author ("Marginalism, Minimum Wages, and Labor Markets," *American Economic Review,* XXXVII [March, 1947], 135-47) that "existing and expected volume of product sales appears to be a factor in firm employment that operates independent of the principle of equating its marginal net revenue productivity and marginal labor cost," Professor Fritz Machlup presumes that I must have in mind the "special case" of the employer who assumes that the demand curves facing him have a "corner" at prevailing prices because competitors would match any price reductions that he initiated (see p. 153 of the same issue of the *American Economic Review*). That the absence of subjective demand schedules and elasticity considerations is widespread in American industry (and is not, therefore, a "special case") is indicated in my article, "Absence of Elasticity Considerations in Demand to the Firm," in the January, 1948 issue of the *Southern Economic Journal.*

(d) interindustry differentials and shifts in them, (e) inter-firm differentials and changes therein, and (f) personal differentials in time rates for the same occupation in a plant.

Case studies of wage structures during the past two decades, and especially under the National War Labor Board, have revealed that the actual size of differentials b, c, d, and e above frequently cannot be justified either by market analysis of the economists or by systematic evaluation of the jobs. Studies of wage structures extending over two to five decades indicate that market forces do not generally tend to equalize wages for comparable or identical jobs in a locality, nor do they bring about rational patterns of geographic wage relationships that can be supported on purely economic grounds. Existing wage scales have seemed rather chaotic not only because numerous noneconomic factors are important in actual wage determination but also because wage theorists generally have had erroneous conceptions of labor markets and incorrect notions of how employers operate and workers are motivated.

In the absence of labor union or governmental intervention, employers have generally been able to select where within a band or range of rates they will establish their wage scales. Some employers seek to be wage leaders in their industry and may establish their wage scales in line with the highest cluster of rates in each community; [1] others seek to pay no more than a cluster for comparable low wage firms or purposely keep their wage scale below the level of the wage leader in their industry.

The factors that have influenced the employers' choices and the limits to the possible range or scope of choice need to be more fully explored. For such exploration, ideas and concepts applied to commodity markets will not provide all the necessary tools, since the actual rates paid for the same kind of work in the same labor market often do not tend to concentrate around a single "equilibrium" rate but may be bunched in a number of clusters and scattered over a whole

---

[1] Which usually includes high wage companies like oil and automobile producers.

range or band of rates. Therefore, new and broader approaches will be needed in searching to discover, for example, what factors limit the range of wage variation for the same work in a labor market, how changes in labor market forces or circumstances serve to confine or expand the possible range of variation, and why wage variability or diversity in one labor market may be double or triple that in another labor market.

Such a "range theory" of wages would provide a frame of reference that would conform to the point of view and the wage policies and practices of employers. It would also permit a more adeqaute explanation of the influences of unions and union policies on wage structures and wage levels. Even more than employers, unions bring political, social, and personal factors into wage problems and wage determination. Through collective bargaining the possible range of rates may, of course, be expanded. Embodying the valid elements in marginal productivity and bargaining theories of wages, a broader "range theory" would allow for factors like noneconomic considerations, special characteristics of labor markets, and differences in business management, that are so neglected by conventional analysis.

So much for the theoretical implications of recent wage studies. What light do such studies shed on the issue of the area of wage determination—whether the appropriate unit for wage policy is the plant, the company, a region, an industry, or the national government?

For much of American industry, the real unit of wage-policy formulation and wage determination is no longer the locality or the company. National unions are organized on an industry, some even on a multiple-industry, basis. One of their objectives is to prevent employers from encouraging interlocality competition in wages and labor costs while minimizing competition between sellers in product markets and buyers within the local labor market. National unions will oppose local wage determination in industries producing for a national market and pricing on a national basis.

Increasingly employers are recognizing that, with national

organization of labor and union wage policy on a national basis, independent company wage policy on a locality-by-locality basis is ineffectual and anachronistic and that genuine collective bargaining with national unions is only possible on a multiple-employer or industrywide basis.[1] Recent developments in the steel industry, which has tended to be a bellwether in wage matters, are significant. Not only have wage negotiations in steel been characterized by industrywide consultation on the employers' side, but twelve steel companies, following a National War Labor Board order, have worked out with the Steelworkers (CIO) a joint job classification plan. The program reduces the number of wage classifications in the industry to thirty, provides standard classifications for equal work on an industry basis, and will presumably result in complete wage uniformity for all twelve companies within each geographical district (Pittsburgh, Chicago, etc.). Undoubtedly, the final result will be a uniform industrywide wage structure under national agreements, which may eventually provide for the same wage scale throughout the country with the possible exception of lower common-labor rates in the South.

Studies of national and regional bargaining show that actual experience lends little support to the popular fear that industrywide wage determination in manufacturing will have untoward economic results, especially for consumers. Investigation of ten to fifty-five years' experience with such bargaining in seven manufacturing industries revealed that, generally speaking, their wage scales were not relatively high, that their wage levels had not risen more rapidly than for manufacturing as a whole, and that wage negotiations had not led to practices restricting economic change or fostering price-fixing.[2] Under industrywide bargaining, wage decisions are

[1] Multiple-employer bargaining has been expanding until now apparently one-third of all organized labor (or between four and five million employees) are covered by agreements with employers' associations. See Moses Shapiro, "Industry-wide Collective Bargaining," in *Proceedings of Industrial Relations Seminar of the Radio Manufacturers Association*, New York City, May 21-22, 1946, pp. 38-39.

[2] See Lester and Robie, *op. cit.*, especially pp. 93-95.

likely to be more sensible and far-sighted, taking into consideration the economic interests of the whole industry, and wages tend to be somewhat more stable, which is particularly desirable where rival unionism helps to give the economy an inflationary bias and expectations of price inflation and deflation aggravate the cyclical swings in business.

Regardless of the area of wage negotiation and determination by management and labor, continued government guidance in wage matters will be necessary. Some national consideration of wage level changes is needed not only because rival unionism stimulates rivalry in wage increases and we lack the foreign-trade check to wage changes that exists in countries more dependent on international exchange (like England, Sweden, or Australia), but also because wages are so important in our economy. The existence of a rational wage structure, with some measure of uniformity in industry wage scales, will facilitate national guidance in wage matters by permitting government recommendation or direction to be confined to broad questions concerning the levels of wages and changes in the level.

CHAPTER NINE

The Meaning of Recent Wage Changes

by *David R. Roberts*

PEOPLE are inclined to allude to the various controls of the wartime period of labor relations as purely temporary measures. In a sense this is true, in another sense completely false. Certain wartime regulations, such as wage stabilization are no longer with us. But their heritage definitely is. Nor is it a heritage that can be disowned with ease. The signs seem to point to the conclusion that the wartime changes will have permanent effects upon future patterns of the American wage structure. Why is this so? What has been the war heritage? What has happened since the war to perpetuate the wartime developments? How have the various groups of workers in America been affected by recent changes in the wage structure? How will the new wage patterns affect the successful operation of the American economy?

The answers to such questions are important for labor leaders and management officials. Both need to know what has been happening to the American wage structure and what meaning recent structural changes have for future labor developments.

WARTIME CHANGES

The war-induced manpower shortage changed the labor market. Instead of the initiative in raising wages devolving on the employees and, in consequence, wage levels in general reflecting bargaining power, the initiative was seized by the employers, who proceeded to drive wage rates upward in order to attract labor. A seesaw between competing em-

226

ployers began to develop, which, if allowed to go on, would have jeopardized the price control program. Therefore, the War Labor Board established a framework of rules within which the upward movement was contained. With both labor and management eager in general to raise rates, this framework of rules became the most important determinant of the pattern of increases, completely overshadowing the normally important factor of union policy. From our present point of view, the significant aspect of that framework was its greater restrictiveness in the high than in the low wage areas. Of the board's major grounds for approving an increase in wages, the Little Steel formula alone was nondiscriminatory in this sense. Both the bracket system,[1] under which 60 per cent of all the board's approvals were made, and the substandard policy [2] were expressly designed to give relief at the low end of the scale. The same effect followed from the consistent awarding of cents per hour rather than percentage increases and the special treatment accorded a number of war-important, low wage industries, whose wage scales hampered the recruitment of needed labor.

Detailed statistical analysis of wage changes [3] can only be made in the manufacturing industries because for nonmanufacturing industries earnings data are scanty and the concept of average straight-time hourly earnings is not equally meaningful, e.g., in agriculture and in transportation. Neverthe-

[1] Under the bracket system particular job rates that were below the bracket minimum, defined in general as a point 10 per cent below the weighted average of such job rates in a particular industry and area, might be raised to the bracket minimum, but rates already equal to or above the bracket minimum might not be increased.

[2] Under the Board's substandard policy wages which were below the substandard rate might be increased to that level but balancing increases further up the scale were required to be tapered progressively to zero at 70 cents per hour, i.e., the higher the rate the smaller the increase and no incease at all was permitted in rates of 70 cents and more per hour. The substandard rate was set initially at 40 cents and increased by steps to 55 cents.

[3] In the following discussion average straight-time hourly earnings will be used as the measure of wage rates because very few rate data are available, and because rate comparisons over time are frequently rendered misleading by changes in job content where piece rates are involved.

less, in order to round out the picture rough estimates of the changes in average straight-time hourly earnings from 1939 to 1945 are presented in the table [1] for the nine major industrial categories.

ESTIMATED STRAIGHT-TIME HOURLY EARNINGS BY MAJOR
INDUSTRIAL CATEGORIES, 1939 AND 1945

	Straight-Time Hourly Earnings (Dollars)		Per Cent Increase 1939 to 1945
	1939	1945	
Agriculture	.153	.439	187
Services	.415	.723	74
Trade	.616	.976	58
Manufacturing	.640	.935	46
Transportation	.626	.851	36
Contract construction	.748	1.264	69
Communications and public utilities	.808	1.029	27
Mining	.829	1.116	35
Finance, insurance, and real estate	.839	1.050	25

Accuracy in detail cannot be claimed for these figures. However, the percentage increases vary so much from one industry to another that the likely statistical error would not be sufficient to make any real difference in the relative magnitudes. The figures show that in general the percentage increase in earnings during the war was inversely proportional to the prewar level of earnings. For example, wages in agriculture and services, the lowest paid fields, rose by 187 and 74 per cent respectively while wages in finance, mining, and utilities, the highest paid fields, rose by 25 to 35 per cent. Hence the whole wage structure was pulled together; its dispersion about the mean was reduced.

Let us now turn to the manufacturing industries where changes in the wage structure can be traced with greater rigor. Here again there is the same marked inverse relationship be-

[1] The basic data used were Department of Commerce figures of annual earnings per full-time employee. These were reduced to average gross hourly earnings by application of estimates of average hours worked from the Bureau of Labor Statistics and elsewhere. In the case of industries where overtime pay is common, a further adjustment was made to eliminate that premium payment.

tween the level of prewar earnings and the percentage increase during the war. Earnings in the five lowest wage industries (textile, tobacco, lumber, furniture, and leather, which averaged 48 cents per hour in 1939) had risen 65 per cent by 1945; earnings in the five highest wage industries (automobiles, petroleum refining, printing and publishing, transportation equipment, and rubber, which averaged 85 cents per hour in 1939) had risen only 38 per cent by 1945. Dispersion, as measured by the standard deviation, was lowered from 21 per cent to 15 per cent of the arithmetic mean during this six year period.[1]

The fundamental character of the inverse relationship between prewar earnings and wartime increases is illustrated by the fact that it overshadows the normal effect of the relative degree of unionization. Earnings in the most highly organized quarter of the manufacturing industries (those with over 60 per cent of the employees under union contract) rose by only 46 per cent from 1939 to 1945 while earnings in the most poorly organized quarter of the manufacturing industries (those with less than 40 per cent of the employees under union contract) rose by 62 per cent. The explanation, of course, lies in the difference between their initial wage levels. The highly organized industries were already paying 70 cents per hour in 1939 compared with an average of 61 cents for all manufacturing. Therefore they found it difficult to qualify for increases under War Labor Board rules. The poorly organized industries on the other hand had relatively low wages, averaging 49 cents per hour, and they found it easier to qualify for increases.

For intra-industry and intra-plant differentials, similar wage data for making comparisons is lacking, but cogent a priori considerations point toward a like narrowing of wage differentials. The records indicate that 60 per cent of the cases handled by the War Labor Board during the stabiliza-

---

[1] Constant employment weights were used throughout the calculations in this chapter in order that changes in the statistical measures should reflect changes in rates and not employment shifts.

tion period [1] (October, 1942, to August, 1945) involved the issue of interplant inequities. During most of that period, such cases were decided according to the bracket principle, and, during the whole period, high job rates were held down relative to low job rates. The large percentage of cases involving interplant inequities leaves little doubt that interplant differentials were narrowed. Such differentials were also narrowed by the operation of the War Labor Board's substandard policy and, especially prior to Pearl Harbor, by minima established under the Fair Labor Standards Act.

The narrowing of differentials between job rates within the same plant may reasonably be inferred from other policies of the government in the face of an over-all labor scarcity. The War Labor Board's substandard policy, it will be recalled, permitted increases up to a minimum rate but required that balancing increases further up the scale be made progressively smaller until they reached zero for 70 cents per hour jobs. The raising of the minimum rate by steps from 40 to 55 cents per hour introduced this differential narrowing device into many plants. The board's consistent awarding of cents per hour rather than percentage increases also had the effect of narrowing differentials.

Data are not available to show how many industries experienced significant narrowing in the range from the lowest to the highest rate in the plant. Testimony at the 1944 textile case before the War Labor Board disclosed that such narrowing had occurred in that industry. The average range from the minimum to the maximum rate in Southern cotton mills was found to be only 27.5 cents; in some mills the full range was as low as 5 cents and in none did it exceed 44 cents. Competition among employers must probably bear chief responsibility for forcing plant wage structures into the patterns approved by the government, although some industrial unions

---

[1] During this period no wage increases could be granted lawfully outside agriculture and railways without board approval, apart from a few numerically unimportant areas which were exempted.

adopted policies that also served to reduce occupational differentials in their industries.

POSTWAR DEVELOPMENTS

Contrary to the view expressed by some, events since V-J Day do not indicate a return to the prewar structure of wage differentials. It is true that the wartime tendency for wages to increase relatively more for low wage than for high wage industries no longer seems to prevail. However, no reverse tendency has become apparent. In fact, there now appears to be very little relationship at all between the wage level and the relative amount of wage increase. Superficially the gains made in late 1945 and early 1946 by powerful unions in a number of basic, high wage industries [1] suggest a widening of differentials between high wage and low wage industries, but wage earners in other lines, without attracting much public notice, have received comparable increases. Hourly earnings in the five industries which were lowest paid in August, 1945, rose on the average by about 14 per cent from that date to July, 1946, compared with an increase of 11 per cent for the five highest wage industries. The dispersion of the individual industry rates about the average for all manufacturing remained virtually unchanged.

No single factor appears to have replaced the relative level of the industry's wages as the major determinant of the magnitude of wage increase. Extent of unionization, which, during the war, was inversely related to the amount of increase has gained in influence. However, the most that can be said at this time is that from an over-all point of view little relationship exists between the extent of unionization and the amount of wage increase. Straight-time hourly earnings in the five least organized and five best organized industries rose by 13 and 11 per cent respectively from August, 1945, to July, 1946. This is not a denial that in specific instances the degree

[1] Automobiles, steel, electrical machinery, slaughtering and meat packing, aluminum manufactures, and petroleum refining.

of organization has been a determining factor in size of wage increases, but it does indicate that the highly and poorly organized industries, as groups, have fared about equally.

With the relaxation of wartime controls, the simple relationships they created are vanishing and the complex of forces normally operative in a competitive society is making itself felt. No simple answer in terms of one or two factors can be given to the question of what is determining the present pattern of wage increases. It is significant, however, that a reversal of the wartime narrowing of interindustry differentials is not evident.

In the long run, indications point toward a slow but progressive narrowing of differentials. First, the public increasingly accepts the proposition that man is entitled to a decent, living wage regardless of where he happens to live or be employed. Such an attitude lends popular support to minimum wage legislation and to government policies like those of the War Labor Board which tended to reduce wage differentials between industries and occupations. Furthermore, the high wage industries are already well unionized so that future expansion in organization will necessarily be confined largely to the middle and low wage industries. The current drives by both the American Federation of Labor and the Congress of Industrial Organizations to organize the South are a case in point. In consequence of such expansion, union pressure will progressively be exerted all along the line rather than at the top of the scale only. Admittedly there are other factors that will help to determine the future pattern of wage increases but the evidence adduced strongly suggests that we should not count upon a restoration of anything resembling the prewar structure of interindustry wage scales.

With respect to the course of intra-industry differentials during the postwar period, there is little definite evidence. A reversal of the wartime changes would depend upon the ability of the low wage firms to insist upon smaller increases than the average for their industries. At least as long as a tight labor market prevails, that will be difficult for low wage firms to achieve. Intra-industry differentials probably have not changed very much since the end of the war. In the long run, minimum wage legislation, union pressure to bring up the low wage firms, and the increasing number of regional and industrywide agreements will militate against any widening of intra-industry differentials. On the other hand, competitive pressures accompanied by unemployment might prove to be, at least in part, an offsetting factor.

Direct evidence is also lacking with respect to the postwar course of wage differentials between jobs or occupations. The net result is difficult to forecast, as the determining forces may be conflicting. A basic influence which antedates the war is the popular feeling already mentioned that a man should earn a certain minimum amount whatever his job may be. This idea finds legal expression in minimum wage laws and less formal acknowledgement in the policies of a number of industrial unions.

Where differential-narrowing policies have been pushed a certain distance they tend to encounter twofold opposition: first, from the employers who take the position that excessive narrowing of differentials destroys the incentive to seek and train for higher jobs and, secondly, from the more skilled workers within the union who feel that their interests are being neglected. The latter condition apparently was reached in the automobile industry by about 1939. Pressure was built up within the United Automobile Workers by the tool and die makers with the result that the union sought and secured wider differentials for the most skilled jobs even during the war. Another case in point is the textile industry. The Textile Workers Union of America, like the United Automobile Workers, had been in favor of raising the minimum rate.[1] By about 1943, when differentials had become drastically narrowed, the Textile Workers Union of America was favoring an increase in the spread, especially in the South. This was granted by the War Labor Board in its 1945 textile decision.

---

[1] However, chief responsibility for the narrowing should probably rest with the Fair Labor Standards Act and the War Labor Board's policies.

In neither of these instances did the reaction set in until narrowing had gone far.

Basic influences like those just mentioned are the long-run determinants of interjob differentials. During 1946 it is likely that some widening did occur in cases where the preceding phase had led to very narrow differentials. Beyond that it is doubtful that very much change in either direction has occurred. Some instances of a return from increases in cents per hour to percentage increases have come to the writer's attention. This would widen job differentials in cents per hour, but it is difficult to estimate in how many cases the percentage basis has been resumed. As to the future, it seems quite possible that some narrowing followed by a reaction may be the pattern that will occur in single industries. The reactions witnessed so far have not restored the prewar width of job differentials and the influences tending to raise minimum rates of pay are probably of such a character that further moderate over-all narrowing is to be expected over the long run. That seems especially likely if a condition of relatively full employment continues to prevail.

IMPLICATIONS OF NARROWED DIFFERENTIALS

Wages are in general such an important element of cost that the extensive wartime narrowing of interindustry differentials implies widespread economic adjustments. First, with the return of competitive markets, the relative prices of various goods and services are likely to gravitate to a structural pattern differing significantly from that for the prewar period. Such a fundamental change in relative prices could only be prevented by (1) an increase in output per man-hour in the low wage industries sufficient to offset substantially the relative increase in their wage rates, or (2) the absorption by these industries of the relative increase in their wage rates, or some combination of (1) and (2). The first cannot be ruled out as a possibility, but the low wage industries as a group have not been conspicuous in the past for technical progress; the high wage industries such as automobiles, electrical machinery, etc., have led the field. It appears unlikely, therefore, that in the foreseeable future industries like textiles, lumber, etc., will offset the relative rise in their wage scales. For them, absorption of increased costs is not very probable. In the "normal" prewar years the low wage industries in general had low profits; some of these, e.g., textiles, lost money quite consistently.

Some notion of the likely changes in price relationships can be inferred from the wage changes that have taken place. Among the nine major industrial categories, wages in agriculture, services, trade, and construction have risen out of all proportion to those in finance, mining, manufacturing, transportation, and public utilities. Within the field of manufacturing, relative increases have occurred in textiles, tobacco, lumber products, furniture, leather, and clothing. In general, industries that provide the basic necessities of food, clothing, services, and shelter will find it necessary to have their prices higher relative to other industries than was true in the prewar period. It is generally agreed that the demand for necessities is relatively inelastic with respect to price. If that be the case, people will respond by spending more money on necessities, thereby maintaining fairly well their physical consumption of these goods at the expense either of purchases of other goods or of saving. Most people probably are not able or willing to meet such higher prices solely from saving so that sales of less essential goods are likely to decline relatively. Whether they will decline absolutely will depend upon the level of national income, which in turn will be influenced by possible reductions in saving. This devious chain of repercussions has been detailed to illustrate the sort of shifts that may be expected. Too little is known of consumers' preference scales to be dogmatic about the precise nature of the shifts in spending patterns. The essential point for the purpose of this discussion is that changes in the wage structure imply changes in the price structure, which will result in interindustry shifts in production and employment and, possibly, changes in the level of national income.

The interindustry shifts just discussed are likely to have their counterpart in shifts of production and employment between firms within industries. Differentials in wage rates between plants compensate, at least to a limited extent, for differences in the efficiency of labor, management, and productive facilities and for advantages of location, etc. The relative rise of wage rates among the low wage firms will leave them at a greater competitive disadvantage unless they are able to compensate by increasing their efficiency. It is doubtful that they will be able to offset fully the narrowing of interplant differentials. Consequently, business will tend to shift to the more efficient firms, when demand slacks off to less than the industry's capacity to produce. The occurrence of such a shift will vary from one industry to another but in many it will not be long delayed. Spot problems of unemployment can be expected to develop even though the industry level of employment may not be greatly reduced.

As already suggested, one of the most important aspects of the narrowing of interjob differentials is its effect upon the occupational distribution of labor. This is a complex problem that can only be touched upon here in passing. Frequently higher paid jobs are more exacting than lower paid ones, and until proficiency is attained, piece-work earnings may drop if job differentials are small. An illustration of the possible consequence of such extreme narrowing is supplied by the cotton textile industry in the South where the range from common laborer to loom fixer was reduced during the war to as little as 5 cents in some instances. Mill managers complained that workers refused promotions. With such extreme narrowing that is understandable. However, the more general problem is how workers would react to a narrowing that was somewhat less extreme. Unfortunately, comprehensive data are not available upon which to base an answer to that question. It does appear, nevertheless, that many prewar differentials were much wider than was necessary to provide reasonable incentive for advancement. Also, there is the intangible factor of desire for status which might be expected to influence workers somewhat to take jobs of greater skill and responsibility. Therefore, the narrowing of occupational differentials might not seriously affect the distribution of labor unless it was carried to extreme lengths.

CONCLUDING REMARKS

Wartime regulation of wages led to a narrowing of wage differentials between industries, between firms in the same industry, and between different classes of work in the same plant. Such effects have been more than temporary. Developments since V-J Day indicate that much of this wartime heritage has become a permanent ingredient of our economy. While the rate of reduction in differentials has been considerably slowed down, the trend in that direction still persists.

An over-all decline in wage differentials is more than a mere change in figures on accounting books. It spells a difference in the pattern of income distribution of the working class. What is more, the incentive of workers to move up the occupational ladder is no longer the same with a decreasing gap between wages for different jobs. On the cost side, narrowed differentials may have a considerable impact on profits and the investment incentive.

We are thus in a transitional era in so far as the American wage structure is concerned. True, the major steps of this transition are now history. But the adjustments to this transition still have to be worked out. That is not an easy task. It will test the mettle of all groups in society, but particularly the trade unions and the employers. There will be the problem and the opportunity to work out the necessary adjustments in the wage and price structure that will permit our economy to function satisfactorily. Knowledge of recent developments and understanding of underlying trends is essential for the development of constructive solutions.

CHAPTER TEN

Unionism and the Marginal Productivity Theory [1]

by *Nathan Belfer and Gordon F. Bloom*

IN 1935, organized labor in the United States numbered less than four millions. In that year, Mr. J. R. Hicks published his treatise on *The Theory of Wages*,[2] a volume which was noteworthy for its assimilation of collective bargaining into general distribution theory without so much as disturbing the imposing edifice of marginal analysis. Whereas earlier writers,[3] considering the problem of wage-employment equilibrium in a free labor market, had held that marginal productivity determined the level of wages, Hicks' modification conceded that union bargaining power could determine wage levels, but marginal productivity still controlled the volume of employment.

Ten years later, unionism had mushroomed into a strong, belligerent movement of fourteen million workers,[4] rambling into office and factory, and honeycombing industry with a mass of restrictions, working rules, and contract regulations, which left some employers fuming, some confused, and some frankly helpless. These union rules and regulations became

[1] The authors wish to express their appreciation to Professor Edward H. Chamberlin for his helpful and stimulating criticisms of this chapter.

[2] *The Theory of Wages* (London, Macmillan and Co., Ltd., 1935).

[3] See for example, J. B. Clark, *The Distribution of Wealth* (New York, Macmillan, 1902).

[4] In 1945, 29 million workers were employed in occupations in which unions were organizing. Of these, 13.8 million or 48 per cent were employed under written union agreements. In manufacturing industry 8 million workers, slightly over 67 per cent of production wage earners, were covered by collective bargaining agreements. ("Extent of Collective Bargaining and Union Recognition," *Monthly Labor Review*, LXII [April, 1946], 567-72.)

238

of increasing concern to labor economists, and a number of scholarly works were published inquiring into their nature, extent, and economic significance.[1] Yet, strangely enough, basic wage doctrine continued on its orthodox path, unconcerned and unscathed by its hostile environment. The marginal productivity doctrine had swallowed collective bargaining without a second glance at its indigestible contents, with the result that reasoning about the effects of wage increases on the one hand, and of union rules on the other hand, went on in more or less separate compartments with little cross-fertilization from the one to the other.

This unsatisfactory dichotomy has constituted a positive impediment in the road to a more complete understanding of current labor problems. It will be the purpose of this chapter, therefore, to examine the effect of union rules and regulations upon the determination of wage-employment equilibria in the individual firm and to inquire into the modifications that may be required in the marginal productivity theory to reconcile it with present-day developments in the labor market.[2]

What is the effect upon the principle of marginal productivity of seniority rules, dismissal wage plans, and union rules and regulations controlling technological change? Is there a need for a new "bargaining theory of wages"?[3] Must every union wage increase induce employers to contract employment or are there "fruits of indeterminateness," which

[1] For example, S. H. Slichter, *Union Policies and Industrial Management* (The Brookings Institution, Washington, 1941).

[2] This chapter will consider only those modifications which may be required by reason of union organization. That other modifications of the theory may be required because of oligopoly, the preference for the full cost principle, the existence of constant marginal costs, etc., has already been the subject of considerable research. See R. L. Hall and C. J. Hitch, "Price Theory and Business Behavior," *Oxford Economic Papers,* No. 2 (May, 1939), 12-45; R. R. Mikesell, "Oligopoly and the Short Run Demand for Labor," *Quarterly Journal of Economics,* LV (November, 1940), 161-66; and R. A. Lester, "Shortcomings of Marginal Analysis for Wage-Employment Problems," *American Economic Review,* XXXVI (March, 1946), 63-82.

[3] The term has been used by John Davidson in *The Bargaining Theory of Wages* (New York, Putnam, 1898). Davidson, however, did no more than to examine various alternative wage theories and to conclude that collective bargaining may increase wages slightly but not above the level set by the worker's marginal contribution.

may be exploited to labor's benefit by reason of its effective bargaining power?

Do unions reduce exploitation of labor,[1] or do they produce a new form of exploitation—exploitation of employer? The persistence of traditional viewpoints in wage theory, deriving from an industrial era characterized by a free labor market, has resulted in a continued interest in the possibilities of exploitation of labor under present-day bargaining conditions, despite the fact that in many firms strong union organization may have actually created a situation in which the employer, and not the employee, is being exploited.[2] In earlier years it was thought that employers were likely to exploit their workers because superior bargaining power, better knowledge of wage conditions, and greater financial resources all combined to tip the scales in favor of the employer in negotiation of the wage contract.[3] Today, in certain industries, the tables

[1] Exploitation of labor will be used in this paper to denote a payment to labor of a wage less than its marginal revenue product. This usage follows that adopted by E. H. Chamberlin in *The Theory of Monopolistic Competition* (3rd ed., Cambridge, Harvard University Press, 1938), p. 183.

[2] Lack of attention to this aspect of the problem has left the concept of "exploitation of the employer" in a clouded and unsatisfactory state. Definition meets with serious methodological difficulties because the concept of "employer" is itself abstruse, ranging all the way from an individual in the personal sense to an aggregation of corporate entities. Furthermore, the entrepreneurial share, in actual fact, is a polyglot accumulation of rent, interest, quasi-rent, wages, and profit. If union organization compels a corporation to pay wages higher than the marginal revenue product of the labor employed, who suffers the exploitation? Obviously, actual disposition of the loss will depend upon the particular accounting procedure adopted. Therefore, the term "exploitation of the employer" will be used in this essay not to focus attention on the factor which pays the extra share to labor, but simply to label conveniently a condition in which labor receives more than its marginal value product. In this usage, exploitation of the employer is synonymous with overpayment of labor in the technical sense. Needless to say, by emphasis upon possibilities of exploitation of employers, the writers do not mean to deny that exploitation of labor exists, nor to minimize the seriousness of the problem. But the changing nature of industrial relations indicates a need for study of an aspect of exploitation theory that till now has been of merely academic interest and, therefore, largely ignored.

[3] Actually these conditions are more likely to affect the level of the wage rate than its relation to marginal revenue product. For a discussion of the conditions requisite to exploitation, see G. F. Bloom, "A Reconsideration of the Theory of Exploitation," *Quarterly Journal of Economics*, LV (May, 1941), 413-42.

have been turned. Many an entrepreneur finds himself sitting across the table from a representative of labor who can draw upon an organization of thousands for financial assistance and legal and technical advice. How does this shift in bargaining power affect marginal productivity equilibrium? Is the employer now likely to be exploited, or will the change in bargaining power simply be reflected in a readjustment of employment, price, and output?

Limitations of space make it impossible to explore all the ramifications that are suggested by these questions. In the following discussion, the problems can only be outlined and tentative conclusions suggested, which may be confirmed by further research. It is the hope of the writers that other investigators will continue the attempt to integrate the practicalities of collective bargaining procedures with basic wage theory to the end that a realistic and logically consistent economic theory of unionism may eventually result.

RESTRICTIONS ON ENTREPRENEURIAL SUBSTITUTION OF FACTORS

In the ideal firm of economic theory, the entrepreneur pulls the strings. He manipulates the personnel in his establishment like so many puppets, hiring and firing at will, rearranging job classifications and valuations, changing men from one position to another. Not only can he adjust wage rates to equal the individual marginal revenue productivities of his various employees, but also, where equation is facilitated by the opposite type adjustment, he can alter individual marginal productivities themselves by regulating speed of output, shortening or lengthening hours of work, selecting more efficient employees for the higher paid jobs, and so forth. So long as these means of adjustment were prerogatives of the employers, a close approximation to the ideal equilibrium of theory was reached in actual business practice.

The advent of unionism, however, has altered this picture in a significant fashion.[1] Unionism is a means of introducing

---

[1] Most writers on labor problems, however, have failed to recognize that

law into industry, but it is law according to union standards. Rules and regulations in union contracts now guarantee safe-guards to employees, which formerly were prerogatives of the employer. No longer are control of speed of output, of hiring and firing, unrestricted privileges of management. The employer still holds the strings, yes; but union rules and regulations have tied his hands. As a consequence, in plants where unions are strongly entrenched, the various workers are not freely substitutable in the manner envisaged by marginal productivity theory. If a workman's output is not a clearly defined entity, these union restrictions make it almost impossible for the employer to determine what part of the total production is attributable to him. Thus, short-run determination of the margins delimiting the individual worker's marginal productivity is encumbered by restrictions imposed by union regulations.

But even if the productivities of individual workmen are clouded by union controls, does not the margin between labor as a whole and capital remain as a horizon upon which the employer can adjust his economic sights? Unfortunately, the answer is no. Even in the absence of unionism, the margin of substitution between labor and capital is complicated by the continual aberrations attributable to technological progress.[1] But unionism renders this even more inexact by its regulations controlling the speed of introduction of improvements, restricting their use in part or entirely, and burdening them with expenses of one kind or the other. The employer is not free to determine the relative efficiency of a man and a

unionism is an institution with far-flung implications, and not simply an organization to make labor more expensive. Thus, numerous books and articles have been written on the deleterious effect of unions on employment, this conclusion being arrived at through application of traditional wage theory; yet the very institution being examined requires major modification of such traditional conceptual tools.

[1] Short-run substitution between labor and capital is, of course, complicated by the fact that the relationship between labor and capital in the short run is more one of complementarity than substitutability. On this point see W. W. Leontieff, *The Structure of the American Economy, 1919-29* (Cambridge, Harvard University Press, 1941), pp. 39-41; and N. Kaldor, "Stability and Full Employment," *Economic Journal*, XLVIII (December, 1938). 642-57.

machine, because the man now imposes regulations hampering the introduction of the machine.[1]

The marginal productivity theory in its traditional form is a theory of equilibrium in the long run. Undoubtedly, at the present stage of union development, union rules and regulations are much less effective in impeding long-run marginal productivity equilibrium than in obstructing short-run equilibrium. But even with regard to the long run, the impediments are considerable and of growing importance, as unionism gains in power and extent of organization.

The term "long run" is perhaps an unfortunate one, but it has become a permanent part of the economists' verbal baggage. The long run is not necessarily a long time. Reduced to simple terms, it is the period within which fixed capital becomes available for reinvestment. What is the long run for a printing press? When the present press wears out and the printer is ready to purchase a new one with the amortized capital? But any printer will tell you that if this is the long run, then union regulations are just as much an obstruction to effective combination of labor and capital in *his* long run as in the short run. Whether he buys a new and improved machine or replaces the old machine with one like it, the union will still tell him how many men he must hire to operate it.

But perhaps the long run is the time at which the printer has amortized all his capital and is ready to invest in an entirely new plant. Now union rules need not restrict him, for he can move to a nonunion area. This was undoubtedly true in years past, but the possibilities are rapidly being narrowed by vigorous union organizing campaigns in the South and other nonunion areas. And if the printer seeks to invest his capital in other industries, he will succeed merely in exchanging one type of union restriction for another. The notion that the optimum combination of labor and capital can be attained in the long run when capital is fluid requires

---

[1] For a description of trade union resistance to the introduction of technological improvements, see Harry Ober, WPA National Research Project, *Trade Union Policy and Technological Change*, Report No. L-8 (Philadelphia, 1940); and Slichter, *op. cit.*, chap. 7.

serious reconsideration in view of present-day industrial organization.

There still remains, of course, the possibility of investing versus noninvesting, and it is upon this alternative, which union rules and regulations cannot very well restrict, that Mr. J. R. Hicks rests his conclusions concerning the effect of union wage pressure.[1] The writers would agree that this is a margin that will ultimately affect the limit to which union leaders can raise real wages. But it is a very ill-defined margin—a margin which is influenced by changing calculations of risk, government policies, and a myriad of other considerations, so that union policies, though having a very marked effect upon the level of wages, have only an ill-defined and uncertain effect upon the decision to invest or consume. Moreover, the Keynesian theory has taught us that consumption too can have a multiplier effect upon investment, so, if the only effect of union policies is to shift funds from investment to consumption, there need be no decrease in the marginal productivity of labor.

This does not mean, however, that unions can push up wages indefinitely without unfavorable repercussions upon employment. Any change in profits affects liquidity preference and an alteration in liquidity preference will ultimately affect employment. But the repercussions of wage increases upon liquidity preference are shrouded in controversy, and few economists would assert that the reaction of liquidity preference sets an effective upper limit to wage increases. Certainly, by comparison with the long-run equilibrium of J. B. Clark,[2] in which the fluidity of capital unerringly determines the marginal productivity of labor, the modern doctrine can set up only an area of uncertainty. Thus, the collective effect of all the restrictive regulations which are part of the mechanism of unionism is to increase the area of indeterminateness in wage determination,[3] both in the long and short runs.

[1] *The Theory of Wages, op. cit.,* pp. 181ff.
[2] As expressed in *The Distribution of Wealth, op. cit.*
[3] For a systematic and thorough analysis of the range of indeterminateness produced by collective bargaining, see W. H. Hutt, *The Theory of Collective*

Obviously, either employer or employees may benefit from the spoils of such uncertainty. Under these circumstances it would seem that a new "bargaining theory of wage determination" is needed to give a realistic explanation of the size of the shares going to capital and labor.

Effect of Seniority Provisions

The difficulties that union rules and regulations present to the determination of marginal productivity are well illustrated by an examination of the effect of seniority provisions. Seniority plans are a common embodiment of the union search for security. Out of three hundred representative trade union agreements negotiated between 1933 and 1939, somewhat over two hundred embodied seniority provisions.[1] Institution of a system of seniority assures three great "securities" to the employee: security from the caprices of foremen as regards promotion, security from unemployment, and security for the older employee. While seniority plans may inspire dissatisfaction among more efficient and ambitious workmen, if wisely administered they probably have a salutary effect upon production. Consideration of seniority lengthens a man's life service in industry, reduces labor turnover, and inspires loyalty to the firm. At the same time, however, by the very emphasis upon length of service, seniority plans introduce into the determination of wages a consideration extraneous to strict calculation of marginal productivity.[2]

Seniority regulations interfere with the strict application of the marginal productivity principle in two ways:

In the first place, there is the obvious fact that manage-

Bargaining (London, P. S. King & Son, Ltd., 1930), pp. 48 ff. Hutt also has an interesting analysis of the development of the concept of "indeterminateness" in the history of economic thought.

[1] Sumner H. Slichter, "Layoff Policy," *Addresses on Industrial Relations* (Bureau of Industrial Relations, Univ. of Michigan; 1939), p. 74. For further evidence of the increasing importance of job security provisions in collective bargaining agreements, see Slichter, *op. cit.*, Chaps. 4 and 5, and F. H. Harbison, *Seniority Policies and Procedures as Developed through Collective Bargaining* (Industrial Relations Section, Princeton Univ., 1941).

[2] Unless, of course, there is a direct ratio between length of service and productivity, which is not likely as a general rule.

ment cannot advance a man and increase his pay simply on the basis of his productive ability alone. If A works harder, learns faster, spoils fewer pieces, and is generally quicker and more alert about his duties than B, according to marginal productivity doctrine, A should receive more pay than B. If both were originally employed at the same job then A should be first to receive advancement to a higher paying position where his productivity will be more adequately remunerated. If, however, B has the longer service and is of average efficiency, application of the seniority principle compels management to reward him, rather than A. One might argue that at the higher rate, B receives a wage equal to his marginal productivity plus an additional reward which his longer service entitles him to command. In strict theory, such a payment of a wage greater than the marginal revenue product would seem to imply exploitation both of the employer and of the more efficient employee.

Actually, however, in his new job, B's wage probably approximates his marginal revenue productivity. The new position will involve new duties and responsibilities which increase his value to the firm, and if B possesses average ability he will be able to perform these new tasks. Therefore, his marginal productivity will rise in accordance with his increased remuneration. If the more efficient employee suffers "exploitation," it is in terms of deprivation of an opportunity to advance,[1] rather than in payment of less than his marginal revenue product in his present occupation.

As far as its effect upon promotion and increase in rates is concerned, seniority does not constitute a serious obstruction to the application of marginal productivity principles. That is true because (1) longer service ordinarily implies greater knowledge and greater efficiency, although not in direct ratio; (2) longer service is rarely associated with a decrease in knowledge and ability (except where age becomes debilitat-

[1] Harry Henig concludes that seniority rules on the railroads do not restrict the opportunities of the more efficient workers to advance to better positions. (*The Brotherhood of Railway Clerks* [New York, Columbia Univ. Press, 1937], pp. 137-42.)

ing) and, therefore, length of service is, in effect, a rough measurement of efficiency; [1] (3) other measures of efficiency are equally rough; and (4) since seniority rarely substitutes for, but rather supplements, the considerations upon which increase in pay and promotion are based, the actual determination of wage rates which results under an enlightened system of seniority is probably not much different from that which would emerge if productive considerations alone were the basis of the calculation.

A second aspect of seniority rules and regulations poses a more serious problem for marginal productivity theory. This is the fact that seniority plans, particularly when they are based on the shop as a unit, interfere with the employer's ability freely to move employees around from one job to another and thus shroud in doubt the marginal productivity of the individual workman. According to marginal productivity doctrine, the increment in product attributable to the addition of the last unit of a factor in use can be determined by removing any one unit, if the units are homogeneous, and ascertaining the consequent diminution in the product.

Even under normal circumstances, such determination is attended with substantial difficulties, but in a unionized plant operating under a seniority plan, the problem of determination is rendered more complex and to some extent insoluble. Consider the problem of the employer who wishes to determine the marginal productivity of Mr. X, a welder in the fender section of an automobile company. In the first place he cannot lay off Mr. X, or any other employee for that matter, without due cause, except at the risk of a strike by the union. It is doubtful whether the union leaders would consider management's interest in marginal productivity theory an adequate reason for even a temporary layoff. The employer might offer to remove Mr. X from the production line, but keep him

---

[1] Dan H. Mater, however, believes that seniority may not be a good measure of efficiency. ("A Statistical Study of the Effect of Seniority upon Employee Efficiency," *Journal of Business of the University of Chicago*, XIV, [April, 1941], 169-204; and "Effects of Seniority upon the Welfare of the Employee, the Employer, and Society," *ibid.* [October, 1941], 384-418.)

on the payroll while determining his marginal productivity. However, the other workers on the job, who will have to re-adjust their work patterns to do without Mr. X, may be suspicious of an impending speedup and prevent the removal of Mr. X from the job, even though he is retained on the pay-roll. But even if the employer is presented with an oppor-tunity to make layoffs during slack times, he may not be able to lay off Mr. X or one of his homogeneous counterparts, for, in this company, the welders may be midway down the sen-iority list and the union rule requires that, when layoffs are made, those employees with the least service must be laid off first. Consequently, to get at Mr. X, the employer must first lay off his maintenance men, some machinists, etc. The result-ing decrease in production is then attributable to the discharge of a conglomeration of men, and Mr. X's contribution becomes lost in the total which itself is an inaccurate index, unduly weighted by the vagaries of the current economic situation.[1]

Still another method is available by which the employer normally can determine Mr. X's elusive marginal productivity. He can exchange Mr. X for a welder in another shop in his establishment, and then observe the change in the output of the two sections that results from this interchange of per-sonnel. Unfortunately, however, if seniority is based upon the shop as a unit, he is prevented from doing this, too. Mr. X will object violently to a transfer to a different shop, as by so doing he will lose his seniority, and the union will back him up in his objections. And if the employer attempts to adopt

[1] A primary difficulty to be encountered in the setting up of a seniority system in a company is the selection of the proper unit—company, plant, or department—as the basis for seniority operation. If plantwide "bumping" is allowed, the problems of marginal productivity determination are magnified. Under such a procedure, when a man is laid off in the fender section, he can bump a man with less seniority in the wheel department, and so on down the line. The resultant loss in production and efficiency attributable to the discharge of the first worker is likely to be much greater than that which would occur in a plant without seniority. Of course, seniority plans can be devised which will not substantially interfere with the employer's ability to rearrange his working force, but, in actual practice, the type of plan which is adopted is more likely to depend on considerations of union politics than upon a concern for the employer's inclination to experiment with marginal productivity determination.

the only other expedient to ascertain this man's marginal productivity—transfer to another job—he will find that other union regulations stand in his way.

The net effect of seniority plans is to solidify job patterns and widen the discrepancy between the fluidity of the model firm of theory and the rigidities to be found in the unionized firm of modern industry. The influence of seniority plans, in this respect, should not be considered *in vacuo*. Considered per se, the divergence from marginal productivity doctrine attributable to seniority plans may not be great, but in conjunction with other restrictive union rules and regulations they significantly modify the normal pattern of wage rates which would evolve from application of the marginal productivity theory.

Restrictions on Dismissals

Unionism is not simply a means of making labor more expensive to the employer who uses it. It is also a means of making labor expensive *even if he does not use it,* for union rules may require the retention of excess men on the payroll.

The marginal productivity theory is a highly elastic theory and it is possible to reconcile it even to practices as remote from marginal productivity principles as "feather-bedding." But it seems more realistic to recognize that feather-bedding, make-work rules, and other similar union regulations seriously qualify marginal productivity determination with regard to employment of individual workmen. For example, Mr. Caesar Petrillo, president of the musicians' union, requires a stand-by crew on a recorded broadcast. He dictates both the wage that is to be paid and the number of men who must be hired. Does the wage paid these men equal their marginal products? What do they add to broadcasters' revenues? It is obvious that their real value consists in the insurance they provide against a strike which would seriously reduce revenues. Then how far can Mr. Petrillo push the wages of stand-by crews? And how many men can he require studios to hire to do nothing?

It may be argued that the marginal productivity principle is operative even here as a tendency, and this contention cannot be denied; for the net effect of the make-work rule is to raise the cost of labor, and at some level of wage rates the broadcasters will refuse to accede to Mr. Petrillo's demands and will risk a strike. But this limit is much more nebulous than the limit ordinarily operative in marginal productivity determination. It is far easier to calculate the additions to cost and revenue incidental to the use of one more man in a factory than the loss of business which will result from a strike called because of the dismissal of one man on a stand-by crew. To be sure, the broadcasters will compensate for the higher costs by raising rates for broadcasting, but even if demand were elastic, it is doubtful whether broadcasters would be able to contract their employment of labor accordingly. The very fact that unnecessary stand-by crews are employed indicates that the number of men employed is not a simple function of cost and productivity, but rather of the strength of the union and the belligerency of its officers.

Thus, rather than attempting to seek an explanation in terms of marginal productivity equilibrium, which undoubtedly can be found if only sufficient ingenuity is exercised, it seems more realistic to admit that we have here another example of the indeterminateness that is introduced by union rules. Marginal productivity principles are operative as a tendency here as elsewhere, but the strength of union organization has widened the limits within which wage rates can be altered without significantly affecting employment.[1]

Organized labor in recent years has shown increasing concern over large-scale unemployment. Among the procedures which have been adopted to minimize such displacement, particularly in times of rapid technological change, is the dismissal wage. Another approach to the problem has been the annual wage. Both annual wage and dismissal wage compensation are likely to become increasingly common in future

---

[1] A somewhat similar effect is produced by full-crew laws and other regulations requiring payment for extra men.

union contracts. An examination of their characteristics and incidence will indicate that they, like other union rules and regulations, impose serious obstacles in the way of traditional marginal productivity calculations.

The dismissal wage is not yet an accepted accoutrement of union organization, but it is placed high on the agenda of union policy. In December, 1944, about 450 dismissal pay plans, covering approximately 135,000 workers, were in existence.[1] The Sinclair Oil Corporation, American Viscose Corporation, Postal Telegraph-Cable Company, Northwestern Bell Telephone, Celanese Corporation of America, the Associated Press, and the United Press are among some of the more important companies that have incorporated dismissal compensation into their union agreements.[2] Philip Murray is a staunch proponent of the dismissal wage, and so are numerous other union leaders, particularly in industries where rapid technological progress creates a serious problem of unemployment. Mr. Murray views the dismissal wage not only as a crutch to assist the displaced worker during a period of unemployment, but also as a club to compel management to minimize displacement of labor. *It is a means of making unemployment costly to the employer.*

This is a statement fraught with significance for the theory of marginal productivity, for it introduces an important qualification to the hypotheses upon which this theory is based. While marginal productivity doctrine has taken account of the effect of various rigidities that restrict the employer's ability to achieve the optimum proportion of the factors, it has always been a basic and implicit assumption that reduction of employment did not cost the employer anything,[3] for it was by

---

[1] U.S. Bureau of Labor Statistics, *Dismissal Pay Provisions in Union Agreements, December 1944,* Bulletin No. 808 (1945), p. 4. A full discussion of the principles of the dismissal wage can be found in Everett D. Hawkins, *Dismissal Compensation; Voluntary and Compulsory Plans used in the United States and Abroad* (Princeton, Princeton Univ. Press, 1940).

[2] *Dismissal Pay Provisions in Union Agreements, op. cit.,* p. 9.

[3] Reduction of employment and output would involve an added cost to the employer in the case of a firm producing under falling marginal costs, but as this situation can hardly persist as a long-run condition, it cannot be considered an exception to the above statement.

this means that he was supposed to compensate for increased labor costs. Obviously, one does not ordinarily compensate for increased costs by incurring new ones, yet the incidence of a dismissal wage presents just this problem to an employer.

To analyze the effect of a dismissal wage upon marginal productivity doctrine, let us avail ourselves of a hypothetical firm in which an equilibrium prevails as regards marginal revenue product and wages. Suppose a union succeeds in organizing this firm and in raising wage rates. The new union, concerned over the rapid displacement of men in the industry, but at the same time anxious to raise wages, includes in the union contract a clause which provides for payment of a dismissal wage. The employer is thus confronted by a situation in which maintenance of the same volume of employment has become more costly, but reduction in the size of the work force, while cutting one kind of wage cost, would add another. What then will be the employer's reaction?

The increase in wage rates invokes a need for economy, but the necessity for payment of the dismissal wage may turn the employer's attention to other means of reducing expenses, rather than taking the most obvious course of economizing on the expensive factor, labor. It is possible that elimination of other waste may so reduce marginal costs of operation that it will not be necessary to raise prices, but this presupposes a backlog of inefficiency which cannot be postulated as a general condition. In the normal case, the union wage increase will produce an increase in prices, but because of the dismissal wage requirement, employment will not be reduced by the full amount indicated by the new intersection of marginal cost and marginal revenue.

The existence of a dismissal wage produces a range of indeterminateness [1] in wage-employment determination. In effect, it lifts the upper level to which, in given circumstances, the wage can be raised without altering the volume of em-

---

[1] Hicks discusses the possibility that the indivisibility of the human unit may produce a range of indeterminateness in wage determination, but he concludes that it is of negligible importance. See *Theory of Wages, op. cit.*, pp. 24-34.

ployment. In our example, the actual number of layoffs that will result from the wage increase will depend upon the size of the wage increase, the elasticity of demand for the product, the elasticity of substitution of capital for labor, the relation of labor costs to total costs, and the size of the dismissal wage.[1] There will be some level of the wage increase and the dismissal wage at which it will be a matter of indifference to the employer whether or not he lays off a man. With a prohibitive dismissal wage, a small wage increase will result in exploitation of the employer by the full amount of the wage adjustment. The smaller the size of the dismissal wage, the less will be the amount of exploitation possible. Since the initial effect of the wage increase will be to produce a rise in price and a fall in sales, the dismissal wage, when effective in the Murray sense, implies that the employer, rather than fire men who are no longer needed because of the reduced volume of orders, keeps them on the payroll and finds some work for them to do. Since the men have become more expensive to the employer whether they are employed or unemployed, it is only logical that the employer should choose to get some work performed for the increased cost. Thus, from the point of view of the worker, a dismissal wage may result in a short-run increase in employment opportunities.[2]

From the point of view of the employer, however, the results are less salutary. Many employers would agree that the dismissal wage has merit as a means of controlling the rate of technological change. When the social cost of lost skills, abandoned towns, poverty, and degradation is taken into account in the balance sheet of technological progress, it is possible that the unrestricted substitution of machinery for labor has produced a rate of progress in excess of the optimum

[1] Thus, unionism adds a new factor to the four conditions that Marshall enumerated as determining the elasticity of demand for labor. See Alfred Marshall, *Principles of Economics* (8th ed., London, Macmillan & Co., Ltd., 1925), pp. 384-87.

[2] In the short run, employers may find it profitable to retain men on the payroll rather than release them and pay the dismissal wage. In the long run, however, this uneconomic operation will decrease employment by forcing many marginal employers out of business.

rate for the community. In so far as a dismissal wage compels employers to adopt a rational plan of technological improvement with a view to minimizing the disturbance to employment and further compels them to assist the men displaced during the transition period, it simply distributes to management a fair share of the burden of the social cost of change. But where, as in the case just examined, the dismissal wage is associated not with technological progress, but simply with a union wage increase, the same justification for the dismissal wage is not applicable. In the latter case, the effect of the dismissal wage is to make it costly for the employer to discharge workers.[1]

In their effort to attain economic security, unions have shown increased interest in the guaranteed annual wage. The Bureau of Labor Statistics estimates that as of January, 1945, 142 manufacturing companies employing 12,000 workers had annual-wage agreements. An additional 30,000 workers in nonmanufacturing industries also were employed under annual-wage contracts.[2] Under the typical annual-wage plan, the employee is guaranteed a weekly income throughout the year, regardless of seasonal fluctuations in output. The number of workers to be hired and guaranteed an annual wage is usually also specified in the agreement.

With a guaranteed annual-wage plan, the marginal productivity concept may be difficult to apply. The annual-wage bill becomes a fixed cost, which can be computed in advance and with the same degree of exactness as rent, taxes on prop-

---

[1] Merit rating in unemployment insurance funds also has the effect of placing a penalty on the employer when he discharges workers. Employers may, therefore, retain workers on the payroll even when wage rates rise, since to dismiss them might increase the payroll tax rate. Moreover, employers will hesitate to employ more workers when demand increases because if they are later forced to discharge them a higher tax rate can result. Merit rating provisions may lead to "stabilized unemployment." See Richard A. Lester and Charles V. Kidd, *The Case against Experience Rating in Unemployment Compensation* (New York, Industrial Relations Counselors, Inc., 1939); and Charles A. Myers, "Employment Stabilization and the Wisconsin Act," *American Economic Review*, XXIX (December, 1939), 708-23.

[2] U.S. Bureau of Labor Statistics, *Guaranteed-Employment and Annual-Wage Provisions in Union Agreements*, Bulletin No. 828 (1945), p. 2.

erty, interest, depreciation charges, etc. Output and efficiency may vary, but the wage bill is fixed and predetermined. Computation of marginal productivity by the employer for the individual laborers constituting the basic work force,[1] becomes well-nigh impossible under such conditions. He loses the freedom to fire and hire workers at will. Under the terms of the union agreement he has agreed to provide a given amount of employment during the year for a given number of men.

The guaranteed-employment and annual-wage agreement introduces a unique monopoly situation. The traditional monopoly of theory sets price at that level which it hopes will yield maximum profits. The monopoly cannot force consumers to purchase more than they wish to acquire at that price of their own free choice. The union, however, controls not only the price but also the quantity of labor. If the trade union is more powerful than the employer, it can force him to hire more workers than he might wish to employ at the quoted wage rate. The strong union can face the employer with two alternatives: hire x workers or no workers at all. If the union offer allows the employer some profit he may find it economical to accept the offer. Otherwise he will have to go out of business entirely. Thus the union, through its monopoly control over the price and quantity of labor, absorbs part of the employer's profit. Theoretically, a powerful union could increase its guaranteed wage bill till the employer's total cost is only slightly less than his total revenue.[2] In actual practice, however, both the annual guaranteed wage and the employment figure have thus far been set at modest limits, but whether this will be so in the future is uncertain.

Guaranteed-employment and annual-wage plans introduce a considerable degree of inflexibility into the employment-wage relationship. Collective bargaining determines not only

[1] With regard to the fringe of workers who are not covered by the plan and whose employment, therefore, will vary directly with changing conditions of demand, the marginal productivity theory may apply with particular vehemence.

[2] For a theoretical, diagrammatic analysis of the effects of the annual wage, see Wassily Leontieff, "The Pure Theory of the Guaranteed Wage Contract," *Journal of Political Economy*, LIV (February, 1946), 76-79.

the wage level but also the number of workers to be hired. The view that, although union bargaining power determines the wage level, marginal productivity still determines the quantity of employment may require revision, if the guaranteed-employment and annual-wage plan spreads over a large sector of the economy.

THE NATURE OF UNION WAGE PRESSURE

Not only does unionism enmesh the employer in a net of restrictive rules and regulations, but also the very nature of union wage demands and wage policies tends to contribute to indeterminateness in marginal productivity equilibrium. Thus, the general acceptance of the across-the-board wage increases, union preference for time pay, and union requirement of premium pay for overtime, have rendered more difficult the payment of the individual worker in accordance with his personal contribution to the revenues of the firm. In this connection, it is indicative of the influence of unionism that not only do actual union organization and union wage increases produce difficulties in marginal productivity adjustment, but also the very threat of union organization may produce disequilibrium in nonunion firms.

General wage increases extending in equal amounts to all employees have long been common in industry, because they lend themselves well to large establishments, create fewer economic grievances, and do not disrupt job valuations. The pattern of uniform wage increases seems well established today.[1] Unions favor uniform general wage increases because they conform to the union policy of "getting something for everybody" and because wage increases which vary in accordance with "merit," or some other immeasurable intangible, breed petty jealousy with consequent disruption of union morale.

The general wage adjustment raises interesting problems for the theory of marginal productivity determination. Ac-

---

[1] F. H. Harbison, "Some Reflections on a Theory of Labor-Management Relations," *Journal of Political Economy,* LIV (February, 1946), 4.

cording to orthodox doctrine, the individual workman is viewed as contributing units of labor which are rewarded by the employer in accordance with the additional value they impart to the revenues of the firm. Thus, an efficient worker who contributes twice as many units of labor as a less efficient co-worker would receive twice the pay of the latter. On the whole, this theory still affords a satisfactory explanation of the derivation of rates of pay in an organized plant where payment is made by the piece. But where hourly rates are in effect, union requirements that the rate of pay for a particular job be uniform throughout the plant and that wage adjustments be general so as to maintain this uniformity, make it almost impossible for the employer to pay each worker in accordance with his marginal revenue product, *even if this could be measured*.[1]

Given a normal distribution of abilities in a particular job classification, marginal productivity doctrine implies a parallel distribution of rates of pay. If such a variation exists prior to unionization,[2] union policy is likely to iron out the differences, probably by raising all rates below the highest. In such a case, the most efficient workers are exploited, not through any loss of deserved increase in pay, but rather by decrease in working opportunities (and therefore in income) as a consequence of the restriction of output which is likely to follow upon a wage increase of this kind. Furthermore, the efficient man cannot be fully compensated for an increase in his output, because a rise in his rate of pay would have to be duplicated for less efficient workers as well.[3] While union pressure is likely to raise the average rate of wages prevailing in a plant,

[1] This condition is added and emphasized because, as has been suggested earlier, union rules and regulations render measurement of individual marginal productivities extremely difficult.

[2] In many cases, it will not. The desire to simplify the wage structure may already have moved management to establish uniformity of rates prior to unionization, in which case the advent of the union serves simply to solidify the *status quo*.

[3] In other words, unionization makes the supply curve of labor units supplied by efficient workers inelastic to the employer. Cf. Paul Douglas, *The Theory of Wages* (New York, Macmillan and Co., 1934), p. 251 ff.

the implication is that the disparity in rate between efficient and inefficient is narrowed.[1]   As a result of the necessity for uniform general wage adjustments, payment of rates in accordance with individual marginal revenue productivity becomes impossible.   Instead, the employer is likely to attempt to equate the average wage of a particular class of employees with its average group marginal productivity.   Such modification of the preciseness of theory does not imply that the employer exploits his labor force considered as a whole.   It is the inefficient worker who gains at the expense of the efficient; the incidence of the union policy of general wage adjustments is borne by the efficient workers who, in effect, are "exploited" by the inefficient.

Whether the general wage adjustment is a salutary wage practice is subject to debate.   At first glance, it appears that maximization of production could best be achieved by individual wage increases based upon merit, which would offer the greatest incentive to efficiency.   But it must be remembered that measurement of individual efficiency and calculation of the marginal contribution of factors in the complex of modern industry is no easy matter.[2]   Despite time studies and industrial rationalization, ability, conscientiousness, and effort are still largely immeasurable attributes, which all too easily can be twisted by foremen to advance their own favorites. Union leaders maintain that any decline in production associated with a loss of incentive is more than offset by the increased output attributable to improved morale.

Union attitudes regarding time and piece pay will vary depending upon conditions peculiar to the individual industry: whether conditions of work can be standardized, the

[1] Whether the most efficient workers benefit absolutely from union organization is open to question.   No doubt, in the reader's experience, cases could be cited to substantiate either view.

[2] For a stimulating analysis of this point, see Richard A. Lester, "Shortcomings of Marginal Analysis for Wage-Employment Problems," *American Economic Review*, XXXVI (March, 1946), 72 ff., and *The Economics of Labor* (New York, Macmillan Co., 1941), pp. 175-84; also, W. J. Eiteman, "The Equilibrium of the Firm in Multi-Process Industries," *Quarterly Journal of Economics*, LIX (February, 1945), 280-86.

extent to which speed of output can be controlled by workers, and the history of wage payment in the industry. As a general rule, unions prefer time pay to piece pay. At the present time, the majority of employees covered by union agreements are paid according to time wage standards.[1] Organized labor's distrust of piece and incentive pay plans rests upon two grounds. The first is that piece pay, by creating differences in earnings corresponding to differences in ability, tends to produce intra-union jealousies and competitive rivalry, which are destructive of union morale and solidarity. The second is that incentive wage plans, particularly in the newly organized mass production industries,[2] have become identified with the speedup and stretchout and have been discredited by employers' cutting of base rates as earnings rise.

The effect upon marginal productivity determination of union preference for time wage payments is a heterogeneous one. On the one hand, to the extent that union organization extends the scope of time payment in industry, the degree of correspondence between the individual worker's wage and ability is reduced. Piece pay measures output; time pay measures time. Obviously, the former means of payment is more likely to produce a wage structure corresponding to individual abilities. Indeed, employers recognizing the desirability of wage differentials that reflect the distribution of abilities have frequently recommended to unions of workers on time pay that they divide their members into classes on the basis of ability and fix a separate rate for each class, instead of setting a single rate for all men engaged in the same kind of work. But unions, on the whole,[3] have rejected such proposals, and wisely so, for union officials entrusted with setting up such

---

[1] S. T. Williamson and H. Harris, *Trends in Collective Bargaining* (New York, The Twentieth Century Fund, 1945), p. 71.

[2] Pressure exerted by the United Automobile Workers was successful in raising the number of automobile workers on time wages to 80 per cent of the total in the industry. See U.S. Bureau of Labor Statistics, *Incentive Wage Plans and Collective Bargaining*, Bulletin No. 717 (1942), p. 3.

[3] Two unions in the building trades, the lathers and the woodcarvers, have adopted such plans. See D. McCabe, *The Standard Rate in American Trade Unions* (Baltimore, Johns Hopkins Press, 1912), p. 95.

plans would inevitably find that they were the object of suspicion and would be accused of playing favorites among the membership.

Of course, since unions ordinarily set only a minimum rate for an hour's or a day's work at a particular job, there is no reason in theory why employers should not reward particularly efficient workers by premium pay. However, employers are generally reluctant to pay such bonuses; they may feel that because of the arbitrary union minimum they are compelled to pay more than the productivity wage to inefficient workers and, therefore, must compensate for this by paying less than the marginal productivity wage to the more efficient men. Thus, union preference for time pay, though it may render marginal productivity payment less exact for individual workers, does not preclude attainment of marginal productivity equilibrium for the group. What emerges is a sort of average equilibrium, in which the standard union rate tends to equal the average productivity of the group.[1]

To some extent, union regulations may actually bring about a closer approximation between earnings and productivity, even for workers paid by time. In the first place, the variations in efficiency within the membership of most unions of time workers are probably not as great as among nonunion men in the same trade, because unions tend to attract the better men and union entrance requirements tend to keep out the very inefficient. More important is the fact that union rules, which limit output and speed of production and prescribe the content of "a day's work," tend to flatten out the curve of individual productivities, regardless of the native abilities of the men, so that, in terms of actual effort expended, individual productivities and the standard union rate are brought into closer correspondence.

[1] Such average equilibria of course antedate unionism. The complexity of operating a company with several thousand workers makes it impossible to set wages varying according to the individual's ability. But unions, by extending the scope of time payment as compared with piece and incentive pay, have thereby increased the relative importance of such average equilibria in the economy as a whole.

In piece-rate industries, even in the absence of union organization, the distribution of earnings will tend to approximate the distribution of abilities, but, here, too, union regulations may actually increase the degree of correspondence between the two. For example, in the garment trades, union officials actively participate with management in setting piece rates and job standards. Such union surveillance and regulation of piece-rate work is likely to remove unfair differentials in rates between workers and to secure better standardization of conditions, so that actual earnings will more closely approximate individual abilities.

Mention might be made of numerous other union rules in the field of wage policy that create difficulties for marginal productivity determination, such as premium pay for overtime, guaranteed average pay for workers on transfer, guaranteed minima for piece-rate work, and so forth. The common characteristic of all these regulations, which is significant from the point of view of marginal productivity determination, is not so much their effect upon the cost of labor as upon the freedom of the employer to react to such increases in cost by recombining capital and labor in the most profitable ratios.

Premium pay for overtime is a case in point.[1] If an employer has been operating 45 hours a week at straight time and a union obtains a contract providing for double pay for overtime over 40 hours, what is the effect upon marginal productivity equilibrium? The mere increase in the cost of labor need not cause any difficulty, for the employer may be expected to react to this stimulus as he would to an increase in the basic wage—that is, by reducing output and employment. However, difficulty is created by the fact that the requirement of premium pay for overtime produces a discontinuity in the supply curve of labor, so that the cost of obtaining 41 hours of labor will be much higher than the cost of securing 40 hours. Consequently, if, at the new higher level of wage cost, the equilibrium position happens to be between 40 and 41

[1] See R. A. Lester, "Overtime Wage Rates," *American Economic Review*, XXIX (December, 1939), 790-92.

hours work per week, it is possible that, at the actual volume of employment decided upon, the marginal productivity of labor will exceed or fall short of the marginal cost of labor. Furthermore, the requirement of premium pay for overtime may prevent the optimum recombination of the factors at a later date when the price of capital alters relative to the price of labor. Suppose, for example, that a plant is operating 40 hours a week, when the price of capital rises. The employer of theory would now find it profitable to work capital more intensively, and one way to accomplish this objective would be to combine more units of labor with his machines by working longer hours. But, if the union penalizes overtime operation by a double rate, the employer may find that, even though his present ratio of capital to labor is not the optimum one, it may be even more unprofitable to work the longer week. Consequently, he will continue to work 40 hours despite the increase in the price of capital, and if an equilibrium existed before, it will not exist any longer. Thus, the net effect of premium pay requirements is to produce an element of indeterminateness in marginal productivity determination by inducing operation at outputs which, from the point of view of marginal productivity theory, are points of disequilibrium. While it is possible that employers will benefit from such disequilibrium, it seems more likely that strong union organization will divert the fruits of indeterminateness into labor's pocket.

The year 1937 witnessed the spectacle of widespread wage increases granted, not as a result of union contracts, but to forestall unions from obtaining such contracts. In 1946 a similar situation developed in the South as both CIO and AFL pushed their drives to organize workers in this area. What is the significance of such wage adjustments? Are the nonunion employees being paid more than their marginal productivities as a result of the wage increases? Or is the additional payment to nonunion labor a form of capital investment to preserve the *status quo*?

Let us consider a hypothetical case in which a condition

of equilibrium exists between marginal revenue product and wages. Then wage rates are raised to deter the progress of union organization. What happens to the previous equality that existed between marginal revenue product and wage? Two possibilities may be distinguished:

In the first case, the entrepreneur compensates for the rise in wage rates by raising prices. If the demand curve has any elasticity greater than zero, the quantity of output that consumers will demand will decrease and, therefore, employment should be correspondingly reduced. But layoffs would only give the union a further arguing point to use in its organizing drive. Therefore, employment is likely to be maintained, and the total value of the wage bill will exceed that which would be dictated by the equation of marginal cost and marginal revenue. Whatever the elasticity of the demand curve,[1] if the rise in labor price is not accompanied by a decrease in employment, the employer will be exploited by the amount of the discrepancy between the new wage and the marginal revenue product.[2]

In the second case, the entrepreneur does not raise prices, but simply pays for the increased wages out of pocket. This might be the situation where the union organizing campaign is directed at one, or a few companies, in an industry selling a standard, unbranded commodity. The price then would be given by the market to this employer and he would be ex-

[1] A possible exception might exist in the case where the marginal cost curve cuts the marginal revenue curve in a perfectly inelastic range—as where a kink in the demand curve has been caused by oligopolistic marketing conditions among the competitors. See Paul M. Sweezy, "Demand under Conditions of Oligopoly," *Journal of Political Economy*, XLVII (August, 1939), 568-73. Professor Chamberlin has pointed out to us that the notion of a discontinuous demand curve can be found in an earlier article by R. F. Kahn, "The Problem of Duopoly," *Economic Journal*, XLVII (March, 1937), 1-20. In such a case, a new equilibrium is established at the higher price without any reduction of employment. Such a possibility, however, is more of a curiosity than a likelihood, and hardly could persist as a long-run condition.

[2] In the limiting case where the demand curve is perfectly elastic, as in pure competition, the rise in wage rates should be reflected entirely in a decrease in output, with no change in price. The threat of union organization, however, may discourage curtailment of output, in which case the employer will be exploited by the excess of marginal cost over price.

pected to contract output in accordance with the rise in marginal cost. To contract output at the fixed price, however, would mean that employees would be dismissed, and that would merely invite union organization. It is possible, therefore, that the employer will go on producing the same volume at a higher level of costs. If the wage adjustment is viewed as an increase in marginal costs, then a condition of disequilibrium will exist and the employer will be exploited. On the other hand, it is possible that the employer considers the wage disbursement in the nature of an investment—an investment in the *status quo*, which will pay dividends not only in savings in labor cost, but also in higher plant efficiency and better employer-employee relationships. On this view, the wage increase is in essence a capital investment which will pay for itself—just like a new machine—in reduced costs of operation over a period of time. Since fixed costs do not affect marginal costs, if the wage adjustment is viewed as an increase in fixed costs, there is no incentive to contract output.

If the mere threat of union organization can produce a condition in which labor may receive more than its marginal value product, it seems logical to presume that actual organization is capable of producing an even larger number and variety of such cases. For, at best, the actual equation of marginal value product and marginal wage cost in the individual firm rests upon a tenuous basis.[1] In a world of monopoly and oligopoly, of fixed and durable capital, where prejudices and lack of knowledge mingle with nonpecuniary motives to confuse the economic milieu in which this equation is staged, the equality between marginal value product and wage can be seen only as a tendency, but a tendency that dominates the delicate interrelationship of wages, employment, and output. To the rigidities, economic and institutional, which retard and distort the influence of this vital economic force, can now be added the paraphernalia of unionism, which fur-

---

[1] W. J. Eiteman contends that it is an impossible task to estimate marginal productivity in modern multi-process production. See his stimulating paper, "The Equilibrium of the Firm in Multi-process Industries," *op. cit.*, pp. 280-86.

ther restricts the ability of the employer to manipulate freely the ratio of combination of the factors of production.

CONCLUDING OBSERVATIONS

The most important fact about unionism is that, on the one hand, by increasing the range of indeterminateness in marginal productivity determination, it creates the fruits of uncertainty; and on the other hand, by augmenting the bargaining power of labor, it enables workers to appropriate the fruits of its own creation. Were it not for the first condition, unions would not be able to raise real wages, unless the increase in money wages had favorable repercussions upon one of the variables of the Keynesian system. In traditional theory, the approximate equality of marginal revenue product and wage would leave no room for absorption of wage increase except through reduction in output and employment.[1] But because unionism has more than a wage dimension, because it alters the nature of industrial organization and control, unions can raise wages without producing unemployment.

Where does the money come from? Who suffers the exploitation? It is perhaps confusing to speak of labor exploiting any other factor, that is, receiving more than its marginal revenue product, when the reason for the existence of the "exploitation" is the very fact that the limits of the marginal revenue product of labor are not well defined. If through superior bargaining power, labor is able to secure for itself a larger share than it would be entitled to if, under the given conditions of proportions of the factors, the marginal product of labor could be ascertained, then it is probable that the extra share is gained at the expense of profits as the residual income recipient.

Thus it appears that union leaders, although unversed in the complexities of economic theory and unaware of the sophisticated economic reasoning necessary to substantiate their claims, nevertheless have exhibited a surprisingly keen insight

[1] Except, of course, when exploitation of labor existed before the advent of unionism.

into the mechanism of the economic system. They have maintained that workingmen, through organization, can divert profits into wages. Economists have argued against this proposition and "proved" that they were in error. The economists were right in theory, but their premises were wrong, for they based their arguments upon a theory that was not directly applicable in its traditional form to the problem of the effect of union organization upon employment in present-day industrial society.

The existence of a margin of uncertainty does not mean, however, that unions have discovered an inexhaustible pool which they can drain to the advantage of union labor. It is a *margin* of uncertainty, not an indefinitely extendible upper limit. Indeed, union leaders have a grave responsibility, for, since the impersonal working of the marginal productivity principle can no longer be depended upon to operate in its traditional fashion, the duty devolves upon union leaders to pursue a wage policy designed to maximize employment opportunities. The welfare of labor, like the welfare of the rest of the community, depends upon a dynamic America, an economy in which the maximum incentive is afforded to seek out and exploit new investment opportunities. The pressure of high costs can stimulate entrepreneurial efforts in this direction, but unions must not push wages so high as to eliminate the prospect of profit. The great difficulty, however, is that even those union leaders who recognize the need for a wage policy designed to maximize production are often compelled to follow a wage policy based on less desirable economic considerations because of the political exigencies incidental to union leadership.

CHAPTER ELEVEN

Some Aspects of Labor Market Structure

by *Lloyd G. Reynolds*

ECONOMISTS in the United States have gone some distance toward describing the kinds of wage structure and the patterns of wage change produced by collective bargaining. These descriptions suggest two questions: First, why *these* patterns rather than others? Why do unions and business organizations pursue certain objectives with respect to wages and why are certain sorts of compromise reached? Second, what does it all matter anyway? What are the consequences of the bargained wage structures? The second question provides our point of departure here.

This question is usually approached via a contrast between the behavior of wage rates and employment under collective bargaining and their presumed behavior in the absence of unionism. It is necessary, however, to be quite clear whether one is contrasting the results of collective bargaining with (a) the results which would be attained under those institutional conditions most conducive to "ideal output," or (b) the results which would be produced by an economy resembling the actual economy (of a particular country, at a particular date) in all respects save the existence of union organization.

The first sort of comparison must start from the familiar assumptions about the existence and perfection of competition, the absence of group association, the rational and informed character of individual action, and so on. The extent to which these conditions do or do not exist in any actual economy is beside the point. The object is simply to construct a formal definition of economic behavior, deviations from which can be detected and described. Judged by this standard, collective bargaining always appears in a rather poor light. The pattern of wages and employment differs markedly from the "ideal" pattern at any time, adjustments to change are slow and incomplete, and so on through a familiar catalog of indictments.

Meditation on this conclusion, however, can lead only to a fruitless yearning for the lost Atlantis of the free market. The practical question is whether the results of collective bargaining in a particular economy are less "ideal" than the results which the same economy would produce in the absence of collective bargaining. This kind of comparison must also be based on an abstract model of the economy but the "realism" of the model now becomes of decisive importance. The model must reproduce the salient features of the actual economy closely enough so that concrete significance can be attached to the results and, consequently, to the divergence between the results and those arrived at under collective bargaining.

Analysis of the economic consequences of trade unionism, in short, requires a reasonably realistic model of the (non-union) labor market.[1] The assumptions must be chosen for their congruence with reality rather than for their mathematical convenience. If it proves impossible to construct a model which gives a satisfactory degree of realism while remaining mathematically manageable, economists will have to admit that they have nothing to say on this issue.

The number of economists who have worked at this task in recent decades is distressingly small, the only major theoretical contribution being that of Pigou. The pictures of the labor market which form the background of our thinking and the substance of our teaching are correspondingly inadequate —so inadequate, indeed, that we are not yet justified in drawing any conclusions concerning the differences introduced by union organization. The models in current use are without

---

[1] The term "labor market" must be broadly interpreted. It is obvious that the demand conditions for labor in an area are influenced by a large number of commodity and factor markets, and that construction of a labor market model rests on open or tacit assumptions concerning these markets.

exception static, noncyclical, full employment models. Virtually all of them assume factor supplies variable in form, i.e., they are long-run constructions. They are insufficiently radical in their acceptance of ignorance, immobility, and noneconomic motivation. Nor are they able effectively to handle the interplay of product markets and labor markets over a period of time.

The object of this paper is to move a few steps toward the kind of labor market model which might be useful as a research and policy instrument. The first three sections have to do with the supply conditions of labor to the individual firm. The fourth section is concerned with the factors influencing the firm's labor demand curve and its choice of a wage rate.[1] The firm is the medium through which the forces operating in product markets interact with those operating in the local labor market. No attempt has been made to draw together the consequences of this analysis for the study of collective bargaining, since to do so would have lengthened the paper unduly. Some of the implications are indicated along the way, however, and others will be apparent to the observant reader.

LABOR SUPPLY UNDER FULL EMPLOYMENT

The supply of labor to the firm was implicitly regarded by neoclassical writers as infinitely elastic at a prevailing wage rate determined under conditions of pure competition in the labor market. Indeed, until recent years, the concept of a horizontal labor supply curve was not questioned even by those who in other respects were critics of accepted wage theory. The critics tended to argue that, because of peculiarities in the labor market, the level of wages in a particular firm would be influenced by the relative bargaining strength of employer and workers. But they do not appear to have challenged the

[1] The substance of these sections has been published in two articles: "The Supply of Labor to the Firm," *Quarterly Journal of Economics*, LX (May, 1946), 390-411; and "Wage Differences in Local Labor Markets," *American Economic Review*, XXXVI (June, 1946), 366-75. This material is reprinted by permission of the editors of these journals.

notion that, once the rate of wages was established, the employer would be able to employ any quantity of labor he chose, i.e., that supply was infinitely elastic at the bargained rate.

The view that labor market imperfections result in a forward-rising supply curve of labor to the firm appears to have been first elaborated by Mrs. Robinson.[1] This conclusion has made its way rapidly into the textbooks and seems well on the way to being generally accepted as a substitute for the horizontal supply curve of earlier days.[2] This is doubtless due in part to the rapid and widespread acceptance of the theory of monopolistic competition. If imperfections in product markets are associated with a sloped demand curve for the firm, it seems reasonable to suppose that imperfections in factor markets result in a similar departure from horizontality.

Doubts arise, however, when one examines the specific explanations offered for the sloped supply curve of labor. Some writers attempt to explain why it is necessary to *raise* wages in order to attract more labor, others why an employer

---

[1] "The supply of labor to an individual firm might be limited for the same sort of reasons. For instance, there may be a certain number of workers in the immediate neighborhood and to attract those from further afield it may be necessary to pay a wage equal to what they can earn at home plus their fares to and fro; or there may be workers attached to the firm by preference or custom and to attract others it may be necessary to pay a higher wage. Or ignorance may prevent workers from moving from one firm to another in response to differences in the wages offered by the different firms." Joan Robinson, *The Economics of Imperfect Competition* (London, Macmillan Co., 1934), p. 296. The discussion is accompanied by the familiar diagram showing rising average cost and marginal cost curves for labor.

[2] See, for example, the following: "A considerable reduction in the wage-rate offered by the particular employer would cause some persons to move into other jobs in the same district or to move to similar firms in other districts. But the employer would not lose the whole of his labor supply. Some of his employees might find it too costly to move into other districts or other trades, or might not realize the opportunities of earning higher wages in other occupations or districts. Similarly, he might have to offer a considerably higher wage in order to attract more labor, because the wage offered must be raised enough to make up for the cost to labor of transferring itself from other less well-paid districts or other less well-paid occupations in the same district." (J. E. Meade and C. F. Hitch, *An Introduction to Economic Analysis and Policy* [New York, Oxford University Press, 1938], p. 153.) See also Richard A. Lester, *Economics of Labor* (New York, Macmillan Co., 1941), pp. 108-109.

can *reduce* wages without losing his entire labor force. In labor markets as in commodity markets, however, it makes considerable difference whether one is looking up or down the supply curve. An explanation which works well in one direction may, when reversed, produce a sharp "kink" in the curve.

Even for movement in one direction—say, up the supply curve—several quite different explanations are offered. The sloped supply curve is sometimes made to depend on the number or size of firms in the market. It is said that an employer who is the only buyer of a certain type of labor in an area will have a sloped supply curve, or that a "large" firm will have a sloped supply curve, whereas a "small" firm would not. Other explanations run entirely in terms of employee behavior —workers are ignorant of the wage rates prevailing in other plants, or hesitate to change jobs because of a desire for security, or are attached to a particular firm by "preference or custom." Again, it is said that higher wages are necessary to cover the cost to labor of moving from other areas.

These differing explanations, while each may apply to a particular situation, cannot all apply at the same time. The various writers have obviously had in mind several different labor market situations. The present section, therefore, distinguishes the main sets of conditions under which the supply of labor to the firm might be less than perfectly elastic, and inquires in each case whether the assumed conditions would produce the continuous forward-rising supply curve currently fashionable, or some other type of curve. Succeeding sections will explore the effect on the labor supply function of removing some of the customary assumptions of wage theory, in particular the assumption of full employment.

"Labor market" will be used here in the ordinary sense of a manufacturing and trading center plus the agricultural hinterland directly tributary to it. The term "wage" will be defined to include all of the conditions affecting the attractiveness of a job, including the basic time-rate or average piece-rate earnings, monetary compensation not included in the base rate— overtime earnings, shift premiums, bonuses, pension benefits, free medical care, sick leave, paid vacations, and the like, together with the social and physical conditions of work. Two plants which are equally attractive to a prospective employee [1] will thus by definition be paying equal wages. The alternative and more conventional approach would be to define the wage as the base rate and to assume either that inducements other than the base rate are equal in all firms under consideration or else that they are of no importance. Since it is obvious that either assumption would be highly unrealistic, it seems better to adopt the definition proposed here and to face squarely the consequent problems of measurement.[2]

It will be assumed throughout this section that there is no involuntary unemployment; that all workers are of equal ability or, alternatively, that labor is measured in efficiency units; and that all jobs are unskilled and all workers therefore interchangeable. The consequences of removing these assumptions will be considered shortly.

A horizontal supply curve of labor to the firm is obtained by adding to these assumptions two others: (a) that all workers are fully informed concerning the wage, as defined above, offered by each firm in the area, and are willing to change jobs for a very small gain in wages; (b) that the firm in question is "small"——that its withdrawal of labor from other firms does not appreciably raise the marginal revenue product of labor in those firms. The object of this section is to examine the principal ways in which these assumptions may be modified, and the type of supply curve which will result in each case. The discussion will be conducted in terms of the relation between wage increases and increases in labor supply, i.e., looking *up* the supply curve, and it will be assumed that we are starting in each case from a wage equal to that of all

[1] Complications resulting from the fact that different workers will have different preferences concerning conditions of work will be considered below.

[2] Application of this definition would require that all attributes of the job other than base rates of pay be reduced to their base-rate equivalent in the worker's mind. This is an intriguing possibility, and it is a merit of the present definition that it pushes one to experiment in this direction. A definition of wages in terms of base rates alone glosses over the difficulties in the problem but does not eliminate them.

other firms in the area. The extent to which this reasoning can be reversed to explain the consequences of wage cuts will be examined at the end of the section.

(a) The assumption that workers are fully informed and completely responsive to wage differences may be altered in three main ways. It may be assumed that workers are ignorant of the wages paid by other employers, or that they are perfectly informed concerning wages but are deterred from changing jobs by considerations of security, or that they are perfectly informed concerning wages but differ in their evaluation of the non-base-rate components of the wage. These possibilities will be considered in turn.

Complete ignorance by all workers of the wage rates paid by other employers would result in a completely inelastic supply curve of labor to each firm. No possible increase in wages would attract any additional labor, since no one would ever hear of it. If part of the workers in the market were informed concerning wage rates while the remainder were not, the supply curve of each firm would have a horizontal section equal in length to the number of "informed" workers and would then become vertical.[1] A gradually rising supply curve could occur only if there were a functional relation between a firm's wage level and workers' information concerning it, i.e., if the workers' ignorance could be dispelled by mere increases in the wage offered *and by nothing else*. For if the workers' ignorance could be dispelled by the passage of time, the rising supply curve would be significant only for short periods and could be flattened out more and more by allowing successively longer periods for adjustment. Or if it could be dispelled completely by a lump-sum expenditure on advertising and other labor recruiting devices, the result would be a step-curve with one rather modest step. Thus, while a continuously rising labor supply curve might conceivably result from igno-

---

[1] Looking *down* the supply curve, there would also be a horizontal section followed by a vertical section. A very small reduction in wages would cause all of the informed workers employed by the firm to leave it, but further reductions would not cause any of the uninformed to leave.

rance alone, this ignorance would have to be of a very special sort hardly likely to be significant in practice.

The worker may be deterred from seeking a new job at a higher wage rate by uncertainty concerning his chance of securing and retaining it. He may be viewed as weighing his prospective future earnings in his present job, discounted to their present value and further reduced to allow for anticipated unemployment, against a similar calculation of prospective earnings in the new job. Workers will differ in their judgment of the wage rates at which it is just worth while to change jobs, because they will differ in the length of the future period taken into account, the rate at which future earnings are discounted, their actual chances of remaining steadily at work in their present job, their estimate of their actual chances, and their estimate of the probable continuity of employment in the new job. As the wage offered in the new job rises, however, it will exceed the "break-even point" for more and more workers. The result is a rising supply curve.

This method of deriving a sloped supply curve, however, involves a departure from the assumption of continuous full employment. Workers will not be seriously influenced by fear of unemployment unless the economy is actually subject to unemployment on a considerable scale. But if unemployment exists, the labor supply curve of the firm may be horizontal over a distance equal to the number of unemployed in the area. This point is stated more precisely in a later section.

"Wages" was defined above to include the base rate of pay, plus "fringe" types of compensation, plus the money equivalent of especially pleasant or unpleasant working conditions. But this yields an unambiguous definition of "equal wages" and a horizontal labor supply curve to each firm only if all workers in the labor market attach the same money value to specified working conditions and fringe compensations. If this is not so, it is no longer possible to say what constitutes equality of wages in the market, since what appears equal to one man may well appear unequal to another. One can say only that, at a specified wage, a firm will attract those workers who value its wage more highly than that offered by any other firm. As the wage offered is increased, the number of such workers will also increase. A sloped labor supply curve may thus be attributed to differences in workers' taste in choosing jobs, in precisely the same way that a sloped demand curve for a commodity arises from differences in consumers' tastes. In both cases the curve becomes horizontal if differences in individual preference are eliminated.

In the case of the labor supply curve, moreover, an additional factor is at work. Part of the satisfaction which a worker derives from his job consists in the social life of the shop, the opportunity for continued contact with well-known associates amid familiar surroundings. Even if specified conditions of work were valued the same by all workers, or even if conditions of work were identical in all establishments, workers might be reluctant to leave a familiar workplace and work group. The wage differential necessary to overcome this reluctance would differ from one worker to the next, and the result would be a sloped supply curve to each firm. This attachment to a particular work group, operating independently of the attractiveness of the job, provides a separate basis for deriving a sloped labor supply curve.[1]

(b) If we remove the assumption that firms are "small," the shape of the supply curve will depend on the reaction of other firms to a change in the wage rate of the firm in question. The problem is analogous to that of oligopoly in product markets, and a similar variety of solutions exists. It is not possible here to do more than mention a few of them, nor is

---

[1] The behavior of individual sellers of labor presents obvious analogies with that of individual buyers of consumer goods at retail. Personal attachment to a particular retailer is analogous to the worker's attachment to a particular workplace. Again, a consumer may habitually buy a particular brand of a product without bothering to reexamine the relative merit of other brands. This is an instance of (deliberate) ignorance, rather than of preference. A comparable case would be that of a worker who decides once for all that his present job is the best obtainable and thenceforth does not bother to inform himself of the merits of alternative jobs.

it possible to go into the dynamics of adjustment from the old to the new equilibrium position.

Looking up the curve from the present wage rate, two extreme possibilities may be distinguished. A wage increase by any one firm might be accompanied immediately by wage increases of the same amount [1] in all other firms. This might happen, for example, if employers followed a practice of consulting with each other before changing wage rates. Under such conditions either the firm proposing a wage increase would be dissuaded from making it or else all firms would advance their rates together. In this case each firm's supply curve will be a small-scale replica of the aggregate supply curve in the market.[2] At the other extreme, wage increases by one firm might be ignored by all other firms. In this case the firm's supply curve would be much more elastic, its slope depending on the extent of workers' attachment to their present jobs. Supply curves intermediate between these two may be derived by assuming that some firms follow a wage increase while others do not, or by assuming time-lags of various lengths between the initial increase and the reactions of other firms.

Looking down the supply curve, similar possibilities may be distinguished. The slope of the curve downward will almost certainly differ from its slope upward, i.e., it will have a kink at a point representing the present level of wages and employment. The actual shape of the supply curve, moreover, may differ from the firm's forecast of its shape. Wage changes may result in surprises to the firm which alter its expectations for the future.

The discussion thus far has ignored the possibility of inter-area migration of labor. This factor may be introduced most

---

[1] Increases of the same *absolute* amount in all firms will not have the same effect as increases of the same *percentage* amount. Which type of increase will be necessary to leave all firms in the same competitive position as before depends on whether workers think in absolute or percentage terms.

[2] This statement assumes that each firm is able to recruit its proportionate share of the additional workers becoming available at higher levels of wages (or, if the aggregate supply curve is backward-rising, that withdrawals from the market are proportionately distributed).

conveniently by considering the case of a firm which is the only employer in its area. The shape of its supply curve will clearly depend on the amount of labor which can be attracted from other areas at various wage levels. Money costs of movement alone would produce only a very slight upward slope in the supply curve. Almost all manufacturing plants in the United States could find many times their present working force within a radius of a hundred miles, and most of the labor migration which actually occurs involves movement of a hundred miles or less. The cost of moving a hundred miles, amortized over the worker's expected period of employment at the plant, would in most cases add only a fraction of a cent per hour to the wage rate. Moreover, a labor supply curve based on costs of movement would not be continuous unless workers were evenly distributed geographically, and this condition is approximated only in purely agricultural areas. Vertical discontinuities in the supply curve on this account are not likely, however, to be of much practical importance.

Probably more important than the money cost of moving is the attachment of workers to a particular locality. Workers ordinarily prefer a familiar community for the same reasons that they prefer a familiar workplace. The intensity of this local patriotism varies, however, from one individual to the next, and it can be overcome by a smaller cash advantage in some cases than in others. This factor thus provides a reason, and the only independent [1] reason, why geographic dispersion might produce a marked upward slope in the supply curve.

This survey of possible labor market situations indicates that one of the reasons frequently given for a sloped supply curve, namely, the desire for security, is inconsistent with the assumption of full employment. Two others—"dispellable" ignorance and costs of geographic movement—do not involve any significant departure from horizontality.

A labor supply curve with an appreciable upward slope

---

[1] Some writers on interarea migration rely heavily on ignorance or uncertainty as obstacles to labor mobility. These obstacles also apply within an area, and the discussion of them in previous paragraphs is applicable here.

must be ascribed to one or more of the following four conditions:

1. Differences in worker preference for specified combinations of money income and working conditions.
2. Attachment of workers to a familiar workplace.
3. Attachment of workers to a familiar place of residence.
4. Large size of employing firms.

Only the first two of these are (or may be) applicable under all circumstances. The third will have a major influence on the firm's supply curve only when the firm is the sole employer in its area and additional labor must come from elsewhere. The fourth is of widespread importance, but it will produce a kinked rather than a continuous supply curve, and in some cases the curve may not even be determinate.

We conclude, then, that there seems to be no reason a priori to regard the continuous sloped supply curve as typical. It will exist under the conditions noted, but supply curves which are substantially horizontal or substantially vertical, or which have a sharp kink at the existing level of employment, may also exist. The relative prevalence of these several situations under conditions approximating those of full employment is a matter for careful inductive study.

THE EFFECT OF UNEMPLOYMENT

The discussion has thus far assumed full employment in the local labor market in question. Let us now assume that the volume of unemployment is greater than the inevitable minimum arising from seasonal and irregular fluctuations in the demand for labor and from defects in the technical organization of the labor market. While this excess of workers will be referred to hereafter as "the unemployed," it includes not only those who would be counted as unemployed under the census definition but also persons not actively seeking work who could be induced to take jobs at existing wage rates by a definite offer of employment.

Let us assume further that employers give first preference in hiring to the unemployed (including new entrants to the labor market) and that they will not, so long as unemployment exists, hire a worker currently employed by any other employer. It is doubtful whether employers anywhere adhere perfectly to such an "anti-pirating policy," but it does form a sufficiently important element in employer action to justify an exploration of its logical consequences.

The assumptions of interchangeability and equal efficiency of labor will be left in force for the time being, but will be dealt with in the following section. Employment in all firms other than the one whose supply curve is being examined will be taken as constant. The wage rates of other firms will also be taken as constant, though not necessarily equal to the wage rate of the firm in question or to each other.

Under these conditions, the supply of labor to a particular firm may be represented as shown in Figure I. The point F represents the firm's current employment (OD) and wage rate (OC). The line AJ represents the lowest wage which the firm can pay and retain its present working force. In the absence of trade union organization or minimum wage laws, it may be taken as the rate below which any reduction would produce a complete and permanent work stoppage.[1] The position of this line at a given moment can never be estimated exactly. It probably depends mainly on the wage rates of other firms, the wage history of the firm in question and its traditional position in the wage structure of the area, and the level and rate of change of employment in the area. It will therefore be different for each firm in the area and will vary from time to time for the same firm.

In order to increase employment beyond D the firm must have recourse to the unemployed, who are represented by the distance DE. If the area in question is regarded as "open,"

---

[1] The reader may object that AJ should slope upward, since wage cuts would cause some workers to leave the firm before others. Under the assumptions made above, however, any worker who left the firm would have to remain unemployed. Some workers might indeed prefer to remain unemployed rather than take wage reductions. It is likely, however, that the great majority would take reductions down to a certain point, below which all would quit in a body. It is thus probably a good first approximation to take AJ as horizontal, at least over relatively short periods.

DE includes not only unemployed persons within the area but all others who can be attracted to the area at existing wage

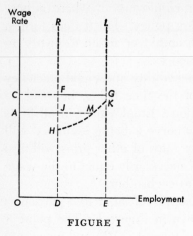

FIGURE I

rates. If there is widespread unemployment in areas close to the one in question, *DE* may consist mainly of potential migrants and may be very large relative to *OD*. *EL* will shift to the left if other firms in this area increase their employment or if employment rises in contiguous areas, and will shift to the right for the opposite reasons.

The supply-price of the unemployed is indicated by *HK*.[1] This curve will be forward-rising for at least three reasons. First, if some of the unemployed have seniority with other employers which they are anxious to retain, a higher wage may be necessary to induce them to forego the chance of returning to their previous employers;[2] this will be particularly important as regards workers with seniority in firms whose wage rates are above those of the firm in question. Second, if there are sources of income other than employment—cash relief, work projects, pension rights, unemployment compensation— some of the unemployed may have a higher reservation price than others on this account. Third, if interarea migra-

---

[1] *HK* has been started below *AJ* because it seems likely that at least some of the unemployed would be willing to take a lower wage than the employed workers would accept, but this is not in any way essential to the argument. The relative position of *H* and *J* would clearly vary greatly from one case to the next, and it is quite conceivable that *H* might lie above *J* on occasion.

[2] If all employers laid off and rehired workers in strict accordance with seniority, if this system had existed long enough for all workers to accumulate substantial seniority, and if all workers valued seniority more highly than wages, the unemployed would in effect be divided into watertight compartments. Unemployed workers "regularly attached" to other firms could not be considered part of the supply available to a particular firm, i.e., the distance *DE* would include only unemployed workers regularly attached to the firm in question.

tion is involved, some workers will require a greater inducement than others to leave their home communities for jobs
in other localities.

The minimum supply-price of labor to the firm, then, is
indicated by *AJMK*.[1] The employer is free to choose any combination of wages and employment which lies above this line.
Once such a combination has been chosen, indicated in this
instance by the point *F*, the firm may be regarded as operating on the supply curve *AJFG*. Wages can be cut to any point
between *C* and *A* with no loss of employees. Looking up the
curve, the firm need not raise wages to secure additional workers until the point of full employment is reached. This would
not be true, of course, in all actual cases. Particularly in very
low wage firms, the reservation price of some of the unemployed might be above the firm's wage level, i.e., *HK* might
intersect *FG*. For the majority of firms, however, it is probably safe to take the supply curve as horizontal up to the point
of full employment.

Several interesting characteristics of this hypothetical labor
market may now be noted. First, the supply conditions of
labor exercise little constraint over the firm's choice of a wage
rate. Within rather wide limits, the firm can raise or lower
wage rates without affecting the amount of labor available to
it or to any other firm in the market. The limits of choice will
be wider for a new firm than for an established firm which,
by its previous wage decisions, has created worker expectations which limit its present actions. The observation that
firms have latitude to pursue a wage policy, of course, raises
more questions than it answers. Why should any firm choose
to pay a wage higher than it is obliged to pay (*A* in Figure I)?

---

[1] Not, as might be thought, by *AJHMK*, since the area *JHM* is of no
practical significance. It is conceivable that an employer might cut wages
below A, lose all his existing workers, and replace them from the unemployed.
In a unionized plant, however, this could be done only with the greatest difficulty, and even under nonunion conditions it would involve such serious labor
unrest that it would not be attempted unless the employer were in desperate
straits. The vertical line *KL* does not form part of the supply curve. When
the point of full employment is reached, the supply curve takes on an entirely
different shape, determined by the factors discussed in the preceding section.

Why should any firm ever raise wages while unemployment exists? No complete discussion of these questions will be attempted here, though some observations on the second one will be made below.

If the firm can vary its wage rate over a considerable range, there are important consequences for the theory of prices and production. The wage rate cannot be taken as given while one examines the firm's decisions on price and output. Decisions on prices are not independent of decisions on wages; indeed, they may be so closely interrelated that they constitute a single policy on prices-*cum*-wages. Looking beyond the firm to the industry, it seems highly probable that different firms will be operating at different wage levels, especially if the industry is geographically dispersed. Moreover, the wage rate of each firm is subject to arbitrary changes. Dispersion and changeability of wage rates introduces serious complications into the theory of pure and monopolistic competition,[1] and still more serious ones into the theory of oligopoly.

Second—and this is merely restating the previous point in another way—differences in the wage rates paid by different firms for comparable work could persist indefinitely without setting in motion any mechanism of adjustment. The labor supply conditions assumed here do not explain why wage differences may arise; such an explanation would clearly have to be sought on the demand side of the market. But once wage differences have come into existence for whatever reason, this type of labor market would permit them to continue undisturbed.[2]

---

[1] Under either pure or monopolistic competition, the constant downward pressure of supply on prices was supposed to encounter the resistance of a firm cost "floor," and between these two millstones the inefficient producer was ground to pieces. But if labor markets are of the type assumed here, the "floor" is different for different firms and is more like a quagmire than firm concrete. Competition may merely push the firm waist-deep into the quagmire, where it dies—if it does die—a lingering death.

[2] One additional assumption is involved here, namely, that young people entering the labor market behave in the same way as the unemployed, and will take a job with a firm which is hiring at the moment rather than remain unemployed in the hope of securing a job with a higher wage firm at some later date. The same result would be obtained by assuming that all new

Third, although the labor market is clearly imperfect, each firm may have a horizontal labor supply curve up to the point of full employment. There will therefore be no tendency to restrict production because of the rising marginal cost of labor and Mrs. Robinson's "monopsonistic exploitation" [1] will not arise, though workers may still be subject to "monopolistic exploitation."

These conclusions rest on the assumption of a substantial volume of unemployment and apply, a fortiori, if unemployment is increasing. How are they affected if unemployment is decreasing, and particularly if the decrease continues until full employment is approached? In this event the supply curve may take on a shape quite different from that shown in Figure I. Looking downward from F, the supply curve will remain vertical so long as employers continue to hire from the unemployed instead of from each other. If the expansion of employment is rapid, however, the "anti-pirating" policy is likely to be abandoned outright or to become seriously attenuated, and workers will also shop around increasingly for new jobs. The firm will then be able to retain only those workers who voluntarily choose its combination of wages and conditions as preferable to that of any other firm in the market. Similarly, looking upward from F, the firm will no longer be able to attract all the unemployed by a mere offer of employment at its present wage rates. Some of the unemployed will now hold back because of a hope of securing employment in a more attractive plant. The more buoyant the demand for labor the stronger will be their expectation of employment and the higher their reservation price. As the market approaches the point of full employment—more accurately, the point at which workers *behave* as if jobs could be chosen with perfect freedom—the firm's supply curve will approximate its "full employment shape" more and more closely.

The factors determining the shape of the supply curve

entrants take jobs in places where friends or relatives are already employed, and that relative wage rates do not influence their choice of jobs.

[1] Joan Robinson, *op. cit.*, Chap. 26.

under full employment have already been examined. To take only one simple case, the supply curve of a small firm enjoying moderate "worker preference" might resemble A_1K_1 in Figure II.[1] This diagram provides at least one reason why employers may frequently be found paying more than they have to at the moment. If the employer expects a return to full employment and a fluid labor market, i.e., if he regards A_1K_1 (Figure II) rather than $AJFG$ (Figure I) as the normal situation, he may consider it risky to drive wages down below A_1K_1 even during periods of unemployment.

The position of F relative to A_1K_1 indicates whether the firm was taking advantage of unemployment to pay wage rates lower than it would have had to pay under full employment. If its full employment supply curve turned out to be A_2K_2, it would clearly have to raise wages in order merely to maintain its present labor force.

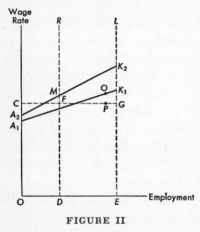

FIGURE II

The firm may feel obliged to raise wages, however, even before full employment is reached. First, the supply curve is influenced, not by the statistical fact of full employment, but by workers' *attitudes* toward the availability of jobs. As soon as workers feel that no risk is involved in changing jobs, the supply curve will assume its maximum slope (A_1K_1 or A_2K_2) and the firm will be obliged to make appropriate adjustments. This may occur some time before unemployment has been reduced to a minimum.

[1] Figure II is perhaps technically incorrect in that it includes both curves from Figure I indicating a condition of unemployment and new labor supply curves (A_1K_1 and A_2K_2) which come into existence only when full employment has been reached (i.e., when DR and EL are identical). This construction has the advantage, however, of illustrating the wage adjustments which may be required to maintain a desired level of employment in the face of the new labor supply conditions.

Second, it may require a lower wage to retain workers already attached to the firm than to recapture them after they have left or to recruit workers employed by other firms. Moreover, it may be easier to hire men while they are still unemployed than to win them away from other firms at a later date. This could be shown diagrammatically in Figure II by vertical discontinuities in A_1K_1 (or A_2K_2), where it crosses DR and EL. Suppose now that the supply curve is A_2K_2 and the firm wishes merely to maintain its present employment. If it waits until EL reaches DR before raising wages, it takes a risk that employment will actually fall below D and that it will have to win these workers back by still larger increases. Prudence will dictate that wages be raised to M before this can happen. Again, suppose that the supply curve is A_1K_1 and that the firm's employment objective is P. This objective can be attained more economically by raising wages to the point O *before* EL moves as far to the left as P, since after this point workers will have to be detached from other firms at greater expense.

Third, if unusually rapid recruiting seems necessary to attain the desired number of workers before the supply is exhausted, and if the structure of the market makes rapid recruiting difficult, it may be desirable on this account to raise wages at a relatively early point in the expansion. Such "preclusive buying" of labor is probably of considerable importance where firms are large and a rapid expansion of employment is under way.

Whether Figure I or Figure II is more relevant to the explanation of actual labor market behavior depends, of course, on how frequently full employment is approached and how long these periods of high employment last. High employment would probably have to last for at least one or two years in order to bring about a considerable volume of voluntary transference of labor among firms and an appreciable reduction in interfirm wage differentials.

EFFECTS OF VARYING EFFICIENCY AND
OCCUPATIONAL SPECIALIZATION

It is necessary now to inquire how far the above results are modified by removing the assumption that all workers are of equal efficiency. Differences in efficiency may be introduced by using the vertical scale of the supply diagrams to indicate *wage cost per worker of standard efficiency*,[1] rather than the wage rate itself. This immediately raises the difficulty that efficiency can be measured only with respect to a particular job. Since the relative efficiency of workers will differ from one job to the next, a supply curve can be drawn only for a single task performed under standard conditions. Moreover, the curves for different jobs can be placed on the same diagram or otherwise compared only on the questionable assumption that "standard efficiency" means the same thing in each instance. The problem will be simplified here by continuing to assume occupational specialization absent. Such an assumption is perhaps not as unrealistic as might appear at first glance, for in many plants a preponderance of the employees are engaged on low-skilled machine-tending and assembly operations which do not differ greatly in the qualities required of the operator.

It is usually argued that differences in individual efficiency will produce a forward-rising labor supply curve even under conditions of unemployment. The argument rests on two main propositions. First, since employers will lay off the poorest workers first, the least efficient of the employed will be better than the most efficient of the unemployed. The wage cost will therefore begin to rise as soon as the first unemployed man is hired. Second, since employers will hire the unem-

---

[1] This comes to the same thing as saying wage cost per efficiency unit of labor, but the above terminology is closer to the current usage of time-study technicians. The problem of defining standard efficiency for repetitive manual operations and evaluating the performance of individual workers in terms of standard is well discussed in Ralph Presgrave, *The Dynamics of Time Study* (Toronto, University of Toronto Press, 1944).

ployed in decreasing order of their efficiency, the supply curve will rise continuously until full employment is reached.[1]

While the logic of such employer behavior is evident, there are important obstacles to the application of an economic calculus in this field. Trade unions are increasingly insistent that layoffs be made on a strict seniority basis; and even where union regulations do not exist, employers usually attach considerable importance to length of service in making layoffs. If seniority is strictly observed, and if there is no correlation between seniority and efficiency, the workers laid off may be just as efficient as those still employed. If an inverse relation exists, as is sometimes contended, the unemployed may actually be more efficient. It should also be remembered that in periods of widespread unemployment the unemployed group is heavily weighted with young people who have just entered the labor market and whose efficiency, at least in jobs requiring little training, is probably relatively high.[2]

The second proposition—that employers will hire in decreasing order of efficiency—will be true only if four conditions are satisfied: the employer must be free from seniority rules and other restrictions on his hiring policy; he must have equal and simultaneous access to all the unemployed workers available for the occupation in question; the tests applied to these workers must permit a perfect prediction of their performance on the job; and hiring must be done in strict accordance with the test results. It is quite unlikely that these conditions would coexist in practice. Indeed, one of them—perfect prediction of job performance—is not technically possible at present. The consequences of failure in one or more of these con-

---

[1] Such a supply curve differs from the usual demand and supply curves of economic analysis in that the units for sale in the market are not interchangeable, but are ranked along the curve in a particular order.

[2] It may be objected that even if efficient workers do happen to be laid off they will not long remain unemployed, for employers will substitute the most efficient of the unemployed for the least efficient of the employed until the possibilities of substitution have been exhausted. In practice, however, such substitution is impeded not only by union rules but by deep-seated worker attitudes.

ditions cannot be traced in detail here. It is evident, however, that a completely unreliable testing system would produce a horizontal supply curve. And a situation in which the employer had access only to successive small samples of the unemployed would produce a more moderately sloped supply curve than a situation in which the whole group could be examined simultaneously.

If the unemployed are hired in decreasing order of efficiency, the slope of the supply curve will depend on the shape of the efficiency distribution and on the system of wage payment in use. A system of increasing piece-rates—hardly ever found in practice—would yield a falling supply curve, proportionate or "straight" piece-rates a horizontal curve, decreasing piece-rates a rising curve, and time-rates a curve of still steeper slope.[1]

In actual practice it is likely that the cost per efficiency unit of the best unemployed man is typically less than that of the poorest man employed. The supply curve of unemployed labor probably does rise in most cases; but if its slope is moderate, the expanding employer may not encounter rising wage costs until full employment is rather close, i.e., HK (Figure I) may intersect FG at a point close to G or may not intersect it at all. There is no empirical basis at present for a judgment on these questions, and investigation would doubtless reveal wide variation from one case to the next. The object here is simply to call into question the strong presumption in favor of one type of supply curve which has been created with scarcely any investigation of actual labor markets.

The introduction of differences in labor efficiency calls for one other footnote to the foregoing argument. Workers of different efficiency probably tend in time to get distributed among employers so that a ranking of firms by average labor efficiency would correspond somewhat with a ranking by aver-

[1] It might be argued that a horizontal supply curve could result even under time-rates, if differences in individual efficiency were exactly offset by differences in the workers' reservation price. This implies, however, that the employer can apply perfect discrimination in hiring—an obvious impossibility in most cases. The point is therefore of little practical importance.

age wage rates.[1] While this tendency has never been empirically demonstrated, it is difficult to doubt its existence. It is effective, of course, only over a period of several decades, because large-scale voluntary movement of labor occurs only at times of high employment,[2] and because the job choices of young people entering the labor force produce their cumulative effect only slowly.

If sufficient time is allowed for adjustment, then, a change in one firm's wage rates relative to other firms' may be partly or even wholly offset by a change in the quality of labor attracted to the firm. A change in the wage rate C (Figure I) may be damped down or even obliterated when the vertical scale is redefined in terms of wage cost per worker of standard efficiency. Again, the slope of the full employment supply curve (A_1K_1 or A_2K_2 in Figure II) will be reduced when the vertical axis is redefined in this way; and the longer the period of time allowed for adjustment, the smaller will be the slope of the supply curve.

A word, finally, about the effects of introducing occupational specialization of the labor force. In order to construct a general supply curve of labor to the firm under these conditions, the vertical axis must be defined as indicating the average level of wages in the plant. The number of additional workers who will be attracted by a given increase in wages (i.e., the slope of A_1K_1 in Figure II) will now depend not only on the factors noted in the preceding section but also on the occupational distribution of the labor force and the supply conditions for each occupation, the occupational rate structure of the plant, the occupational rate structure of other plants in the area, and the way in which the wage increase is distributed among the various occupational groups.

---

[1] The labor force may be thought of as strained through a series of sieves. The firms with highest wage rates get first choice and are able to strain out workers who meet strict hiring specifications, while low wage firms must take the residue. The level of labor efficiency which a firm desires is doubtless one of the major factors influencing its choice of a wage rate.

[2] In the few labor markets which the writer has had occasion to observe, voluntary movement of workers on a large scale occurred only during the periods 1917-20 and 1941-47.

The concept of a general labor supply curve thus becomes more difficult to define and also less useful; for where occupational specialization is important, a company does not want merely so many more workers, but rather a balanced expansion of the working force. Any general wage increase must be sufficient to attract the required number of the scarcest type of worker, even though the increase also attracts many more workers of other types than are needed. A general supply curve may thus be quite misleading about the wage increase involved in a given expansion of employment, tending to understate appreciably the size of the increase that would be required.

Another aspect of the same problem appears if one attempts to use separate supply curves for each occupation. Workers in a particular occupation may be in short supply, even though there is extensive unemployment in other occupations. If the scarce occupation requires a lengthy training and if the absence of trained workers is impeding production, it may be necessary to attract workers from other firms. The firm may thus be operating on a full employment supply curve for one or more occupations, while continuing to enjoy a horizontal supply curve for other occupations. An increase in wage rates for the scarce occupation, however, may necessitate a general wage increase throughout the plant. This provides an additional reason why general wage increases may occur in spite of general unemployment.[1]

What can be said in summation about the usefulness of the continuous forward-rising labor supply curve? It is clear that the shape of the supply curve is much influenced by one's assumption about the level of employment. Under full employment, the labor supply curve will normally be forward-rising, but there is strong reason to doubt that it will be con-

---

[1] In terms of Figure I, the distance JF is much less for a single occupation than for all workers in the plant, because workers in any occupation will resist any marked reduction of their *relative* earnings. An increase granted to one occupation will raise the wage expectation (A) of workers in other occupations and may thus require increases in those occupations as well.

tinuous. In most labor markets, the buyers of labor are "large." [1] The determination of wages then depends on the reaction of the oligopsonists to each others' decisions. A supply curve of the *ceteris paribus* type is inapplicable, and a usable supply curve can be drawn only on rather complicated assumptions about interfirm reactions. Such a supply curve will certainly display kinks and may not even be determinate. [2] Even where a determinate supply curve exists, to suppose that its position can be known by the employer implies that he is singularly gifted in predicting the behavior of other employers and of the workers in the market.

Any reasoning about labor supply which is based on full employment assumptions, however, is of strictly limited usefulness. If one is attempting, not to develop propositions about ideal allocation of resources, but to construct a general theory of how labor markets operate, the possibility of involuntary unemployment must be admitted. No model of the labor market which excludes the pervasive influence of unemployment on worker and employer behavior can provide even a first approximation to reality. Reasons have already been given for thinking that, even where the supply curve of the unemployed is forward-rising, most employers will be faced with rising wage costs per efficiency unit of labor only when full employment is quite near—i.e., only for a short time during a cyclical upswing which carries close to the point of full employment. If, then, one has to choose a single supply curve for purposes of reasoning about "typical" labor market behavior, a horizontal supply curve will give more realistic results than any other. The neo-classical assumption on this point turns out to be reasonable after all, though for quite different reasons than those usually advanced.

[1] This is obviously true in small cities; and even in large cities it is likely to be true either because employers are large in an absolute sense or because only a few employers compete for particular specialized skills.

[2] This possibility is analogous to the possible indeterminacy of the oligopoly demand curve. Cf. Benjamin Higgins, "Elements of Indeterminacy in the Theory of Non-Perfect Competition," *American Economic Review*, XXIX (September, 1939), 468-79.

THE DEMAND FOR LABOR AND THE
DETERMINATION OF WAGES

While the supply conditions described in previous sections will *permit* wage differences to exist, the conditions which will actually *produce* wage differences must be sought on the demand side of the labor market. The remainder of this chapter will be devoted to exploring these demand conditions. In order, first, to isolate the effect of different types of competitive situation in product markets, let us assume (*a*) that each firm knows the location of its "minimum wage," and that the minima of all firms are the same; [1] (*b*) that the supply of factors other than labor is perfectly elastic to each firm; (*c*) that the local labor market under consideration is completely isolated from all other labor markets. The effect of removing these restrictions will be considered in a moment; it is obvious that the result will in each case be to render wage differences more likely. We shall assume throughout that union organization is absent. It will also be assumed that only one occupation exists in the market and that differences in individual efficiency either do not exist or are taken into account through the use of efficiency units.

The average and marginal net value productivity of labor for any firm in the market may be represented, as in Figure III, by curves of the type *ANP* and *MNP*, while *AB* represents the minimum wage. It is possible to introduce discontinuities into the marginal productivity curve by assuming similar discontinuities in the firm's marginal revenue curve. [2] The results

[1] By "minimum wage" is meant that level of wages which would provoke the workers to quit work in a body, and at which the supply curve becomes horizontal (*AJ* in Figure I).

[2] Vertical discontinuities in *MNP* may be obtained by assuming that prices are not varied continuously with changes in cost—for example, that prices are never changed by less than 5 per cent, or that prices are set only in certain "brackets" or "price lines," or that prices are changed only at fixed intervals of time. Horizontal discontinuities can be introduced by assuming that the demand curve for the product is itself discontinuous and that marginal cost is constant over the relevant range; if a horizontal section of the marginal productivity curve happened to coincide with a horizontal supply curve of labor, the equilibrium employment of the firm would be indeterminate over this range. These complications will be ignored here.

which can be obtained in this way, however, are probably of rather short-run significance, and results derived from a continuous marginal productivity curve can be taken as approximately correct over considerable periods of time.

It is clear that the figure does not represent an equilibrium position for any firm in an industry to which entrance is open, whether the situation is one of pure competition, monopolistic competition, or oligopoly. If new firms can enter at wage rate A, then ANP and MNP will be forced down until AB becomes tangent to ANP. Thus even if a firm had established a wage rate above A while profits in the industry were temporarily high, it would not be able to maintain this wage rate but would be forced back to A.[1]

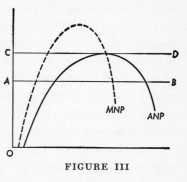

FIGURE III

If, however, the firm in question is a monopoly, in the technical sense, it will be free to pay any wage rate between A and C. As the wage rises toward C output will decline, the price of the product will rise and profits will diminish. At each wage rate the monopolist can choose a rate of output which will maximize profits, but the maximum of these maxima will be obtained at wage rate A.[2] The possible reasons why the management of a monopoly might choose to forego maximum profits and pay a wage rate above A need not be discussed, though some suggestions on this point are offered

[1] A wage higher than A can be established permanently if, while the industry is out of equilibrium and profits are above normal, a union enters the industry and enforces a wage greater than A from all firms, at the same time preventing any new firm from entering the industry at a lower wage. But this amounts to saying that the minimum wage A has now been raised by trade union action and does not constitute an exception to the statement just made.

[2] If profits were introduced into the figure as a third dimension, MNP would resemble the backbone of a mountain range sloping downward on either side and also running downward as one goes from AB toward CD. MNP is a locus of profit maxima, and the greatest of these maxima will occur at its intersection with AB.

below. It is sufficient here to indicate the existence of a range of managerial discretion and the stability of any wage rate within this range.

The preceding paragraph relates to a monopoly whose prices and profits are limited only by the position of its demand curve. A public utility limited by law to a fixed rate of return on its investment could pay any wage between A and C with complete indifference, provided that the costs deducted in arriving at MNP include the legal maximum profit. A monopoly selling to a government agency on the basis of cost plus a fixed fee or cost plus a fixed rate of return on capital could also, without affecting its profits, raise wages to any level which the purchasing agency could be induced to accept. If the price included cost plus a profit calculated as a fixed percentage of cost, the firm's profits would be increased with each increase in wages. Thus in these cases there is no reason to expect A to be selected as the wage rate.

The case of oligopoly with closed entrance is somewhat more complicated. If producers do not cooperate with respect to product prices, then prices must fall to equality with average cost, and the wage rate of each produced must be A. If, however, there is price cooperation—which may mean anything from a close-knit cartel agreement to simply taking account of the probable reaction of other firms in the industry to a price change—the resulting price, demand conditions permitting, will be somewhat above average cost. Each firm will then have something of the monopolist's latitude with respect to wage rates: it can pay anything between A and the wage which would just reduce its profits to normal. The freedom of each producer is qualified, however, by the necessity of maintaining cordial relations with other producers. If most firms in the industry choose to pay wages considerably above A, then a firm which pays only A may be suspected of undermining the price agreement and pressure may be put on it to come up to the general industry level. One would, therefore, expect a certain clustering of wage rates rather than an even distribution over the possible range. The oligopolists may even agree to pay the same wage as a means of buttressing the price agreement. If they seek also to maximize their profits, the agreed wage will be A; but other motives may dictate selection of a higher wage.

Under the conditions assumed, then, the wages of firms operating under conditions of pure competition, monopolistic competition, or oligopoly with either free entrance or uncontrolled prices, will tend toward equality at A. Monopolies and members of oligopoly groups with closed entrance and controlled prices will also pay A if they wish to maximize profits; if they are willing to accept a lower level of profits, however, they can choose to pay wages above A by amounts varying with the position of their demand curves. Firms whose prices are set by government acting either as purchaser or regulator are still more likely to pay wages above A. Thus, in any labor market containing firms of these latter types, one would expect to find some dispersion of wage rates for comparable work.

Let us now consider the consequences of removing some of the assumptions made at the outset. Suppose, first, that a firm in a competitive industry is able, because of imperfections in the market for a factor other than labor, to purchase that factor more cheaply than its competitors.[1] Suppose further that this advantage is not open to would-be entrants to the industry. Then part or all of the surplus income accruing to the advantageously situated firm may, at the discretion of management, be transferred to labor through higher wages. Thus even firms subject to pure or monopolistic competition in product markets may have something of the monopolist's latitude with respect to wage rates.

Second, suppose that the labor market under consideration is only one of many, and that these markets have differing "minimum wages." This implies that movements of labor and capital are not sufficiently rapid to eliminate interarea wage

[1] This may mean purchase of a higher quality of a factor at the standard price rather than payment of a lower price for the same quality. It seems likely, for example, that especially able managers will receive less than their full contribution to production, particularly in a situation in which individual income-tax rates are high.

differences within the period of time taken into account. Now suppose the firms in a competitive industry are distributed among these markets in such a way that their minimum wages form a statistical array resembling the so-called "bulk-line cost curve." Then the price of the product will tend to settle at a level sufficient to cover the minimum wage of a firm at, say, the ninth quartile of the array. If costs other than wages are uniform throughout the industry, all firms below the ninth quartile will have some latitude with respect to wage rates. Each of these firms can pay anything between the minimum wage in its own area and the minimum wage of the "marginal" firm; the lower the minimum wage in a particular area, the wider the range of discretion of firms in that area. This situation is stable, of course, only if there are obstacles to new firms entering the industry in the areas with the lowest minimum wages; otherwise, the industry would become concentrated increasingly in those areas, and dispersion of wage rates arising from geographical dispersion of the industry would disappear. If one brings into the picture not one industry but a large number of industries, each with a somewhat different geographical distribution, then it is clear that each labor market in the economy may have its own pattern of interfirm wage differences, which will not be reproduced exactly in any other market.

The individual firm is caught between the area and the industry. Conditions within the area, particularly the wage levels of other firms, determine the minimum which it must pay. The wage rates of other firms in the industry, *ceteris paribus*, will determine the maximum which it can afford to pay. If the latter figure is less than the former, the firm will in time be forced out of operation; but if it is greater, the firm can be guided by the wage level either of the industry or the area. Developments in the industry may lead the firm to make wage changes independently of any developments in the local labor market. Indeed, for firms in competitive industries which are geographically dispersed, it appears that the industry is normally the dynamic influence in bringing about wage changes, while the influence of the local labor market is merely passive or permissive.

Third, let us admit the possibility that different firms in the same labor market may have different minimum wages. One reason for this is that wage differences which have persisted for some time become customary and workers tend to presume that they should continue. A wage rate which would be accepted if paid by a traditionally low wage firm may provoke a revolt if adopted suddenly by a high wage firm. Each firm thus has its own minimum wage which is related to its present and previous actual wage rates. These minima lie one above the other like steps on an escalator. The relative ranking of the various firms doubtless changes gradually over long periods of time, but at any one time it is rather firmly fixed in the minds of both workers and employers.[1] Any attempt by one firm to drop its wage rate below the minimum expected of it, or to retain the same wage rate when the wage escalator is moving upward, will cause serious labor unrest.

This circumstance helps to explain not only why wage differences persist but also why they may widen with the passage of time. Once a set of differentials has become customary, a management gains no credit with its workers by merely doing what is expected of it. It can add fresh luster to its reputation for generosity only by *increasing* its wage differential over other firms. But this new differential will in time become customary, and so on. The differentials presently existing in most United States labor markets are clearly too large to have been attained in one jump, and can only be understood as the outcome of some such historical process.

Under the assumptions made at the outset, one would expect to find in any locality a "prevailing rate" of wages, from which only monopolies or quasi-monopolies could deviate.

---

[1] Witness the large number of cases in which a firm requested the War Labor Board to approve a wage increase in order to enable it to maintain or restore its "historical position" in the area wage structure. Such requests were uniformly refused, and had to be refused under the wage stabilization policy. There can be no doubt, however, that this refusal frequently worked severe hardship on the firms involved.

When the three assumptions just discussed are relaxed, however, the likelihood of a "prevailing rate" is removed. There is now no reason why each firm in the market should not have a different wage rate. Moreover, there is no longer any reason to expect a clear relation between a firm's wage level and the type of product market in which it deals. The effect of differing types of product market, while still present, is mingled with the effect of conditions influencing each firm's cost position in its own industry—notably the wage levels of other areas in which rival producers are located, and the cost of factors other than labor to this firm as compared with others. Added to these factors affecting each firm's ability to pay are differences in managerial judgment concerning the wisdom of paying as much as one can. The actual wage structure of an area reflects the composite effect of these influences. The effect of each can be gauged only approximately and only through studies which reach beyond the area concerned to the cost-price structure of each industry represented in it.

With these considerations in mind, it is possible to suggest one or two reasons why a firm may choose to pay a higher wage than it has to at the moment. The firm is likely to be uncertain about the precise location of its wage minimum, particularly under dynamic conditions in which the minimum may change very frequently. If it can afford to do so, it is likely to "play safe" by paying somewhat more than its estimate of the minimum. Different firms may thus be at differing distances above their wage minima because of differences in the accuracy of their estimates and also because of differences in the safety margin which they feel able to afford.

The degree of uncertainty is increased if one takes into account a factor hitherto excluded from the discussion, viz., variations in individual efficiency. A reduction in wage rates will lead to a less than proportionate reduction in wage cost per efficiency unit of labor; for efficiency will fall both through a lowering of the grade of labor which the firm can recruit and through a reduction in the efficiency of those already employed. The wage level which would actually yield minimum cost per efficiency unit could perhaps be determined by successive wage reductions. But since such experimentation is dangerous, it may not be undertaken unless the pressure of competition compels it, and the firm may continue at a level of wage costs somewhat above what is strictly necessary,

A monopoly or a closed oligopoly group may pay more than the minimum wage in order to render the industry less attractive to potential competitors. It has frequently been pointed out that a monopolist may for this reason charge a price below that which would maximize profits. But profits can be held at a moderate level by paying high wages instead of by charging low prices. Provided potential competitors take the wage level of established firms as an indication of what they would have to pay to secure labor, this technique may be highly effective.

Payment of a relatively high wage may also simplify the problems of personnel management by facilitating recruiting of labor, stabilizing the working force, stimulating efficiency, improving labor cooperation with management, and so on. Maximizing profits is hard work. Some sacrifice of profits in order to make the job of management easier may be perfectly "economic" action from the standpoint of the managers, though not from the standpoint of the owners.

The argument of this section has been directed toward explaining the long-run persistence of differences in wage *levels* within a local labor market. But it is also relevant to the problem of how wage *changes* occur and how changes in one labor market are transmitted to others. Under usual assumptions about labor market structure one would expect that, during a cyclical upswing, wages would rise in an area *only* when full employment had been reached. The area would then begin to draw labor from other areas and, as full employment was reached in more and more areas, wage increases would become general throughout the economy. During periods of cyclical decline this process would be thrown into reverse. In either case, local labor markets would be linked together primarily by interarea movements of labor, and the rapidity with which wage changes were transmitted throughout the system would depend on the rapidity of this movement.

This sort of model, however, does not explain the fact that wage rates frequently rise in an area while heavy unemployment still exists,[1] and that wage impulses are transmitted within and between labor markets much more rapidly than could be explained by actual or even potential movement of labor. These facts can perhaps be more nearly explained by the considerations set forth above. Suppose that the leading firm of a "controlled oligopoly," located in labor market A, raises wages—perhaps as prelude to or aftermath of a price increase. The wage increase is followed by another member of the industry, located in labor market B. This action will raise the estimates which other firms in area B make of their own minimum wage; as demand conditions permit, some of them will make increases to maintain their historical position in the wage structure. Thus the whole escalator of minimum wages in the area moves upward, carrying actual wage rates along with it. But the firms in area B have competitors in areas C, D, etc., some of whom will be influenced by the wage changes in B, and so on. A symmetrical explanation can be offered for the transmission of wage decreases.[2]

Thus, through industry linkages, a wage change in one area may be transmitted rapidly to distant and apparently unrelated areas. This need not involve any actual or even threatened movement of labor between areas. Interarea movement of labor appears indeed to perform, not its traditional function

---

[1] Indeed, statistics of average hourly earnings by industry indicate that wage rates tend to rise first and fall last in industries in which cyclical unemployment is greatest. See the discussion of this point in John T. Dunlop, *Wage Determination Under Trade Unions* (New York, Macmillan Co., 1944) pp. 130-43. It would be interesting to make a similar analysis on an area basis, but wage statistics are not now organized in such a way as to permit this.

[2] The only important difference in the two cases is that the firm initiating a wage decrease is likely to be a member of a competitive industry. Dunlop's observation that "declines in product prices and not unemployment constitute the effective downward pressure on wage structures" (*op. cit.*, p. 146) is entirely consistent with what has been said here.

of equalizing wage rates, but the quite different function of equalizing unemployment ratios in different areas. During recession and depression labor mobility declines greatly and, because of differences in the cyclical variability of different industries, unemployment piles up more rapidly in some areas than in others. As recovery gets under way, movement sets in once more toward areas in which the unemployment ratio is relatively low.[1] But the areas in which unemployment is low are not necesarily those in which wage rates are high.

Industry linkages have undoubtedly been greatly strengthened, particularly in manufacturing, by the growth of collective bargaining. The wage level and wage structure of the unionized firm is oriented forcibly toward the industry pattern even where this involves considerable divergence from the area pattern. Wage changes are transmitted rapidly throughout industries dispersed from New England to the Pacific Coast. When one considers that the wage strategies of several of the major industrial unions are coordinated increasingly through the CIO, it is easy to understand why the genesis and transmission of wage movements need have nothing to do with actual or virtual mobility of labor.

CONCLUSION

The wide gap between the accepted models of the labor market and the actual behavior of wage rates and employment has inhibited systematic research in this field. This chapter has attempted to advance hypotheses around which the wealth of data available in any local labor market may profitably be organized. It has been suggested that attention should be concentrated primarily on the supply conditions of labor to the individual firm, the characteristics of the product market in which each firm deals and its cost position relative to other firms in its industry, the considerations influencing the exercise of managerial discretion with respect to wage rates, and the

---

[1] See on this point the studies of the Oxford Institute for Economic Research, reported in *Oxford Economic Papers,* October, 1938, and September, 1940.

way in which changes are transmitted among firms and labor market areas. It is important also to make accurate measurements of wage rates, appropriately defined, and to extend these measurements over as long a period as possible.

PART THREE

Labor and Full Employment

CHAPTER TWELVE

Trade Union Policy Under Full Employment[1]

by *Eugene Forsey*

I DO NOT propose to discuss here the problems of the transition from war to peace, or how unions can help to get full employment in the first place. I am concerned with the more fundamental problem of the place of unions in a society that has achieved full employment in peacetime, without sacrificing any of the essential freedoms, and that wants to keep both full employment and freedom. I am assuming that full employment involves planning. I am assuming also that unions are not just nuisances but, in one form or another, permanent and desirable social institutions. Can we plan production without planning wages, hours, and conditions of work? If full employment involves planning these also, where do the unions come in? Must they sacrifice their traditional freedom to bargain collectively on behalf of their members, and suffer a sea-change into something, if not rich and strange, at least very different from what they have ever been before? Or can the community do this part of its planning through collective bargaining? Can we continue to have purely sectional bargaining, plant by plant, industry by industry, or must the various unions act as a unit according to a general wage policy laid down by some central organization? Must trade unionism change its functions, or its structure, or both?

---

[1] The problem with which this essay deals raises issues that are basic to the very existence of the trade union movement, and on such issues a mere trade union civil servant has neither the right nor the power to commit anyone but himself, and even himself perhaps, only rather tentatively.

Most of the essay appeared in the August, 1946 issue of the *Canadian Journal of Economics and Political Science*, XII, 343-55.

These questions have been much more widely discussed in Britain than in the United States and Canada. If we mean business when we talk of full employment, especially full employment in a free society, it is high time such matters were thoroughly discussed and analyzed. For they are not by any means minor questions. Mrs. Wootton goes so far as to say that "Of all the possible points of conflict between conscious planning of priorities and traditional freedoms, the regulation of wages is likely to prove the most stormy"; [1] and of course in this context "wages" include hours and conditions of work —not only what is paid, but what it is paid for. In the United States and Canada, freedom to bargain collectively can scarcely be called one of the "traditional" freedoms; for most workers it is still a recent, hard won, and imperfect conquest. But it is none the less prized for that, and it will not be easily surrendered, even as the price of full employment. For of all the freedoms, this is perhaps the one that comes closest home to the ordinary worker. He knows from experience that without it he can have little freedom from want or fear, and not much freedom of speech about some of the things that matter most to him. But he knows also that collective bargaining cannot prevent depressions and mass unemployment; and he knows what depressions and mass unemployment do to freedom from want and fear and freedom of speech. Must he choose between free collective bargaining and full employment? Or can he have both?

A full employment economy has three main labor problems: (1) a general level of wages which will not involve a continuous process of wages and prices chasing each other up in an inflationary spiral; (2) relative levels of wages in the different industries and occupations which will distribute the labor supply in accordance with the requirements of the national plan; and (3) mobility of labor so that the whole plan will not be dislocated by a surplus of jobs in some industries and places

[1] Barbara Wootton, *Freedom Under Planning* (Chapel Hill, N. C., University of North Carolina Press, 1945), p. 102. This and subsequent quotations reprinted by permission of the University of North Carolina Press. Copyright, 1945, by the University of North Carolina Press.

and a surplus of workers in others. Each of these, and especially the first two, raises important problems of trade union policy.

GENERAL LEVEL OF WAGES

In considering the general level of wages, we may perhaps best begin with one point on which there appears to be wide agreement: full employment can be maintained only if there is adequate effective demand for consumer goods. High wages are one way of assuring this. But high wages do not fall like the gentle rain from heaven. They are largely, though not of course entirely, the result of trade union action.

It may be objected that, especially in the United States and Canada, where farmers form a large proportion of the population, and where the majority of the wage earners are still unorganized, unions have only a very limited power to ensure adequate effective demand for consumer goods. This view, however, overlooks three factors. In the first place, unions raise the wages of unorganized workers as well as organized. Nonunion, or even anti-union, employers have to give some increases to keep from losing labor and to head off the unions. In the second place, unions have done, and are doing, a good deal to induce governments to adopt social security measures which raise and stabilize consumer expenditures generally. In the third place, high industrial wages, if combined with high productivity and reasonable prices, mean higher incomes for farmers, as war experience has shown. In both the United States and Canada, therefore, trade unionism can be a powerful force in raising and maintaining consumer purchasing power. It cannot do the job by itself, and what it can do may, as we shall see, be largely nullified by other factors. But what it can do makes it a positive factor for full employment, and there can be little doubt that if it disappeared, or were shorn of the power to bargain collectively for better wages, hours, and conditions of work, the task of maintaining effective consumer demand would be harder to accomplish.

It is implicit in this argument that the general level of wages must at least keep pace with increasing productivity of labor, and it is generally agreed that if it does no more, no difficulties will arise. But there is, of course, no guarantee that unions will keep their demands within these limits. On the contrary, it is highly probable that they will not. For to do so would be to admit that the present distribution of income between wage earners and other classes is right and must not be changed. Few, if any, unions will subscribe to that proposition. All of them will be much more inclined to the counterproposition that in every industry the distribution ought to be changed in favor of the wage earners; and they will be practically unanimous that in certain particular industries the existing distribution constitutes, to use the language of a Canadian order-in-council, a "gross inequality and gross injustice" which can only be rectified by wage increases far exceeding any increase in productivity since any given base year. Nor are such opinions mere self-interest or prejudice. As Lord Beveridge says, an increase in the wage earner's share of the total product of industry "is desirable from the economic as well as from the moral point of view"; [1] and even the highly conservative League of Nations Delegation on Economic Depressions, in warning that "inflationary processes are likely to begin whenever wages increase more than productivity," adds the "important" qualification, "unless . . . excessive profits are being earned and the profit margin can be cut without hindering enterprise." [2]

There is, however, general agreement that wage increases greater than the increases in productivity raise serious problems. Full employment makes the labor market "a seller's market rather than a buyer's market," and this "will perma-

[1] Lord Beveridge, *Full Employment in a Free Society* (New York, W. W. Norton and Co., 1945), p. 200. This and subsequent quotations reprinted by permission of W. W. Norton and Company, Inc. Copyright, 1945, by the publishers. See also Kenneth B. Williams, "Employment and Wage Policies," in the Federal Reserve Board's *Postwar Economic Studies,* No. 4 (May, 1946), p. 34.

[2] *Economic Stability in the Post-War World* (Geneva, 1945), p. 204.

nently and markedly increase the bargaining strength of labor." [1] "The fear of under-cutting of wages by non-union unemployed is absent. At the same time, any one employer can only increase his staff by reducing the staff of another, and he may try to entice labor by offering higher money wages." [2] On the face of it, this looks like a perfectly delightful situation for labor. But actual experience would probably lead the wage earners and their unions at least to echo the words of Mr. Pepys about his "new crucifix": "mighty fine, but not so fine as I expected." They might discover that it was not fine at all. Traditional sectional collective bargaining, union by union, plant by plant, industry by industry, would undoubtedly raise money wages. But unless there were effective price control and an appropriate taxation policy, the indirect consequences of such bargaining might snatch away most of the gains. To quote Lord Beveridge again:

Particular wage demands which exceed what employers are able to pay with their existing prices and which force a raising of prices, may bring gains to the workers of the industry concerned, but they will do so at the expense of all other workers, whose real wages fall owing to the rise in prices. The other workers will naturally try to restore the position, by putting forward demands of their own. There is a real danger that sectional wage bargaining, pursued without regard to its effects upon prices, may lead to a vicious spiral of inflation, with money wages chasing prices and without any gain in real wages for the working class as a whole. . . . inflationary developments which bestow no benefits upon the working class; spell expropriation for the old age pensioner and the small rentier; and which endanger the very policy of full employment whose maintenance is a vital common interest of all wage-earners.[3]

This is oversimplification. Even without price control, sectional bargaining, as Mr. Worswick has pointed out, may lead to a small permanent rise in real wages, though of course at

[1] Beveridge, *op. cit.*, p. 199.
[2] G. D. N. Worswick, "The Stability and Flexibility of Full Employment," in *The Economics of Full Employment: Six Studies in Applied Economics* (Oxford University Institute of Economics, Oxford, Blackwell, 1944), p. 63.
[3] Beveridge, *op. cit.*, p. 199.

the expense of people with fixed or slowly rising incomes.[1] But there is no doubt that Beveridge's statement of the position is substantially correct. Is there any remedy?

Five, not of course mutually exclusive, appear to have been suggested: (1) price control; (2) coordination of union wage policies by the central labor organizations; (3) where unions and employers are unable to reach agreement, submission of the wage question to arbitration, the award to be final and binding, though without legal penalties for strikes or lockouts in breach of it; (4) as a correlative to (3), acceptance by employers of an obligation to put all the facts as to profits, costs, and margins unreservedly at the disposal of the arbitrators and their expert staffs; (5) self-restraint by the unions.

Price control is clearly indispensable. As Lord Beveridge says, "It would be unreasonable to expect the unions to abstain from using their bargaining strength to the full, unless the Government can give them some assurance that it is pursuing a policy of stable prices." [2] The General Council of the British Trades Union Congress was very emphatic on this point, in its answer to Beveridge's questionnaire on the subject in 1943:

As regards the Trade Union Movement, there is no need to fear such a spiral if the Government can convince the Movement that in genuine pursuit of a policy of full employment it is determined to take all other steps that are necessary to control prices and can convince the Trade Union Movement of the need to secure equivalent guarantees that wage movements will not be such as to upset the system of price control. In those circumstances it would be the duty of the Trade Union Movement to give suitable guarantees about wage settlements and reasonable assurances that such guarantees would be generally observed. . . . We would in all cases insist that reliance must be placed upon the ability of the Unions to secure the general compliance of their members and that the possibility of individuals or small groups refusing to conform to general settlements should not be made the excuse for the imposition of legislative sanctions. Existing statutory provisions regarding the observance of wage rates, impose upon employers *only* the

[1] Worswick, *op. cit.*, pp. 64-65. See also Charles O. Hardy, "Prospects of Inflation in the Transition Period," *Postwar Economic Studies, op. cit.*, pp. 24-25.

[2] Beveridge, *op. cit.*, pp. 202-3.

obligation to observe those rates *as a minimum.* We should expect a continuance of statutory provisions of this kind and the making of similar provisions for the general enforcement of measures of control over margins, costs, profits, etc.[1]

Lord Beveridge proposes that price control should concentrate on essential goods and services and commodities in short supply.[2] Mr. Worswick goes farther. There are, he suggests, two methods of control. The first calls for: (*a*) pegging the cost of living by the use of subsidies; (*b*) increasing income tax faster than wages "to cover the increase in the cost of subsidies and to allow for the fact that a given amount of tax will not reduce consumption *pro tanto,* because it falls partly on savings"; and (*c*) designing taxation so that it will not "interfere with the incentive to private investment."[3] The second involves freezing all prices by law. Assuming for the moment the practicability of this, he points out that employers will now be forced either to reduce real costs or sacrifice part of their profits. Marginal producers will be driven out of business; the rest will expand their production, taking up slack in their production organizations and probably cutting down on selling costs, notably competitive advertising, for which full employment, by guaranteeing a steady market, will have reduced the need. If this does not absorb the increase in labor costs, then there will be a redistribution of gross income, a shift from profits to wages; this will lead to increased total effective demand, which of course cannot be satisfied and must therefore be reduced again by increasing progressive taxation or cutting deficit spending on public investment. He favors a combination of the two methods, "operated together industry by industry in such a way as to produce the over-all stability of the price level."[4]

[1] General Council of the Trades Union Congress, *Post-War Reconstruction: Interim Report* (London, 1944), pp. 30-31.

[2] Beveridge, *op. cit.,* p. 203.

[3] Worswick, *op. cit.,* pp. 65-66.

[4] *Ibid.,* pp. 66-68. On possible methods of price control, see the very interesting and detailed proposals in *Employment Policy and Organization of Industry after the War,* a report of conferences at Nuffield College, Oxford, by employers, unionists, and economists (London, 1943).

Both Lord Beveridge and Mr. Worswick, however, insist that a policy of constant increases in money wages accompanied by price control will produce the desired results (a stable full employment economy and redistribution of income in favor of wage earners) only if the unions can achieve a unified wage policy and strategy. Sectional bargaining by particular unions will continue, and will "obtain relative advantages for the members" of the unions concerned. But it will have to be supplemented by pressure for

increases in taxation on non-wage earners (to finance subsidies and to control total effective demand), in order to permit of a rise in the real consumption of workers. Clearly this second function cannot be fulfilled upon sectional lines. . . . Stabilization of full employment depends upon hitting an *average* rate of increase of wages which is not more than can . . . be compensated by increases in taxation on non-wage earners. It is improbable that the outcome of a multitude of separate wage-bargains will prove to be just right. . . . It is desirable that sectional policies should be coordinated sufficiently to ensure that the *average* rate of increase in money wages is not more (nor less) than can be compensated by increases in taxation upon non-wage earners. Ideally, a central body, presumably the T.U.C., would draw up a scheme of priorities for wage increases. Such a central body might, for example, exert greater pressure for scaling-up the wages of the lowest-paid workers, than, say, for further improving the standards of the relatively well-to-do skilled workers. It would be for the Unions themselves to determine the degree of freedom which can be left to individual Unions for modifications of wage-rates within the general framework. In preparing its wage policy the central body will want to know, and have to know, more about the financial position of industry than has been made known in the past, and this may involve certain institutional modifications in the conduct of industry.[1]

In other words, in a full employment economy, the unions will have to superimpose upon their traditional, sectional, direct bargaining with employers for money wages a new type of indirect bargaining through government for redistribution of real income. Wage bargaining will become, in part, as Mr.

[1] Worswick, *op. cit.*, pp. 68-70.

Worswick says, "a political problem . . . to be settled on a political plane." [1]

If Lord Beveridge and Mr. Worswick are right, then the trade union movement, even in Britain, and still more in the United States and Canada, will have to undertake a drastic revision of both structure and policy. Beveridge is optimistic about the prospect in Britain. Organized labor there, he says, "has sufficently demonstrated its sense of citizenship and responsibility to justify the expectation that it will evolve, in its own manner, the machinery by which a better co-ordinated wage policy can be carried through." [2] He may be right, especially now that Britain has a Labor government. But it is significant that the TUC reply to his questionnaire, already quoted, says nothing about "coordination"; that it is vague and noncommittal about the means by which the "guarantees" and the "reasonable assurances" that they will be generally observed (surely a most curious use of the two terms?) are to be translated into fact. It is also significant that, despite the efforts of the General Council over a number of years, comparatively little has been done even to bring together the often numerous unions in related trades. Mrs. Wootton, certainly no ignorant, incompetent, or unfriendly critic, is by no means as optimistic as Beveridge. She points out that the TUC is purely consultative and advisory, and that it has no power to "make its affiliated unions toe the line in wage policy," and she questions whether it seriously wants any effective power of the sort.[3]

None the less, despite the jealously guarded economy of the particular unions, there is some ground for sharing Beveridge's hope for British unionism. The British unions are, with minor exceptions, united in a single Congress. They have long experience. They have large resources, not least in the way of expert advisers. They enjoy an unquestioned position

[1] *Ibid.*, pp. 70-71.
[2] Beveridge, *op. cit.*, p. 200.
[3] Wootton, *op. cit.*, pp. 105-6.

in the British community. They are accustomed to political action. They have great political power.

Canadian unions, on the other hand, are divided among three central organizations, and some of the most important do not belong to any central organization. Most Canadian unions have only a relatively short experience. Their resources are far from large. They have very few expert advisers. They do not enjoy an unquestioned position in the Canadian community. They are less accustomed to political action and have far less political power than their British counterparts. On the other hand, the unions in the Canadian Congress of Labour at least have established a wage policy coordinating committee. This indicates a recognition that some unified planning of grand strategy is necessary, though of course this committee is not dealing with the problems which would arise under full employment.

The position in the United States is different from that in either Britain or Canada. American unions, like Canadian, are divided, though the added complication of a Catholic union movement is absent. Many of the large American unions are still young. But most of them have large resources and fair-sized staffs of expert advisers. Their position in the community, though still less well established than that of the British unions, is better than in Canada. They have had some experience of a kind in political action, and they enjoy very considerable political influence. The CIO unions have been fairly successful in coordinating their wage policies, though, as in Canada, they have not had to deal with the problems of a full employment economy.

In both the United States and Canada, therefore, the chances of the unions achieving a unified general wage policy do not look very bright, though it is well to remember that by the time either country really establishes stable full employment the unions may well have changed considerably. The climate of public opinion in which they must operate may also have changed. At present, in the United States, as Dr. Braunthal says, "public opinion . . . hardly seems ready to go very far in approving the continuation or establishment of price controls, price subsidies or very large public investments." [1] This is largely true of Canada also, though both Canadian unions and the Canadian public generally have begun to emancipate themselves from the doctrinaire devotion to "free enterprise" which still holds most Americans in its thrall. The prospects of success in Canada would, however, be better if the government were able and willing to adopt a policy of permanent price control, instead of being constitutionally debarred from it and consumed with eagerness to get rid of all existing price controls as fast as it can.

If the unions accept the policy of coordination, individual unions, like individual nations, will have to sacrifice their "sovereignty" to save their essential freedoms. They will have to give their central organizations real power in matters of common concern. They will have to assume new functions. In Canada at least, they will have to provide themselves with a much larger, and highly competent, staff of expert advisers. But the union movement as a whole will still be free. It will not have become the creature of the state or the puppet of the employer, private or public. It will not have been reduced to the status of a mere advocate or adviser. In short, it will still be doing, and still able to do, though in part by new methods and much more effectively, the job it has always tried to do.

Acceptance of the proposal for arbitration with the award final and binding would probably be less satisfactory to both the unions and the community. It would not deprive the unions of the opportunity to bargain with the employers, but it would seriously restrict their powers in such bargaining; and where the question did go to arbitration, the unions would become mere advocates pleading a case. This is an important and socially necessary function; it is one of the functions which unions already perform; and it is possible that at least in certain industries and services it is a function with which some unions will be satisfied. But it will only be accepted where

---

[1] A. Braunthal, "Wage Policy and Full Employment," *International Postwar Problems*, III (January, 1946), 48.

the unions are either very weak or very firmly established or subject to special laws which prevent them from using their economic strength to the full. In other words, its application is likely to be patchy. There is also the possibility that under this system both unions and employers will adopt the maxim, "Agree with thine adversary quickly whiles thou art in the way with him, lest he deliver thee to the judge"; it may be profitable for the two parties to agree on a mutual exploitation of the consumer. This would mean industrial peace in the industries concerned; but it might be bought at a pretty heavy price. Moreover, even if arbitration were very generally accepted, unless the arbitrators thoroughly understood the necessities of the situation and the type of wage settlement required to make the full employment economy work, the results might bear no resemblance at all to a rational wage policy. Arbitrators working only on the traditional basis of what is "fair" and "reasonable," or what workers in comparable industries or jobs are getting, or a health and decency or minimum subsistence budget, or the particular industry's ability to pay, will produce satisfactory results only by accident, because they will be shooting at the wrong mark. It need hardly be added that arbitrators of the right kind will not be too easy to find. From the unions' point of view, it would certainly seem better to accept the self-discipline involved in the policy of coordination rather than the degree of outside control involved in the policy of arbitration.

Undoubtedly the policy of arbitration could not work at all unless the employers accepted the obligation to make all the relevant facts available to the arbitrators. Indeed, as Mr. Worswick hints, it is doubtful whether the policy of coordination will work either unless the employers are prepared to furnish far more information than they usually do now. In view of the attitude of some leading American employers in the recent past, this is not a very hopeful prospect for the United States; and in Canada the matter is further complicated by the fact that some of the largest corporations, being wholly owned subsidiaries of American firms, do not publish any financial statements at all. However, it must again be noted that on this continent we appear to be still a long way from a stable economy of full employment, and that by the time we get there industry, like unions, and like public opinion, may have changed a good deal.

The policy of self-restraint by the unions is Dr. Braunthal's specific, and he offers it only for the United States and in view of the present state of public opinion there. "Under these circumstances," he says, "restraint in wage demands would appear a safer way of maintaining a system of full employment than an increase in governmental intervention beyond the extent to which it would be needed to keep a system of full employment working." Despite the fact that under full employment excessively high wage rates could no longer be checked by unemployment he is optimistic about the prospects for union self-restraint. First, there are "patriotic motives . . . and . . . pressure of public opinion." Secondly, there is "the feeling of economic security": with "extreme fluctuations of business conditions the workers' demands for higher wages in upswing periods stem to a certain extent from their desire to make good for their income losses in the preceding depression period and to profit from the rare and short-lived opportunities of boom conditions. In a full-employment economy, this important motive for excessive wage demands will be eliminated." Thirdly, in each particular industry there would still be "economic penalties and sanctions for excessive wage demands." Too high a level in a particular industry "may cause a permanent shrinkage in the volume of employment in that industry, which in turn would threaten part of its workers with the loss of their jobs, temporary unemployment, and later a certain down-grading, that is to say, employment in other industries for which they would be less well trained and in which they would get lower wages. Nor would such a wage policy lie in the material interests of the labor unions involved. No union . . . likes to see its own basis narrowed down by a shrinkage of the industry under its control."[1]

[1] *Ibid.*, pp. 48-49.

Dr. Braunthal tempers his optimism, however, by the admission that employers and workers may not behave "in accordance with the rules of rational wage policy." In that event, the problem would arise "whether proper wage policy should be secured by governmental wage control in extreme cases or whether governmental controls should not rather be applied in the field of prices and investments. The decision in such a dilemma," he concludes, "would ultimately depend on the distribution of political power." [1]

To this it is only necessary to add that when government control of wages enters, free collective bargaining on that subject disappears, and only the most urgent and evident public necessity will induce British, American, or Canadian unions to accept such control.

Can we count on the unions to act reasonably as a general rule? That is the essential question. If we can, then the problem of the general level of wages in a full employment economy will probably be solved without any serious diminution of unions' freedom.

There are, however, at least three serious threats to a unified wage policy or a policy of self-restraint by individual unions. They all arise from the fact that at present, as Mr. Hardy says, "The decision whether to demand wages so high as to force higher prices is made by each industrial union separately; the price consequences are spread over the whole community. No union's successful demands will raise its own members' living costs by nearly as much as it [sic] will increase their incomes." [2]

Some unions might be dominated by men who understood little and cared less about the dangers of an inflationary spiral or the shrinkage of their own industries, or who, even if they saw the dangers, might feel that it was still "good policy for each union to try to get its increases first and make them bigger than the average." [3] In industries with an inelastic

[1] *Ibid.,* p. 50.
[2] *Op. cit.,* p. 24.
[3] Hardy, *loc. cit.*

demand, the danger of shrinkage would be small and remote, especially under conditions of full employment generally,[1] and a strong union might feel confident of its ability to keep its own wages always one jump ahead of prices. Such unions would not be likely to accept either a unified wage policy worked out by the labor movement as a whole or a policy of self-restraint. On the contrary, they would probably go out for all they could get for their own craft or industry regardless of the effect on other workers, regardless of the effect on costs of production, the cost of living, or the maintenance of full employment.

Other unions might be dominated by men who believed that only revolution could bring full employment. Such men would look on inflationary spirals and other dislocations of the existing economic system with equanimity. That wage increases beyond a certain point might lead to the collapse of capitalism would not deter them from demanding such increases; rather the opposite. Unions of this kind also, though for different reasons, would be likely to go in for a "devil-take-the-hindmost" scramble for higher wages.

If even one or two important unions did this, and won substantial success, there would be strong pressure from within the others to make them do the same. If their leaders resisted, they might be thrown out of office, or pushed aside by "unofficial," rank-and-file revolts such as have occurred recently in several British unions. This is the third and most serious threat to a unified wage policy or a policy of self-restraint.

Can these threats be met? It would be rash to prophesy; but my own opinion, based on an admittedly limited experience, is that if the public, including the union public, is sufficiently educated; if the government shows that it really means to get and keep full employment; if it controls prices; if it takes the unions into its confidence, and gives them a real share in the formulation of its whole industrial policy; and if the employers accept unions ungrudgingly and wholeheart-

[1] See Hardy, *op. cit.*, p. 25.

edly, instead of dreaming of the lost delights of the open shop and individual bargaining, and scheming to bring them back; then the unions will as a rule act reasonably. Union members and union leaders are on the whole pretty decent human beings, and about as intelligent as other people, and, like other people, will respond to decent treatment. But, like other people, they hate to be lied to or swindled.

APPROPRIATE WAGE RELATIONSHIPS

So far we have been considering the problem of the general level of wages. But the problem of relative levels in different industries is no less important. Indeed, Mrs. Wootton makes hardly more than a passing reference to the former, and devotes almost her whole attention to the mobility of labor (a subject to which we shall return presently) and the question, whether free collective bargaining can "regulate wages and conditions of employment in such a way as to match labour supply with the requirements of public plans." [1]

Here also there is no guarantee that the results of a series of sectional bargains will come out "just right." Even if the sectional bargaining is modified by the policy of coordination, and that policy produces the "right" general level of wages, it does not follow that the wages in particular industries or occupations will be just high enough to attract just the number of workers required, neither too many nor too few; and this will be just as true under complete public ownership or a mixed economy as it is now. Even the modified, "coordinated" form of free collective bargaining may result in rates which will entice workers away from jobs of high social priority to jobs of low social priority, and so frustrate some of the most important of the community's plans. It may also result in rates which will keep people hanging about industries to which they are redundant, and so help to create and perpetuate pockets of unemployment in particular industries or places. (This latter effect, however, can be better dealt with by other means than changes in the wage rates. We shall consider it in

[1] Wootton, *op. cit.*, p. 113.

a moment or so, when we are dealing with mobility of labor.)

Mrs. Wootton concludes that it is quite hopeless to rely on anything like traditional, sectional collective bargaining to bring about the right distribution of labor. This is not the fault of the unions. They exist to look after the interests of their members, and "They are no more to be blamed if they do this job, and this job only, than a lawyer engaged for the defense is to be blamed if he does not urge upon the Court the social importance of imposing an adequate penalty upon his client. . . . It is the business of a Union to . . . put sectional interest first. . . . These sectional societies are doing an important job in looking after interests which might easily be overridden or neglected if there were not such organized channels through which their claims might be heard."[1] But the fact remains that:

Where wages are settled by free collective bargaining, such factors as the strength, or degree of monopoly, enjoyed by the organizations on both sides, together with the skill of the negotiators, must necessarily play a big part in pushing rates up here, or down there. These influences will themselves operate within the limits of a certain social and economic environment (the most powerful Union or the cleverest negotiator cannot perform miracles); and that environment will in turn be shaped, on the one hand, by external economic circumstances like the rise and fall of demand for particular products, or the coming and going of different techniques of production, and, on the other hand, by the immense weight of conservatism which overhangs all our notions of what different skills and types of work ought to be paid. None of this has anything to do with the rational regulation of wages in accordance with the labor demands of a determinate production plan.[2]

In effect this means that conscious determination of production priorities implies also conscious regulation of relative wage rates. There must in fact be a plan for wages.[3]

How is it to be worked out? There would seem to be four possible methods: (1) government regulation; (2) arbitra-

---

[1] *Ibid.*, p. 107.
[2] *Ibid.*, p. 108.
[3] *Ibid.*, p. 104.

tion; (3) a further development of the policy of coordination by the unions themselves; and (4) self-restraint by the unions.

The first could, and in a democratic society presumably would, include discussions by the official wage-fixing body with the unions before fixing or changing wage rates. Some people might call this a form of collective bargaining. But, as Mrs. Wootton observes, "if the plans are to be fulfilled, the discussion must be conducted on terms which guarantee that the employing side is bound in the last resort to win every time: which is not what is generally understood in this country by free collective bargaining." [1] Under either government regulation or arbitration, also, the unions might negotiate with the employers (private or public) "the allocation between various grades and skills of a planned total wage fund for each industry," [2] but this again is not what is generally understood by free collective bargaining either in Britain or in any other western country.

The method of government regulation would abolish genuine collective bargaining and would probably involve an attempt to impose legal penalties for breach of the regulations which it would be difficult, if not impossible, to enforce. The method of arbitration to settle relative wage levels is open to much the same objections as the same method to settle the general wage level, unless, of course, it is made compulsory by law, when it becomes just a form of government regulation. The further development of the method of coordination to provide also for the right distribution of labor supply would seem to be the best solution of the problem, provided the unions can be persuaded to accept it.

The method of self-restraint has certain possibilities. To quote Mrs. Wootton again:

If we retain completely free collective bargaining, we should have somehow to induce a quite revolutionary change in the attitude of the parties to those bargains. It would, moreover, be a change which would completely do away with bargaining in the present

[1] *Ibid.*
[2] *Ibid.*, p. 118.

sense of a tussle of economic strength and wits; and which would do violence to the fundamental *raison d'être* of the organizations which now make these bargains. Trade Unions, and their counterparts on the employers' side, exist, as we have said, to get all they can for their members. They would be turned upside down and inside out, if they renounced this function in favor of the task of helping to regulate wages and conditions of employment in such a way as to match labor supply with the requirements of public plans.

Conceivably, since freedom of collective bargaining is much cherished in this country, the best way of retaining this freedom, as the scope of economic planning extends, would be frankly to invite the co-operation of the Unions in their own metamorphosis in this way. The success of any such plan (which looks impossible on paper) would be entirely dependent upon a large dose of goodwill, commonsense and understanding. It would be one of those cases in which a freedom was retained on condition that it was exercised with exceptional discretion. Not all plans that look impossible on paper are unworkable in practice. On paper it is impossible that the British Commonwealth, at least since the Statute of Westminster, should have hung together as long as it has. But it has.[1]

The fact of the matter is that as yet we have almost no experience to go on either in regard to the general wage level or relative wage levels under full employment in a free society. We have never had stable full employment in peacetime; and wartime experience, like Russian, though suggestive, cannot be conclusive. British experience in the next few years will be highly instructive. But it will offer only partial guidance to those countries which are determined to preserve a private enterprise system as nearly unsullied as may be, and the very special difficulties of Britain's economic position may further reduce its applicability on this side of the Atlantic, particularly in the United States.

DISTRIBUTION OF THE LABOR SUPPLY

The question of mobility of labor is one with which Lord Beveridge and the League Delegation on Economic Depressions also are much preoccupied. With the rise of new

[1] *Ibid.*, pp. 113-14.

industries and the decline of old ones, it is perfectly possible to have enough jobs for everybody and yet to have large pockets of unemployment: a shortage of jobs in some industries and some places, and a shortage of men in others. With the increasingly rapid pace of technological change, this problem is likely to become more, rather than less, serious. The men and the jobs have to be brought together. One way is to bring the jobs to the men, by controlling the location of industry. Lord Beveridge rightly lays great emphasis on this, and it is even more important in the United States and Canada than in Britain. But it is, as Beveridge recognizes, not always feasible, and it does not touch the problem of mobility between industries. Even the most Beveridgean of governments, therefore, would have to take steps also to get the men to the jobs, in other words, to encourage mobility of labor.

Unions can encourage mobility of labor in several ways. (a) They can make it easy for members to transfer from union to union. This is obviously much less necessary if the prevailing type of union is nationwide and industrial, rather than local and craft; and where transfers are necessary, they can be carried out more easily if the various unions all belong to the same central organization. (b) They can put pressure on the government to provide for retraining for men whose skills have become redundant and to provide financial aid for workers who must move to other localities. This latter is, of course, of special importance on this continent, where the expenses of movement are very high. (c) They can accept, as the British TUC is prepared to do,[1] limitations upon unemployment insurance designed to make sure that workers in a declining industry or area do not obstinately cling to that industry or area for an indefinite period, refusing to take other work in the same area or elsewhere even at standard rates and under standard conditions. (d) They can accept control of juvenile employment through the compulsory use of the official employment exchanges for all engagements of boys and girls up to eighteen. "Controlling the flow of adaptable juve-

[1] Trades Union Congress, *Post-War Reconstruction, op. cit.*, pp. 31-32.

niles," says Lord Beveridge, "is the simple, painless way of adjusting the total supply of labour in each industry to changes in demand; in all normal cases it should enable a contraction of demand in a particular industry to be met by checking new entrants without displacing existing workmen." [1] (e) They can accept compulsory notification of all engagements, possibly of all vacancies. Mrs. Wootton declares roundly, for reasons which are not clear to me, that the latter "would necessarily involve industrial conscription"; [2] but even she can find no fault with the former. [3] (f) They can press for higher wages in the expanding industries. (g) In declining industries, they can refrain from pressing for wages higher than the industries can afford to pay (with or without subsidies), or, alternatively, can accept limitation of entry into such industries and so avoid the necessity of relative or absolute wage reductions. Limitation of entry would seem to be the more sensible policy. As Mrs. Wootton says, if there is a 10 per cent surplus of labor in some industry, the other policy "demands a relative reduction in the wages, not only of the surplus 10 per cent, but of all the workers employed in the industry. In a prosperous and expanding economy we might . . . hope that 'relative reduction' will generally mean nothing worse than staying put where you are, while others rise. Even so, since 90 per cent of the workers in [the] industry are, by definition, wanted where they are just as much as ever they were, it seems a little hard that their wages should be held back by the necessity of inducing those who are now superfluous to leave." [4]

Unions can discourage mobility by doing the opposite of all these things, and also by attempting to maintain restrictive rules and practices which, in a full employment economy, would lose most or all of their justification. Lord Beveridge has much to say on this subject, but he is very careful to

[1] Beveridge, op. cit., p. 171.
[2] Wootton, op. cit., p. 91.
[3] For an excellent treatment of mobility in relation to social security, see Gertrude Williams, The Price of Social Security (London, 1944).
[4] Wootton, op. cit., p. 89.

make it clear that "Many of the rules and practices evolved by organized labour . . . are essential to a progressive society. They serve to maintain or to promote high standards of skill, . . . integrity, efficiency and quality. They are the only way in which . . . labour can bring order out of disorder and can co-ordinate activities which, if unco-ordinated, may lead to social waste and needless acrimony." But many of the rules are "purely negative" and "born largely out of a spirit of self-defence" against the insecurities inherent in our present unplanned economy.[1] This matter is probably much more important in Britain than on this side of the water, because British unions are older, more numerous, and more powerful than ours. In North America, probably only a relatively few old established craft unions are in a position to exert any appreciable influence in this respect, though their strategic position in certain key industries may make their influence of greater importance in certain contexts. In Britain, Lord Beveridge thought the matter important enough to include it in his questionnaire to the TUC. He got a rather Delphic response. Subject to some vaguely stated conditions, "Trade Unions," the TUC said, "may well be expected not to impede the achievement of full employment by the rigid maintenance of demarcation practices which were themselves designed to ensure the continuity of employment of their own members during periods of industrial insecurity." It added that the "Trade Union Movement . . . cannot commit itself in advance to the relaxation or modification of any of its practices nor can it give pledges as to its future actions in the absence of firm undertakings about the policy of the Government and the obligations to be entered into by all other parties." [2] This seems to me reasonable enough; and where the TUC has refused to tread, I do not propose to rush in, especially as on this continent most of the workers concerned in anything like restrictive practices belong to the rival federations, and any criticism might smack of the pharisaical. It should perhaps

---

[1] Beveridge, *op. cit.*, p. 174.
[2] *Ibid.*, pp. 31-32.

be added that the TUC thinks that the problem of mobility
of labor under full employment "may prove to be very small
indeed," [1] and that Mrs. Wootton, though admitting that it is
"all guesswork," is "inclined to think that . . . excessive mobility is more to be feared than undue sluggishness." [2] My
own guess would be that in Canada, especially if there is no
positive and vigorous policy of controlling the location of
industry, the immense distances and the cultural differences
between the main bodies of workers in the two great industrial
provinces would make the problem of mobility very much
more serious than in Britain, and force Canadian trade unionism to give it a much larger place in its policy than the British
TUC or its constituent unions have ever done. The problem
might also be of considerable importance for the United
States, although it has a much less marked concentration of
industry in certain areas than does Canada.

FACILITATING CONDITIONS

All the problems we have been discussing will be solved
much more easily if certain conditions are fulfilled. The first
of these is adequate statistics of productivity. The second is
a marked increase in the political power of the unions. We
shall never get stable full employment at all unless the unions
keep pressing for it day in and day out; and when we get it,
we shall never have adequate price control unless the unions
keep pressing for that. The third condition is a considerable
extension of public ownership, with workers' representation
on the boards of publicly owned enterprises. Public ownership is in many cases the only effective method of controlling
prices; public ownership with workers' representation may in
many cases be the only effective way of giving workers access
to the economic facts which they need as a basis for reasonable wage policies, and the only effective way of securing
maximum productive effort from the workers. The fourth
condition is a national minimum wage and maximum hour

[1] Trades Union Congress, *op. cit.*, p. 31.
[2] Wootton, *op. cit.*, p. 94.

policy, to put a floor under wages and a ceiling on hours. This, with full employment itself, will make unions far less likely to go in for demands which cannot be met without serious damage to the economy as a whole. The fifth condition is the development of a comprehensive system of social services and security. This extension of "socialized wages," by making the worker less dependent on his individual wages for the basic necessities of life, will encourage him and his unions to be reasonable.

CHAPTER THIRTEEN

The Labor Force and Economic Change[1]

by *Clarence D. Long*

AS THE WAR drew to a close, the season for economic fore-casting opened. Among the contenders were experts in government bureaus, who entered the field with a warning that at least eight million persons would be unemployed in 1946. It is now well known that the unemployed turned out to number hardly more than two million.

Part of the error seems to have derived from an insufficient appreciation of American industry's ability to reconvert quickly and of people's postwar desire to consume. A bare possibility offers itself that this poor grasp of consumption possibilities had a subconscious basis in the dim earnings future of Washington economists facing a return to the universities! Whatever its basis it led to an underestimate of the employment demand for labor. The other part of the six million exaggeration of unemployment appeared to be due to an excessive appreciation of the population's postwar desire to work. This overappraisal of people's eagerness to labor is less easy to explain from what I know of my fellow economists. But its consequence was an overestimate of the size of the labor force.

[1] The present essay is a prospectus, rather than a report, on the statistical supply curve of labor. The ultimate study will rest upon a rather more exhaustive and rigorous analysis of the behavior of the labor force and its components among different places and under varying economic conditions. The writer is preparing the study for publication by the National Bureau of Economic Research as part of the series of the Conference on Research in Income and Wealth. Much of the research for this essay was accomplished during 1946 while the writer was a member of the Institute for Advanced Study, Princeton. Harry Eisenpress and Janette Rainwater have carried a large part of the statistical burden. Fritz Machlup was kind enough to read the proof and to make some helpful suggestions.

The labor force error represented in part a failure to anticipate the speed with which those who were expected to leave the labor force would withdraw after V-J Day. But it represented also a belief, held in the face of considerable historical evidence to the contrary, that the labor force would be a substantially larger proportion of the population as a result of the war.[1]

In view of the many frustrations that delight in stalking the forecaster, these overestimates of labor force and unemployment are no doubt pardonable. Nevertheless they demonstrate the utility of understanding the forces affecting the proportion of the population available for gainful employment under changing economic conditions.

Other illustrations come readily to mind. Goals of full employment, or high employment, require knowledge of the number of candidates for work when an unusually large proportion of the labor force has already acquired jobs. Advance plans for the relief or useful reemployment of the idle, when factories slash payrolls and builders pigeonhole their plans, depend on whether the number of unemployed will increase more or less than the number of workers who receive pink dismissal slips. Appraisals of the potential national product must rest on some notion of the potential force of workers or work

---

[1] C. D. Long, *The Labor Force in Wartime America*, Occasional paper 14 (National Bureau of Economic Research, 1944). "The outstanding peacetime characteristic of the labor force is its stability of size relative to the population" (p. 23). "Finally, judging from the past stability of the labor force propensity, most of the war additions to the labor force seem likely to go out with the war's end, leaving the labor force larger only by reason of the growth in population" (p. 65).
Compared to 1940, the post-war labor force (including armed forces) is a slightly higher proportion of the population. In April 1947 it was 56.2% of the population 14 and older, or a net excess of 1.7% (1.8 million workers) over 54.5% in April 1940. This excess is probably due, not to permanent effects of the war, but to the present inflationary demand for labor; for the persons involved are elderly men over 55, or boys and girls under 20 many of whom are employed after school and on Saturdays because such jobs are now easy to get and are often conveniently located. It is amusing that by April 1947 the war excess over "normal" of working women had turned into a deficiency—contrary to the expectation, widely held during the war, that women would stay on working. The decline in the labor force in the months after VJ Day was nothing short of remarkable. No less than 5½ million persons had departed by April 1946.

seekers. The present essay seeks therefore to learn the behavior of the labor force in times of great economic growth and upheaval.

Appreciation of this problem is by no means new. For at least several centuries economists have speculated upon the aggregate supply of labor; and have explored their own minds or examined the statistics to answer several questions, still interesting and practical, about the response of the laboring classes to the increased or decreased rewards of toil.

THREE QUESTIONS

A primary question has always concerned whether the supply of all labor to all employers might actually decline as average real wages rise; and, conversely, as real wages decline, whether a larger aggregate stream of labor might pour into the market from workers struggling to maintain their standards of life.

This question concerns also the magnitude of the response. Suppose it turns out to be certain, as many economists perhaps from occupational cynicism have surmised, that more pay brings really less work to market. How great relatively might be the fall in supply that accompanies a given rise in real incomes? Could it be so great that labor may be said with some truth to desire only a constant living standard and to show no more gratitude to the industrial system than to reduce its availability for work in equal proportion to the rise in its wages? This position was taken by the ancient mercantilists. It is still defended by some employers of native labor in areas remote from civilization and of Negroes in parts of the United States less remote from the centers of culture.

In partial contrast, might modern labor, while substantially reducing its offerings, nevertheless temper its desire for leisure by withdrawing labor in smaller proportion than the real wage increase? A statistical conclusion of this sort was reached by Paul Douglas in a pioneer study of several years ago, and has been accepted generally by economists as showing that the short-run supply curve of labor is mainly inelastic and yet does have considerable (negative) slope.[1] If that conclusion were sound, it would mean that increases in income would be accompanied by declining percentages of the population in the labor force. Such reductions would hold back somewhat the increases in the real national product. Future rises in income would thus be partially, though perhaps not greatly, self-limiting.

The second question is: If the labor force falls, as wages move upward, how promptly does it fall? Douglas at first implied that the response would occur in the short run. We ask whether his intercity comparisons of a moment of time yield any promise that a fall in labor supply will follow quickly, within months or a few years, an increase in labor incomes. On the other hand, may the response delay years, perhaps decades, after the income change? Does a decline occur perhaps only in the short run? Is it possible that the labor force rises again to its former level, as standards of life subsequently catch up with the rising incomes and workers feel the pressure to maintain installments on the furniture or to buy license plates and insurance for the car.

A third question has possibly never caught the full attention of theoretical economists. Nearly all investigators, Douglas among them, have concerned themselves implicitly with supply of labor under high employment. Since Douglas wrote, the great depression planted a notion that has achieved a surprisingly firm hold upon opinion, in view of its rather weak grasp on fact.

This notion is called "the additional worker theory."[2] It

---

[1] Paul H. Douglas, *The Theory of Wages* (New York, Macmillan Co., 1934), Chap. XI; Erika H. Schoenberg and Paul H. Douglas, "Studies in the Supply Curve of Labor," *The Journal of Political Economy*, XLV (February, 1937), 45-79.

[2] The following articles cover an early controversy on this subject, between W. S. Woytinsky favoring the notion and D. D. Humphrey opposing it, as well as some later studies of my own also opposing it. The Woytinsky view seems to have become the general opinion; but I believe that the statistics of the past and the events of the future will demonstrate it to be wrong. See W. S. Woytinsky, *Additional Workers and the Volume of Unemployment in the Depression* (Social Science Research Council, Pamphlet Series No. 1, 1940), pp. 1, 17, 26; D. D. Humphrey, "Alleged 'Additional Workers' in the Meas-

rests on the supposition, more plausible than scientific, that a drastic decline in demand for labor compels many dependents (housewives, students, and retired elderly persons) to enter the labor market in search of jobs. The purpose of their search is, of course, to restore the family income, reduced by the unemployment of husband and father. The argument presumes that the chief breadwinners continue their own hunt for reemployment. It implies therefore that a downward shift of the demand induces, or is somehow interrelated with, an upward shift in the supply. Labor supply and demand are not independent but have powerful (negative) reactive effects upon one another. If the argument were sound, if there were many additional workers in depression, the already large problem of reemployment in depression would assume an even more formidable aspect. An additional and effective argument would become available to many persons in a mood to deprecate the quantitative seriousness of depression unemployment. A basis would exist for charging that many of the unemployed are actually such additional workers.

A contrary statement of this third question bears on the full employment controversy. Economists occasionally suggest that large numbers of persons may enter the labor force as the demand for labor rises under a full employment program.[1] The entrance of many persons ordinarily unemployable or undesirous of employment would add to the task of providing jobs for all. Contrary to the additional worker theory, if the demand for labor should rise (shift upward), the supply of labor would do likewise.

The following preliminary investigation divides for convenience into three parts. Each part deals with one of the

urement of Unemployment," *Journal of Political Economy*, XLVIII (June, 1940), 412-19; Woytinsky, "A Reply to Mr. Humphrey," *Journal of Political Economy*, XLVIII (October, 1940), 735-39; C. D. Long, "The Concept of Unemployment," *Quarterly Journal of Economics*, LVII (November, 1942), 9-10; and *The Labor Force in Wartime America, op. cit.*, pp. 24-26.

[1] J. H. G. Pierson writes in *Full Employment* (New Haven, Yale Univ. Press, 1941), pp. 18-19, note 22: "For it is probable that, if society were committed to providing job opportunity for all those able and wanting to work, however numerous, certain fresh supplies of labor not apparent at present would shortly be uncovered."

three questions posed above and summarized here:

(1) Is the proportion of the population in the labor force truly smaller in areas where real earnings are higher? If such spatial association exists, is it as pronounced as Douglas suggested?

(2) As incomes of labor increase over time, does the proportion in the labor force decline? If so, does it decline quickly, or after long delay? Was Douglas justified in fact, even if not in theory, in describing his association as the short-run supply curve?

(3) Does the entire labor force rise in depression, in accordance with the additional worker theory? Or does it fall in depression, and then rise in subsequent recovery as demand for labor shifts upward toward full employment? Or is the labor force unresponsive, perhaps even to great fluctuations in demand for labor?

This essay opens an investigation to frame statistical answers to these three questions. It aims therefore to revise and extend what is known, or believed to be known, about the aggregate supply of labor. Statistical measurement requires us to treat the supply as consisting of three components: number of persons in the labor force; number of hours in the full-time work week; and efficiency of labor due to its own efforts. These pages deal entirely with the labor-force component.

THE LABOR FORCE

A reasonably precise definition of labor force is "the number of persons during a given week reported to have a job or business, or to be doing or seeking full-time or part-time work for pay or profit, including work without pay in a family enterprise." A handier, though perhaps deceptively simple, definition is the "number of persons having jobs or seeking them."

The labor-force concept has several characteristics that ought to be made explicit. It includes both the employed and the unemployed and leaves out the man who is in full-time school or retirement, or who has better things to do at the moment than gainful employment. It covers General Eisenhower and his civil service secretary, the beauty parlor operator who fixes the secretary's hair, and the owner of the parlor who collects the price of the coiffure at the door. It covers the dentist who is to repair the lady's teeth in the morning, the president of the company that made her car, and the farmer's boy who works without pay at his father's roadstand and sells the secretary her week's supply of eggs on her way home. It covers one of her brothers who is working his way through college but not her other brother who goes to high school full time. It covers her brother's wife who sells real estate in her spare time, but not the wife's sister who spends all of her own time (and no doubt some of her husband's) in caring for home and family. It also omits the occupations of uncaught criminals and (after 1930) the employment, however useful or gainful, of persons in jails and asylums and of children under fourteen.

It bases its unit of measurement on a person rather than an hour of work, counting the newsboy who works a few hours after school equally with the physician who labors a sixty-hour week. It magnifies therefore the size of the labor force at the expense of the remaining population. It allows only one status, a labor-force status, for persons leading double economic lives, chiefly working students and housewives in the labor force on a part-time basis.

This concept, used since 1940 and occasionally before then, has the theoretical advantage of focussing on the activities of a single week. Activities of the previous month or season are omitted and the duplication of adding together past and present employment and unemployment is avoided.

The census does not attempt to weigh the employed by the efficiency of their work or the unemployed by the intensity of their need for work. Nor does it reveal how variations in wages or in labor demand would affect work-seeking. The current data cannot reveal directly, therefore, what would be the labor force and its composition under different economic conditions, say those of depression. The search for behavior under variable conditions engages our attention in this chapter.

THE LABOR FORCE AT A MOMENT OF TIME

A number of years ago, in his treatise on *The Theory of Wages,* which with all its many faults is one of the great books in economics, Paul Douglas asked whether the labor force tended in actual fact to be less numerous where the population from which it was drawn was more prosperous. He sought to answer this question by associating two oppositely varying sets of data in each of 38 to 41 large United States cities. Each city furnished one observation. The first set of data was the average wage and salary earnings of adult male factory workers in 1919 adjusted for intercity differences in the cost of food; the other was the proportion of the population in the labor force in January, 1920. A later study by Douglas and Schoenberg covered the census of 1929-30.[1] We begin here by launching similar explorations for 1899-1900 and 1939-40.

Age and sex are basic determinants of labor-force participation at any income level. Douglas made separate comparisons, therefore, for each age and sex group, associating adult male income with the number, say, of girls aged 17 in the labor force in every 1,000 girls of that age in each city. First he correlated the detailed age-sex groups. Next he compared— again always with adult male earnings [2]—the combined number of all ages and both sexes in the labor force in each 1,000 persons. He did this by standardizing or reweighting each city's population. While varying in size, each city was made to have the same distribution of boys and girls, of young and middle-aged men and women, and of elderly persons. Thus the difficulty was eliminated that one city might have larger proportions of its population in the labor force merely because

[1] Douglas and Schoenberg, *op. cit.*

[2] He used adult male earnings partly because they are the main source of family income and the main determinant of labor force even for women and children, and partly because there is less part-time employment of males and less of a problem of comparing earnings for similar effort.

it had larger proportions of its population in the ages when persons are most likely to seek work.

Douglas's general conclusions from the two censuses obtain a good deal of support from my study of the 1900 and the 1940 enumerations. They are:

(1) Among the large cities a decided inverted relationship existed between the relative real earnings and the proportions who were in the labor force (employed or unemployed).

(2) This negative relationship marked particularly the cases of the young, the women in the central age group, and the older groups. (Actually it did not appear at all in the case of males of the central age groups.)

(3) Cities where male incomes were $100 higher tended to have 5 or 6 fewer persons in the combined labor force in each 1,000 persons of standard age and sex.

(4) Cities where male incomes were 1 per cent higher tended to have 1/6 of 1 per cent fewer persons in the combined labor force of both sexes and all ages.

Douglas took pains in his second study to mention that the inverse association applied only to large cities of the United States at a moment of time. Economists have inferred from his *The Theory of Wages*, however, that the association measured the supply curve of labor in all areas and over short-run periods of time. (The long run receives attention in Douglas's subsequent chapters on population changes occurring over generations and even centuries.)

The research for the present section had two missions. It sought first to confirm whether the direction and magnitude of the inverse correlation, remarked by Douglas for 1919-20 and 1929-30, would appear also for 1899-1900, as well as for 1939-40 for which more accurate and complete labor-force and income data are available.

It strove secondly to ascertain whether rural areas, and rural and urban areas combined, revealed the inverse association. This study could not be made at the regular censuses earlier than 1940 for lack of detailed data on rural incomes. It was conducted by correlating the proportion of each state's population in the labor force in March, 1940 and the median income of its males who worked 12 months in 1939. Each of the urban or rural areas of the 48 states was taken as a separate observation. Additional, and very interesting, inverse relationships appear for married women: between their number in the 1940 labor force (per 1,000 of standard age) and the 1939 incomes of their individual husbands. The latter studies compare different income groups in the same area or any area, and do not depend upon geographical variations. Separate comparisons are presented, however, for large cities, small cities, and rural nonfarm areas. They all show a steep and almost uninterrupted decline in wives' labor-force propensities, as husbands' incomes increase. The inverse association appears especially distinct and smooth in the urban areas. Comparisons for both area and direct data yield altogether the following results:

(1) High male earnings are accompanied by low labor-force propensities among the young, the elderly, single women in the central ages, married women, and the combined age and sex groups. Inverse association appears not only for large cities but also for the urban areas (above 2,500 population) of the 48 states.

(2) No significant correlation is manifested in the relation between adult male incomes and adult male labor force (age 25 to 64).

(3) Little or no correlation with income appears for rural and urban labor forces combined. A slight inverse correlation appears when family incomes (per member) were substituted for male earnings. It remained, however, far from strong.

Except among young and elderly persons and married women, labor-force proportions vary with incomes only faintly and inconclusively. The urban labor force by itself manifested rather strong inverse affinity with income. It has not been strong enough when diluted with the low rural association, to have a very pronounced effect on the whole United States labor force. Such an association would have been in any case timeless or spatial, and could not have been called a short-run supply curve. The latter term ought to imply that a rise in income would be followed shortly (in several months or a few years) by an appropriate decline in the labor force. The spatial relationship discovered by Douglas, and partially confirmed in this study, may have taken decades and even generations to come about. (Douglas regarded "the long run," however, as occurring over generations and as reflecting the effect of real wages on the birth and survival rates of the population and thus, eventually, upon the aggregate size of the labor force.)

The next section investigates whether the labor force has actually fallen in proportion to the population, as real incomes have risen from one census to another. (Comparisons are restricted to years of high employment.)

THE LABOR FORCE OVER TIME, UNDER CONDITIONS OF RISING INCOMES AND HIGH EMPLOYMENT

Paul Douglas undertook to demonstrate, for a moment of time, that the labor force proportion tended to be smaller in cities where wage and salary earnings were higher. The present study supports strongly his demonstration for the large cities. It obtains similar results for all urban areas. But it has uncovered no inverse relationship among the nation's rural areas. It fails also to obtain positive results from the combined rural and urban population. (The latter data were standardized so as to have the same age and sex and rural-urban composition in each state.)

Douglas did not make an inquiry over time. We require one here, however, our purpose being to ascertain if the labor force declines as incomes rise. The study compares labor force and income from one census year of high employment to another.

Comparisons of the labor force between different censuses present many problems and some hazards. Censuses may have somewhat different concepts of the labor force, and may vary in completeness even under the same concept. Although census labor-force data of the period studied are probably more reliable than the vast majority of economic statistics, we refrain from drawing conclusions that cannot weather a good margin of error.[1]

Our income–labor-force comparisons over time rest on several rather extensive adjustments, which do not, however, produce results that are significantly different from those derived by comparing raw data.

One adjustment standardizes the population in order to eliminate the variations in age and sex and in rural-urban residence. Its purpose is to prevent them from obscuring the income–labor-force association. The adjusted data measure the number of persons in the labor force (employed and unemployed) per 1,000 population of similar age and sex or rural-urban residence.[2]

A second adjustment compensates for differences in season of the year when the labor forces were originally enumerated. The 1900 labor force counted in June, needs a slight reduction, and the 1920 labor force, counted in January, needs a slight increase, to make them comparable with the 1930 labor force, counted in April.

A third adjustment adapts the income data to represent the real wage and salary earnings of adult male workers.[3] That

[1] For an excellent discussion of the problem of distinguishing between the labor-force and non-labor-force elements of the population in order to obtain comparability over time, see Solomon Fabricant, "The Changing Industrial Distribution of Gainful Workers: Some Comments on the American Decennial Statistics for 1820-1940," Conference on Research in Income and Wealth, November, 1946 (soon to be published).

[2] There is a theoretical problem involved in such standardization. In strict logic a different pattern of fluctuation will emerge for every base that is used for standardization purposes. In the present type of problem, however, the choice of the base year, or area, has little practical significance, because the population age-sex groups showing the greatest variation in proportion to total population have relatively small labor-force propensities. For example, the pattern of labor-force change from one census to another from 1890 to 1930 is substantially the same whether the base is chosen as 1890 or 1930. A contribution, however, to standardization theory has been made by E. D. Goldfield, "Method of Multiple Standardization and Allocation of Interactions," Appendix B of a forthcoming monograph by J. D. Durand, "Growth of the U.S. Labor Force, 1890-1960."

[3] Simon Kuznets, National Product since 1869 (New York, National Bureau of Economic Research, 1946), p. 119. Decade estimates: 1884-93, 1894-1903, 1914-23, 1924-33.

involved expressing annual income in terms of the gainfully occupied adult male population. Separate data for adult males were not available for 1919, 1929, or 1939. Earnings, therefore, were converted to an equivalent adult male basis on assumption that the earning power of two adult males equalled that of three women, three boys, or four girls. Total income data were then divided by a gainfully occupied figure that was the sum of these various earnings groups so weighted. To reduce the data to figures of constant purchasing power, incomes per worker were divided by an index of the cost of living. The U.S. censuses from 1890 through 1930 occurred when unemployment was comparatively low (not more than approximately six per cent of the work force).

The initial step of the present inquiry involves testing whether the timeless or spatial associations of labor force with income among the large cities—discovered by Douglas for 1919-20 and 1929-30 and by me for 1899-1900 and 1939-40—have shifted downward as the median real incomes of adult male workers have moved upward, over that period of four decades. In his second study Douglas compared the relative steepness of the slopes of the timeless associations of 1919-20 and 1929-30. He did not compare, however, the absolute levels of the curves to ascertain whether, as earnings rose over time, the labor-force proportion fell in conformity to his negatively sloping supply curve, or perhaps rose in contradiction of it.

STABLE LABOR FORCE PROPORTION OVER TIME

The present investigation found that the static curves sloped downward *spatially* at each of the four census dates. They did not tend on net balance to shift downward *in time* as incomes rose over the high-employment decade dates, 1900-1930.[1] The male labor-force curve was lower in 1930 and the female labor-force curve was higher. But both sexes combined had slightly higher proportions in the labor force in 1930 than

[1] The labor force of each city has been standardized on the basis of the population, age and sex distribution of Chicago in 1930.

1900.[1] It is most likely that there was a nearly horizontal trend during the period when real incomes rose under high employment.

Whether the proportion of standard population available for work diminishes from one decade to another, as incomes of male workers rise, is examined also in the over-all labor-force proportions in various nations. These nations, selected because they had censuses of population that occurred at high-employment dates, were the United States (1900-1930); Germany (1925, 1939); Great Britain (1911, 1939); Canada (1911, 1941); and New Zealand (1901, 1926). The list will be extended in our subsequent study.

Two types of comparisons were made for each nation between the high-employment dates. One was the change in number of persons in the labor force. This number was taken as a ratio to the number of $100 rises (from the earlier date) in real annual incomes of adult male workers. The comparison measured the rough slopes of the labor-force—income curve over time.

The other comparison was the percentage change in labor force from the previous census. This was taken as a ratio to the number of one per cent increases in incomes. It measured the crude income elasticities of the labor force over time. Over-all labor force was compared to male incomes in each nation. U.S. national income per equivalent adult male worker was compared to male and female labor force in rural and urban areas separately. Some disagreements appeared in the various relationships between labor-force changes and income changes. The disagreements appeared not only between the different areas in the United States, but also between the United States and the other countries. Certain similarities nevertheless stand out.

(1) In each nation a small net number of males tended to leave the labor force (the employed and unemployed) and a

---

[1] Both "static" and "dynamic" are used here with much latitude. Actually the static curves are not static, for many differences may develop as one proceeds from one area to another; the dynamic curves are not dynamic, for they connect only a series of static curves.

rather smaller number of females to enter it. A net exodus of 3-8 males, and a net entry of 4-11 females, per 1,000 standard-age persons of each sex respectively, coexisted with each $100 rise in male incomes. In percentages, a decline of $\frac{1}{30}$ to $\frac{1}{6}$ of 1 per cent in male labor force and an increase of $\frac{1}{10}$ to $\frac{9}{10}$ of 1 per cent in female labor force (per 1,000 females) coexisted with a male income rise of 1 per cent from the previous date compared. This inflow of females into the labor force over time was opposite to the static outflow noted by Douglas and myself for spatial increases of income.[1]

(2) The greatest rise in the labor-force propensity of females, as incomes rose over time, seemed to occur among married women. At least this was true in Germany between 1925 and 1939 and in the United States between 1890 and 1930. United States married women increased three times as much in the labor force as in the population; related to each 1 per cent rise in male incomes, the proportion rises 1.5 per cent. Yet it was among married women that the greatest *declines* occurred in 1940, as the incomes rose in a spatial or timeless sense from one locality or income group to another. Married women in the 1940 United States labor force were 1/6 of 1 per cent to 1 per cent fewer in those groups where incomes of husbands were 1 per cent higher.

(3) All the countries showed net tendencies for boys and girls and elderly persons to retire from the labor force and for females to enter it.

(4) In the United States (except the large cities) and in New Zealand, the outflow of males overshadowed the inflow of females, and the combined labor force of both sexes tended to decline, though almost imperceptibly. The decline in numbers in the United States was 1 person (in 1,000 of standard age and sex) for each rise of real male incomes of $100. The decline in percentages was 2/100 of 1 per cent for each increase in income of 1 per cent, over that of the previous census date.

[1] See also the supposition by R. A. Lester in *The Economics of Labor* (New York, Macmillan Co., 1941), p. 204.

(5) In Germany, Great Britain, Canada, the 38 large United States cities, and in the rural and urban and overall U.S. labor force of 14 and older, the inflow of females dominated, and the combined male and female labor force grew, again almost imperceptibly. The growth in numbers was 1 to 4 persons, and in percentages was 2/100 to 3/100 of 1 per cent.

(6) For the 5 countries as a whole a mean rise appeared. It was insignificant, however, and the labor-force proportion everywhere manifested a high degree of stability in over-all size.

The addition to this study of other countries and earlier and later periods may tip the trend more definitely in an upward or downward direction, although, either because the individual groups sometimes conflicted in their movement or because the groups manifesting marked change in propensity were smaller than those exhibiting stability, none of the 5 nations studied showed much individual labor-force variation in either direction. The trends appearing in this study may stem, moreover, from social and institutional developments rather than from income increases. An attempt will be made in the final study to assign their true causes. The present data make it moderately safe to say that the over-all labor force tended neither to rise nor to fall significantly as incomes rose from one high-employment period to another.

THE LABOR FORCE DURING DEPRESSION AND RECOVERY

Our study now drops the high-employment condition. It proceeds to examine the effect on the net labor force of the great depression of the 1930's and the subsequent recovery. The prevailing theory of the additional worker assumed that children and women would seek jobs in deep depression because their fathers and husbands became unemployed. With the family heads presumably continuing to seek work, the net number of unemployed would enlarge from two directions: a decline in the employed and a rise in the labor force. The difficulties of reemploying the idle labor force would thus appear in exaggerated form.

Presumably, the recovery would witness a converse decline in labor force. The main supporter of each family would recover his job, the family would no longer need the earnings of its women and children so desperately, and the latter could give up their search for employment. If they had located jobs, they could resign their actual employments. The labor force might return to normal proportions.

Complete decline of labor force to predepression levels during recovery is not, of course, a necessary part of the additional worker theory. Some of its adherents contend that many additional workers might remain in the labor force permanently once they secured jobs.

Nationwide census data offer scant material for testing what happens to the labor force as employment falls. All the regular U.S. population censuses during the period from 1890 to 1930 happened to be taken in years of high employment; even the 1940 census was taken after the worst phases of the depression of the 1930's had passed. Census data are not, however, completely lacking for depression periods. At least eight censuses of population and of the labor force occurred during the 1930's in this country and abroad.[1] Four were statewide censuses in industrial commonwealths in this country, and occurred in the darkest years of the 1930's. They included Massachusetts and Pennsylvania in early 1934, Michigan in early 1935, and Rhode Island in 1936. A fifth was the nationwide sample enumeration of unemployment taken in December, 1937, during the 1937-38 recession. Part of its

[1] *Michigan Census of Population and Unemployment*, "Age, Sex, and Employment Status of Gainful Workers, etc.," 1936, pp. 2, 33 (inside covers).

The Pennsylvania Census of Employable Workers in Urban and Rural Non-Farm Areas (State Emergency Relief Administration, 1936).

Report on the Census of Unemployment in Massachusetts as of January 2, 1934, Labor Bulletin No. 171, pp. 5-8, *passim*.

Rhode Island Decennial Population Census of 1936. *Story of the 680,712* (Department of Labor), pp. 10, 23, 26.

Census of Great Britain, 1911 and 1931. "The Industrial Distribution of the Population of Great Britain in July, 1939," *Journal of the Royal Statistical Society*, Parts III-IV, 1945.

Seventh Census of Canada, 1931, Vol. VI, *Unemployment*.

Statistik des Deutschen Reichs, Band 453, Heft 2, p. 5. *Census of Partial Employment, Unemployment, and Occupations: 1937, Final Report*, Vol. IV.

purpose was to obtain independent information on unemployment and part to check the results of a voluntary postal card survey of unemployment made several weeks earlier. The remaining depression censuses were regular censuses of population and gainfully occupied in three foreign countries. These were Germany, 1933; Great Britain, 1921 and 1931; and Canada, 1921 and 1931. Administrations of no two of the eight enumerations were interrelated.

The depression labor force could be compared in all cases with the labor force of both previous prosperity and subsequent recovery. The recoveries were partial in Great Britain in 1939 and in the United States in 1940, but fairly complete in Germany in 1939 and Canada in 1941.

Labor-force comparisons in any one of these eight areas have doubtful reliability. The 1934-36 censuses of the four industrial states are compared here with the U.S. census for those states at the previous (1930) and the subsequent (1940) census, in order to show what happened to the labor force as conditions changed from high employment to depression and back to partial recovery. However, the various State Emergency Relief Administrations conducted the state depression enumerations and based them on formal definitions of the labor force that differed somewhat from the U.S. census concept and varied among the states themselves. Three of the state censuses occurred in the slightly less active month of January, rather than in April or late March, the date of the U.S. census. Although the Pennsylvania data occur in more nearly the same season (February-April) as the U.S. data, they do not command great reliance, since no 1934 population data were gathered in that state and, therefore, they had to be supplied by interpolation between the 1930 and 1940 censuses.

The enumerative check census of 1937 had to be compared with the U.S. census of 1930 and 1940. The data of the 1937 census are open to question because its conduct was in the hands of postal carriers, not census-trained enumerators, its definition of labor force was comparatively restrictive, and it was a large sample instead of a complete count. Moreover, the sample failed to represent about 18 per cent of the nation's population, namely those residing off postal routes in many rural areas.

The regular census data of the three foreign countries may be more comparable from one enumeration year to another than were the U.S. state data; nevertheless they bear the conceptual weaknesses of the gainful worker definition that had prevailed in the United States census through 1930. Theoretically the earlier gainfully occupied included persons claiming a usual occupation, even if they did not work or seek work on the enumeration date (as the U.S. data have stipulated since 1940 and in some cases since the middle 1930's). Classification of people thus by their past, rather than current, work status might fail to register all of the changes in labor force that occur under varying economic developments.

A tendency has existed to exaggerate this undoubted difference between 1940 labor-force concepts and those of earlier censuses. Tests conducted by the census itself have suggested that enumerators tend in practice, when not under discipline of scientifically arranged schedules, to report the person's activity as of the moment he is being enumerated rather than of his past or even of the census week. If this very human practice is general, it wipes out much of the practical difference between census-week-status and customary-status concepts of the labor force. Nevertheless it should be admitted that the labor force might possibly have changed more in depression than the data show.

We have pointed out that no single area commands complete trust in its data. Yet if all the different state and national data behave similarly, that behavior may deserve some confidence. Nearly all of the data, except for the U.S. check census of 1937, do manifest the following similar behavior in depression and recovery:

(1) Even virtual collapse in employment demand for labor, and of course in labor income, has little apparent effect on the net over-all labor-force proportion. Enumerated on the basis of status in the census week, the depression labor force

might decline more than did the data gathered on a customary-status basis. On the other hand, when corrected for having been taken in the winter months of inactive agriculture, the labor-force statistics might decline less than the present data. However, declines are not great even in those states, Michigan and Pennsylvania, using a concept more similar to the current-worker definition of the 1940 census. It may be possible to say here, subject to later revision, *that the labor-force proportion seems largely independent of the fluctuations in employment.*

(2) Any changes manifested here were in disobedience to the postulates of the additional worker theory, and in the same direction as the movement of employment. The labor force declines a bit as employment of labor falls, and rises a bit as employment recovers. The conceptual weaknesses of the data do not suggest that more accurate statistics might support the additional worker theory by reversing this positive tendency. Indeed it is worth mentioning that new or inexperienced persons were counted in the depression labor-force data of the four U.S. states, though not formally in the 1930 census. In spite of this fact, and the fact that unemployment was more heavily concentrated in new workers, labor-force proportions were lower in deep depression than in 1930 when the census concept excluded such workers. Our findings give little support to the existence of substantial numbers of additional workers, under either depression or full employment conditions.[1] No doubt some additional workers do appear in de-

[1] The check census of 1937 was the one real exception to this evidence, for it seems to show a substantial rise in the over-all labor-force proportion under depressed employment conditions. No satisfactory explanation can be found for this manifestation—certainly none in the concept used, which was unduly restrictive rather than too comprehensive. The most plausible explanation would be the one that any special unemployment census is apt to over-count both unemployment and labor force. While it is true that the four U.S. state censuses were also special unemployment censuses and open to the same objections, it is possible that they gave less of an impression to the public that the unemployment census was part of a job-finding or relief-giving program. There is also the possibility that the depression rise in labor force measured by the check census actually occurred but was a temporary result of the sudden 1937 recession. The check census occurred at the bottom of that recession, and it is conceivable that, after four months of one of the

pression; there is equal likelihood that many other candidates for the labor market, especially new workers on the unskilled level or dislodged elderly workers, withdraw after becoming discouraged by the severe competition for jobs and by the low pay and harsh discipline that prevail in the work that is available.[1]

(3) To the minor extent that the labor force varies with economic cycles, both males and females appear to be in the labor force (working or work-seeking) in smaller numbers when the employment demand for labor is very low. This mildly positive relationship between labor demand and labor force stands out in a little better relief if adjustment is made for the fact that the long-run trend of the labor-force proportion has been downward for males and upward for females. A similar positive pattern marks the labor force of individual population groups. These groups include the primary wage earners (males, age 25 to 64) and young persons, elderly persons, and women (25 to 64).

SUMMARY AND CONCLUSIONS

Our analysis of labor-force behavior under changing economic conditions has reached several conclusions, that may, of course, need correction as additional research extends the materials and refines the methods.[2]

most rapid employment recessions on record, many dependents may have entered the labor force in search of work who later retired when they discovered that jobs were scarce, pay was low, and work rules were severe. We must regard the check census as a possible and apparently inexplicable exception to the case against the additional worker theory.

[1] If this conclusion of substantial invariability of labor force in depression proves to be sound, it will justify the intuitive judgment of Pigou: "In this book in the main I shall take the number of would-be wage earners in a given situation as a fixed datum, so that the quantity of unemployment and the quantity of employment are simply complements of one another." (*The Theory of Unemployment* [London, Macmillan & Co., Ltd., 1933], pp. 7-8.)

[2] Wassily Leontief writes his belief that "Further progress must be made along the line of analysis which, first of all, concentrates its attention on individual households and explains the variation of labor supply in terms of factors such as family size, age composites, potential earning power of principal and secondary earners, etc. The aggregate market supply curve will have to be obtained through summation of individual schedules in the range of significant variation of all these basic independent determinants." I agree

First, it supports Douglas's demonstration that the labor-force proportion (total number employed and unemployed per 1,000 persons of working age) tends to be somewhat smaller in cities or state urban areas where adult male wages and salaries are higher.[1] It does not, however, reveal significant variation among rural areas or among rural and urban areas combined. Douglas himself was apprehensive that his conclusions might have limited scope. Certainly the available facts do not justify generalizing Douglas's city labor-force curves to represent all types of localities. As for the interpretation to be placed upon the urban associations, Douglas in a later study repudiated the notion, acquired by economists from the title of his chapter in *The Theory of Wages*, that his static association represented the "short-run supply curve" of labor.

Second, in this country and elsewhere, the over-all labor force displays very little change in its peacetime proportion of population standardized for age and sex. Its stability seems to hold despite the fact that the main supporters of families, the adult males, receive steady increases in income over long periods under high employment and that both income and employment fluctuate in major economic cycles. While showing, at times, considerable turbulence in its composition, the labor-force proportion is remarkably constant in over-all size.

Third, some slight downward inclinations in the labor force are manifest, although minor refinements of data or method might easily eradicate them. These changes are of two sorts. On the one hand, very small declines in the labor force may accompany large increases in the real incomes of males between high-employment episodes. This inverse relationship obtained in the United States for urban and for rural areas, although rural areas showed some rise between 1890 and 1900

with Professor Leontief that such an analysis is necessary. Indeed I plan to make it if I can obtain the requisite data from the census files. However, we shall never be able to dispense with the aggregate studies of the kind I have made, for we need them to check the summations of the individual schedules and to furnish a full account of the residual interactions.

[1] In the case of the cities it was possible, except for 1900, to adjust the male income data for intercity differences in cost of living.

in labor-force propensities of males or of both sexes combined.[1]
So slight is the change in over-all labor-force proportion that,
on net balance, only 1 person in every 1,000 population 10 and
older, appears to leave the labor force as annual real earnings
of males rise $100. In percentages the U.S. labor-force pro-
portion seems to fall only 3/100 of 1 per cent as real labor
incomes rise 1 per cent. This fall might be expressed as
reflecting a crude elasticity of the dynamic labor-force curve
of the amount of −0.03.

On the other hand, the labor force tends to decline slightly
as income and employment fall drastically in depression, falling by 5 or 10 persons as 100 persons lose their jobs. Conversely, it may increase by small amounts as incomes and
employment enjoy major recoveries. This tendency contributes no support to the additional worker theory that the labor-
force proportion rises on net balance as the large-scale unemployment of primary wage earners forces housewives, students,
and elderly retired persons into the labor market; it seems,
if anything, to reverse that theory slightly.

The supposition of reversal does not, of course, deserve
great confidence. Depression enumerations of the four states
took place largely in midwinter, when agriculture is slightly
less active and school attendance is somewhat higher, than in
April, the month when the U.S. census made the enumerations
of 1930 and 1940. Seasonal differences could thus account for
part of the apparent depression decline; and this fact, in com-

---

[1] Louis Ducoff advances the interesting point that, if the labor-force data
are to be adjusted for shifts from rural to urban residence, the income data
should also be so standardized. He argues in effect that the income data so
standardized would increase less rapidly than the unstandardized income and
that the labor-force curve would be more steeply inclined. Some attempt
will be made in the final report to standardize the income data for rural to
urban shifts, but on the whole very little can be done in this direction either
statistically or conceptually. The income–labor-force association would still
be highly inelastic even if standard income were shown to rise much less than
unstandardized. Simon Kuznets observes in this connection that, since the
rural-urban standardization of income is difficult to bring off, it might be best
also to compare labor force without the rural-urban standardization. This
suggestion may have considerable merit. The final study will, in fact, present
an additional separate comparison without the rural-urban standardization for
either income or labor force.

bination with the smallness of the decline, limits us to saying merely that the aggregate labor force may be largely independent of cyclical fluctuations in the peacetime demand for labor (loosely indicated by employment).

The war did not violate this peacetime record of stability, even though greatly enlarging the labor force (including armed forces) temporarily. Careful study shows that the changes in the over-all labor force were closely associated, month by month, with the size of the armed forces, rising with the draft and falling with the demobilization. Under the April, 1947 situation of almost full employment, the labor-force proportion of the standard population was only 2 per cent larger than in April, 1940. Of the 14 large cities whose labor forces in late 1946 were estimated on a sampling basis by the census, the labor-force proportions were generally lower than in April, 1930, the most recent prewar month of high employment. They were appreciably higher (2 per cent or more) only in Newark and Chicago. An analogous return to approximately prewar proportions of the population has occurred in the British labor force.

Fourth, the labor-force propensity has held fairly constant in over-all magnitude. It has been constant also among males from 25 to 64. Among the other age-sex groups of the labor force, rather marked changes seem to have occurred over the decades. Propensities have fallen greatly in the case of young and elderly persons and have risen in the case of women, the rise having been especially great among married women. The variations of the individual groups do not seem closely associated in time with income or indeed with any other single factor. Elderly persons sought early retirement because of income rises, increased pensions, or large-scale unemployment. Children left the labor force in largest numbers when educational opportunities became plentiful or when unemployment made job competition excessively severe for persons without experience or training. Women entered the labor force in spite of the large rises in real income. Indeed these income rises should, on the basis of the static association, have suggested their large-scale exit. The paradoxical rise has been due no doubt to the great social upheaval that occurred over the decades and made it at once feasible, respectable, and possibly compulsory, for women to work gainfully.

It is even conceivable that compensatory developments helped stabilize the labor force. As large numbers of young and elderly people left the labor force, many women may have entered it to contribute support to the retirement of their parents or the education of young husbands, brothers, or older children. Great reductions, moreover, in hours of work since 1890 have occurred variously under rising income or depression unemployment; these fewer hours of work doubtless operated as an escape for persons desiring to work less as their incomes rose,[1] or served as a means of spreading the smaller number of jobs over the labor force. They also had much to do presumably with making it possible for many more women to work at outside employments and still perform their home duties. Such compensatory interrelationships would, if we could demonstrate their existence, give some additional assurance that the labor force would be a stable proportion of the population in future decades.

Our tentative conclusion is that the over-all labor force may remain a fairly invariable proportion of the standard working-age population, at least relative to fluctuations in other important economic magnitudes. If further research supports this stability, then economists and economic policy-makers may proceed more confidently in their theoretical speculations and practical plans.

Economic theory would benefit from the knowledge that the over-all, labor-force dimension of the aggregate labor supply curve is not only inelastic with respect to income change, but does not vary much with employment fluctuations. Such

---

[1] See Leo Wolman, *Hours of Work in American Industry*, Bulletin 71 (National Bureau of Economic Research, Nov. 27, 1938). Average full-time hours of work, computed by weighing Professor Wolman's hours data with number of occupied persons attached to each industry of the decennial census, show that for 1890 to 1930 full-time hours of work dropped 19 per cent, or more than six times the percentage decline in persons occupied.

stability is probably rare in economics. Fairly certain knowledge of a case of this importance would narrow the analytical search for equilibrium wage and employment levels and relieve us of the toil, or the nearly unfulfillable obligation, of analyzing and measuring subtle and complicated reactions between supply and demand.[1] It would help to solve problems both of general equilibrium and of partial adjustments of individual firms and localities, within the general adjustment.[2]

For research and policy-making, a stable labor force would have practical implications to economic planners and business forecasters. It is true that forecasts of the number of unemployed, secured by deducting forecasts of employment from the labor-force projection, would yield rather variable results; an error of 1 per cent in the labor-force projection might amount to a large percentage of the unemployed residual. It is also true that a watch must be kept for social changes and for developments in administration of relief, social insurance, unemployment compensation, veteran benefits, and other institutional factors that might conceivably have perceptible effect on the labor-force propensity. Nevertheless, if the labor force should prove to be relatively unfluctuating under changing economic conditions, its size in years hence could be approximated with no more than moderate error by projecting into the future the slowly changing structure of the population in the past. Estimates of the potential real national product, which enjoy a brisk output among forecasters and planners, rely heavily on labor-force projections; if the latter could be

---

[1] Such a finding would justify the position taken by brute force by many economists. Hicks says: "For the question of the total number of labourers available in a community is one which modern economists are content to treat as lying outside the theory of wages (differing in this from their predecessors of a century ago). It may be regarded as belonging to the theory of population." (The Theory of Wages [London, Macmillan & Co., Ltd., 1932], p. 2.) Pigou follows the same practice (The Theory of Unemployment, op. cit., p. 7).

[2] See for example, R. A. Lester, Economics of Labor (New York, Macmillan Co., 1941), Chaps. 7, 8; "Shortcomings of Marginal Analysis for Wage-Employment Problems," American Economic Review, XXXVI (March, 1946), 63-82; Lloyd G. Reynolds, "Some Aspects of Labor Market Structure," supra.; J. T. Dunlop, Wage Determination under Trade Unions (New York, Macmillan Co., 1944), chap. 3.

made fairly accurate, the potential income projections would be somewhat less risky.

Full employment goals also rest on labor-force estimates. We have far to go before achieving a sound definition of full employment and this study has given little direct help toward an ideal definition. But whatever the accepted level (say 55 per cent of the standard working-age population), our preliminary conclusion is that full employment may not fluctuate seriously with levels of income and labor demand, that unemployment and employment figures are not necessarily padded with millions of additional workers in either depression or full prosperity—unless, of course, drastic changes in the administration of relief and unemployment compensation payments should create false incentives for people to register in the labor force contrary to their normal inclinations. If this preliminary finding receives support in our future research, it will mean that somewhere there is a statistical goal of peacetime full employment which may stand fairly firm throughout great economic perturbations.

About the Authors

NATHAN BELFER received his Ph.D. degree from Harvard University in 1946, and is at present Assistant Professor of Economics at Brooklyn College. He has taught at Tufts College, Simmons College, and the Massachusetts Institute of Technology, and was a Sheldon Fellow at Harvard University in 1941.

GORDON F. BLOOM received his Ph.D. degree from Harvard University in 1946, and is at present a student in the Harvard Law School. He has been a Fellow of the Social Science Research Council and has worked in the Office of Price Administration. He served in the United States Navy during the war. He has contributed to the *Quarterly Journal of Economics, Economica,* and the *American Economic Review.*

ROBERT K. BURNS received his Ph.D. degree from the University of Chicago in 1942 and is at present Associate Professor of Social Science and Executive Officer of the Industrial Relations Center, University of Chicago. He has served with the National War Labor Board and the Veterans Administration. He is the author of *Unionization of White Collar Workers* and a contributing author to *How Collective Bargaining Works.*

NEIL W. CHAMBERLAIN received his Ph.D. degree from Ohio State University in 1942, and is at present Research Assistant and Assistant Professor at the Labor and Management Center, Yale University. He has been employed by the International News Service, and during the war served in the United States Navy. He has been a Research Fellow at the Brookings Institution and is the author of *Collective Bargaining Procedures* and *The Union Challenge to Management Control.* He has contributed to the *Quarterly Journal of Economics,* the *Journal of Political Economy,* the *American Economic Review,* and the *Brooklyn Law Journal.*

ROBERT DUBIN received his Ph.D. degree from the University of Chicago in 1947 and is at present Assistant Professor of Industrial Relations and Manager of the Industrial Relations Center, University of Chicago. He served with the Labor Branch of the War Department from 1941 through 1946. He is coauthor of *Patterns of Union-Management Relations: The UAW-CIO, General Motors and Studebaker.*

JOHN T. DUNLOP received his Ph.D. degree from the University of California in 1939, and is now Associate Professor of Economics at Harvard University. He has lectured at Stanford University and has served with the Temporary National Economic Committee. He has held positions in the National War Labor Board, the Office of Economic Stabilization, and the Office of War Mobilization and Reconversion. He is the author of *Wage Determination Under Trade Unions* and coauthor of *Cost Behavior and Price Policy*. He has contributed to the *American Economic Review*, the *Quarterly Journal of Economics*, the *Journal of Political Economy*, the *Review of Economic Statistics*, the *Economic Journal*, and the *Review of Economic Studies*.

LLOYD H. FISHER is a Wertheim Fellow in Industrial Co-operation at Harvard University. He has done graduate work at the University of Paris and the University of Pennsylvania, following receipt of a B.A. degree from the latter institution in 1931. Formerly he was Research Associate in the Institute of Industrial Relations, University of California, at Berkeley, Wage Stabilization Director of the Tenth Regional War Labor Board, Director of Research for the International Longshoremen's and Warehousemen's Union, and an Economist with the United States Departments of Agriculture and Interior. Mr. Fisher has contributed to the *Journal of Farm Economics*, *The New York Times Magazine*, *Proceedings of the National Conference of Social Work*, and to government publications.

EUGENE FORSEY received his Ph.D. degree from McGill University (Canada) in 1941, and is at present Director of Research for the Canadian Congress of Labor. He also holds the M.A. degree from Oxford University, England, where he was a Rhodes Scholar from 1926 to 1929. He has taught at McGill University and the University of British Columbia, and was a Fellow of the Guggenheim Foundation in 1941 and 1942. He is the author of *Economic and Social Aspects of the Nova Scotia Coal Industry*, *Social Planning for Canada*, and *The Royal Power of Dissolution of Parliament in the British Commonwealth*. He has contributed to the *Canadian Journal of Economics and Political Science*, *Politica*, the *Canadian Historical Review*, the *Canadian Bar Review*, the *Nation*, the *Dalhousie Review*, *Maclean's Magazine*, and the *Canadian Forum*.

FREDERICK H. HARBISON received his Ph.D. degree from Princeton University in 1940, and is at present Associate Professor of Economics and Executive Officer of the Industrial Relations Center of the University of Chicago. He has been connected with the Office of Production Management, the War Production Board, the War Department, and the Petroleum Administration for War. He is the author of *The*

Seniority Principle in Union-Management Relations, Seniority Policies and Procedures as Developed Through Collective Bargaining, Seniority Problems During Demobilization and Reconversion, and a contributing author to *How Collective Bargaining Works.* He is also coauthor of *Patterns of Union-Management Relations: The UAW-CIO, General Motors and Studebaker.* He has contributed to the *Journal of Political Economy.*

EVERETT KASSALOW received his B.S.S. degree from the College of the City of New York in 1938, and is at present Director of Research for the United Rubber, Cork, Linoleum and Plastic Workers of America. He has worked for the United States Bureau of Labor Statistics and the Research Division of the Congress of Industrial Organizations. He has contributed to various issues of the *Monthly Labor Review.*

CLARK KERR received his Ph.D. degree from the University of California in 1939, and is at present Associate Professor of Economics and Director of the Institute of Industrial Relations, University of California, at Berkeley. He has been on the faculty of the University of Washington and has served with the National War Labor Board as well as Impartial Chairman in the contract between the Waterfront Employers' Association of the Pacific Coast and the International Longshoremen's and Warehousemen's Union. He is the author of *Migration to the Seattle Labor Market Area* and is coauthor of a forthcoming volume of readings in labor, and has contributed to the *Monthly Labor Review.*

RICHARD A. LESTER received his Ph.D. degree from Princeton University in 1936, and is at present Associate Professor of Economics and Research Associate in the Industrial Relations Section, Princeton University. He has been on the faculties of Duke University, University of Washington, and Haverford College. He has held positions in the National War Labor Board, the War Production Board, the War Department, the United States Treasury, and the Committee for Economic Development. He is the author of *Economics of Labor, Providing for Unemployed Workers during the Transition,* and *Monetary Experiments,* and coauthor of *Wages under National and Regional Collective Bargaining, Labor and Social Organization,* and *The Case Against Experience Rating in Unemployment Compensation.* He has contributed to the *American Economic Review,* the *Journal of Political Economy,* the *Review of Economic Statistics,* the *Southern Economic Journal,* the *Harvard Business Review,* the *Journal of Farm Economics,* and the *Social Service Review.*

CLARENCE D. LONG received his Ph.D. degree from Princeton University in 1938, and is now Professor of Economics at the Johns Hopkins

University. He is also a member of the research staff of the National Bureau of Economic Research. He has taught at Wesleyan University and has been a member of the Institute for Advanced Study and a Fellow of the Guggenheim Foundation. During the war he served in the United States Navy. He is the author of *Building Cycles and the Theory of Investment* and *The Labor Force in Wartime America.* He has contributed to the *Quarterly Journal of Economics,* the *Review of Economic Statistics,* the *Harvard Business Review, Editor and Publisher,* and *Dun's Review.*

HERBERT R. NORTHRUP received his Ph.D. degree from Harvard University in 1942, and is now Assistant Professor of Industrial Relations at the New York School of Social Work, Columbia University. He has been on the faculties of Cornell University, New York University, and Columbia University, and has served as an economist with the National War Labor Board. He is the author of *Organized Labor and the Negro* and *Unionization of Professional Engineers and Chemists.* He has contributed to the *Quarterly Journal of Economics,* the *Journal of Political Economy,* the *American Economic Review,* the *Southern Economic Journal,* the *Journal of Business,* and the *Political Science Quarterly.*

LLOYD G. REYNOLDS received his Ph.D. degree from Harvard University in 1936, and is at present Professor of Economics and Associate Director of the Labor and Management Center, Yale University. He has been on the faculties of Harvard University and the Johns Hopkins University. He has also held positions in the Office of Price Administration, the War Food Administration, the National War Labor Board, and the Bureau of the Budget. He is the author of *The British Immigrant, The Control of Competition in Canada, Labor and National Defense,* and *Trade-Union Publications.* He has been a contributor to the *Quarterly Journal of Economics,* the *American Economic Review,* the *Canadian Journal of Economics and Political Science,* the *Journal of the American Statistical Association,* the *Journal of Farm Economics,* and the *Advanced Management Quarterly Journal.*

DAVID R. ROBERTS received his Ph.D. degree from Harvard University in 1941, and is at present Assistant Professor of Economics at Carnegie Institute of Technology. He has been on the faculty of Alleghany College, and has served with the United States Department of Commerce, the War Production Board, and the National War Labor Board. He has contributed to the *Quarterly Journal of Economics,* the *Journal of the American Statistical Association,* and the *Survey of Current Business.*

JOSEPH SHISTER received his Ph.D. degree from Harvard University in 1943, and is at present Research Associate and Assistant Professor at the Labor and Management Center, Yale University. He has been on the faculties of Cornell University and Syracuse University. In 1944 and 1945 he was associated with Dr. W. M. Leiserson in a study of trade union government and structure, sponsored by the Rockefeller Foundation. During the war he served in the United States Army. He has contributed to the *Quarterly Journal of Economics,* the *Journal of Political Economy,* the *American Economic Review,* the *Southern Economic Journal, Dun's Review, Personnel,* and the *Canadian Journal of Economics and Political Science.*

INDEX

Amalgamated Clothing Workers of America, 93n., 126n., 199
Amalgamated Iron, Tin and Steel Workers Union, 182
American Association of Engineers, 145
American Chemical Society, 136, 138, 149-50
American Federation of Hosiery Workers, 87, 199
American Federation of Labor, 135
American Federation of Teachers, 135, 144-45, 157
American Institute of Architects, 149
American Medical Association, 138
American Nurses' Association, 136, 142-43, 149, 151-56
American Society of Civil Engineers, 136-37, 140-43, 146-48, 152, 156
American Viscose Corporation, 251
Arbitration, cf. collective bargaining; full employment
Associated Press, 251
Attitudes, influence on labor-management relations, 14-15; influence on trade union development, 175, 184, 187-89

Bahrs, George, 25n., 53n.
Bakke, E. Wight, 7n., 104n., 111n., 115n., 123, 163n., 178n.
Ballard, B. J., 154n.
Bargaining power, influence on labor-management relations, 16
Barkin, Solomon, 131
Barnett, G. E., 42n., 55n.
Bauder, Russel, 164n.
Beard, Charles A., 163n.
Beveridge, William, 308-13, 323-26
Black, Martin L., Jr., 219n.
Bloom, Gordon F., 240n.
Boughton, V. T., 148n.
Braunthal, A., 314-15, 317-18
Bridges, Harry, 26

British Trades Union Congress, 310, 313, 324-27
Bryce, James, 79n.
Building Service Employees' Union, 136
Bury, J. B., 163n.

California State Nurses' Association, 151-56
Capital requirements, influence on labor-management relations, 13-14
Celanese Corporation of America, 251
Chamberlin, Edward H., 238n., 240n., 263n.
Chemists and collective bargaining, cf. industrial research, professional societies, trade unions
Clark, J. B., 238n., 244
Collective bargaining, arbitration and, 129-31; grievance proceedings and, Chapter 3; importance of distinction between grievance proceedings and, 81-85; job evaluation and, 131-32; new economic approaches to, 120-26; new patterns of, Chapter 5; new role of specialist in, 127-32; prices and, 120-22; professional societies and, Chapter 6; public and, 115-20; cf. employers' associations—administrative type, full employment, marginal productivity theory, professional societies, trade unions, trade union development, union-management cooperation
Collins, Orvis, 96n.
Commager, Henry Steele, 184n.
Commons, John R., 165n., 169n., 171-72, 190n., 192n.
Congress of Industrial Organizations, 314
Cost conditions, influence on labor-management relations, 13-14
Cross, Ira B., 26n.
Curti, Merle, 187n.

363